Fiona Phillips is a television presenter who until recently presented *GMTV* for twelve years. She has presented numerous television and radio programmes, has appeared in two feature films, writes a weekly column in the *Daily Mirror* and is a columnist for *Tesco* magazine. Fiona has written widely on Alzheimer's in newspapers and magazines, and campaigns for more support from the government for carers. In January 2009 she made the Channel 4 programme *Mum, Dad, Alzheimer's and Me* and in January 2010 followed it up with *My Family and Alzheimer's*. She lives in London with her husband and two children.

BEFORE I FORGET

In August 2008, television presenter Fiona Phillips quit the job she loved, after twelve years in GMTV, interviewing the most famous and influential people on the planet. She was going to devote more time to her father, Phil, who had been diagnosed with Alzheimer's — a year after her mother had died of the same disease. *Before I Forget* is an account of growing up in the 1960s and '70s within a complex family. Fiona reveals her parents' pride when she landed the job at GMTV. She describes watching them fade away as both parents succumb to Alzheimer's: one moment interviewing George Clooney, the next taking a call from Pembrokeshire Social Services to say that there was trouble at her parents' house, hundreds of miles away.

FIONA PHILLIPS

BEFORE
I FORGET

Complete and Unabridged

CHARNWOOD
Leicester

First published in Great Britain in 2010 by
Preface Publishing
An imprint of
The Random House Group Limited
London

First Charnwood Edition
published 2011
by arrangement with
The Random House Group Limited
London

British Library CIP Data

Phillips, Fiona.
  Before I forget.
  1. Phillips, Fiona. 2. Women television personalities
  - -Great Britain- -Biography. 3. Television personalities- -
  Great Britain- -Biography. 4. Phillips, Fiona- -Family.
  5. Alzheimer's disease- -Patients- -Family
  relationships.
  I. Title
  791.4′5′092–dc22

  ISBN 978–1–4448–0872–8

Published by
F. A. Thorpe (Publishing)
Anstey, Leicestershire

Set by Words & Graphics Ltd.
Anstey, Leicestershire
Printed and bound in Great Britain by
T. J. International Ltd., Padstow, Cornwall

This book is printed on acid-free paper

To Mum and Dad for giving me so
many wonderful things to remember.

But I, being poor, have only my dreams;
I have spread my dreams under your feet;
Tread softly because you tread on my dreams.

'He Wishes for the Cloths of Heaven'
W. B. Yeats

Introduction

I loved my job on the *GMTV* sofa, but when I decided to quit in the summer of 2008, it was because I loved my family more. I know I'm not alone in believing that family should always come first, but how many of us actually manage to put our loved ones in pole position? And how many of us suffer with a huge burden of guilt because we don't achieve it?

It was something I'd been mulling over for a long time: I had two very young children, a mum who was suffering badly with Alzheimer's disease and a dad who, to say the least, was behaving oddly, all combined with 4 a.m. alarm calls and the fear that my own mind was dissembling, so even finding the time to ponder was a luxury I didn't have. I thought a lot about changing things, worked, a lot, and didn't sleep very much at all. Over the years the agonising, the guilt, the lack of sleep and the absence of a proper social life became my life. And when I finally realised that it was not much of a life, my mind was made up.

It wasn't a decision I took lightly. I couldn't believe I'd got the top job on that famous red sofa in the first place, never mind that I'd still be sitting there after twelve years. I'd worked from the age of eleven, when I took on two paper rounds — lugging huge bags of newspapers around and popping them in letter boxes at the crack of dawn and after school. My mum used to say, 'You're so bloody independent.' I suppose I was. So bloody independent I was desperate to work so I wouldn't have to rely on Mum and Dad for handouts. They worked hard and it rubbed off on me. I have worked and worked and worked ever since, determined to prove myself and to achieve, so to give up a job that I never really dreamed I'd ever have to begin with was a massive life-changing decision. It could have been professional suicide too — it still might, who knows?

What I do know is that I loved every minute of *GMTV*. It was such a privileged position. I was allowed into millions of homes every morning, while people were getting ready for work and school. It enabled me to travel and, for well over a decade, to talk to those involved in the biggest news and entertainment stories of the day. It's rare for anyone to look forward to going to work every day, but I can honestly say that there was not one day when I didn't relish the thought of chatting away on that famous red sofa — well maybe one or two days, but I'll tell you about those later!

But there were big stories going on in my life too, and in a way the scales tipped from 'My work is my life' to 'My life is my work'. As family concerns got bigger, in my mind the job got smaller, and hand in hand with the enormous pleasure I gained from my work, was a chronic sleep deprivation which robbed me of living life to the full, of being able to handle the extra burdens that having chronically ill parents, two babies and 4 a.m. starts brought with them. After fifteen years of being constantly knackered, I wanted a bit of my life back. My children deserved to see me looking alive and fresh and wanting to play with them after school, rather than being so deadbeat by school pick-up time that I felt like I was on drugs. My husband was worthy of more than a snapped 'I'm shattered, I've been up since three thirty' when he arrived home from work at 8 p.m. and asked how I was. I even started resenting him having more sleep than me and 'just going to work' when I got up before dawn, worked *and* saw to the house, the children, the shopping, the fridge, the cupboards, the homework, the doctor, the dentist, the haircuts, my parents — you get the picture.

When I quit, I hoped I wasn't giving up work altogether. I couldn't — we still had a mortgage to pay and children and my dad to take care of. That's the reason I took so long to make my mind up. I'd thought about going for at least three years, ever since my old sparring partner Eamonn Holmes packed his trunk and said goodbye to the breakfast circus. I'd thought about it while I was with Eamonn too, when we had our downs — there were quite a few of those! I'd thought about it while I was interviewing self-important self-publicising 'me, myself, I' celebrities. I'd thought about it when I'd chatted to ordinary selfless people who made time for others — foster parents, charity workers, social care professionals — people I admire the most. More and more I felt the treadmill of my crack of dawn starts cramping what I really wanted to be. More importantly, increasingly I couldn't carry on with the burden of guilt which had been growing and growing since my mum was diagnosed with Alzheimer's disease and became heavier and heavier when my dad fell prey to the same condition. It weighed me down so much that, in the end, I guess I just gave in. It was so unlike me. I felt ashamed of myself, that I was weak for not being able to do it all.

I had to give a statement to *GMTV*'s head of press, Nikki Johnceline, a great friend who'd shared many long chats with me in my dressing room after the show came off air each day. We both filled up as I tried to put my reasons for leaving into words. A statement was finally released to the press which included the lines: 'This has been the hardest decision I have ever made. I love the job but I've got other responsibilities — children, a home life and an elderly dad who needs me — and I've recognised that I can't have it all.' Not quite the whole package perhaps, but enough to explain why I felt it was time to go.

With my life teetering so precariously to maintain a balance, anything that tipped the scales just slightly would be enough to bring it all crashing down. I can remember screaming silently to myself, heart racing, when an extra-curricular something happened that I just didn't have time to deal with — when social services phoned with a problem concerning my mum and dad, or if I was asked to change the lead story of my *Daily Mirror* column while I was already on the way to Wales to deal with my

4

parents. Ahhh! I felt I wasn't doing anything properly. The notes that often came home from school asking for parents to help on the latest trip filled me with anxiety and guilt and sorrow because I just didn't have the time. If I was dealing with my workload I felt I should be spending more time with the children. If I was with the children I felt I should be in Wales with my parents. If I was with my parents I felt . . .

Well, it doesn't need any more explanation does it? It was such a personal decision and *GMTV* was so much part of the TV furniture — not a huge starry vehicle, no pretensions of grandeur — that I really didn't anticipate the headlines that my decision would generate. I phoned Richard Wallace, my editor at the *Mirror*, before the *GMTV* statement was released. I wanted him to know what I was doing before anyone else. He's always been very loyal to me and I wanted to tell him in case he felt that it affected my job at the newspaper — he might not want me to write my weekly column, I thought, once I'd left *GMTV*. I dropped my two boys off for the day at a Chelsea soccer summer school, got a coffee from Starbucks, went back to my car and called him. 'I just wanted to tell you first that I'm leaving *GMTV*,' I think is what I said. 'Hang on, let me sit down,' was Richard's reaction, which sort of brought home the enormity of my decision. 'Look, I'll completely understand if you don't want me to write my column any more,' I rather pathetically offered. 'Don't be stupid,' he said. Phew! That was the reaction I'd hoped for but feared I wouldn't get.

I'll always be so grateful to Richard for that.

The next day, Friday 29 August 2008, it was front-page news: I QUIT — FIONA PHILLIPS LEAVES GMTV AFTER 15 YEARS. Bloody hell, what have I done? I thought. But it was a fleeting emotion batted away by my growing conviction that in the beginning, in the end and for that huge great bit in the middle all you've really got is family. I wrote my own version for the Mirror the day after the story broke which began, 'As I write this I actually feel physically sick. My decision to leave GMTV after twelve years on the sofa is the hardest I have ever had to make — like jumping off a cliff and hoping someone will save me halfway down. And yet hoping they won't. So right now I'm somewhere between the top of the cliff and the ground, feeling bilious about cutting my ties with the job I love, yet knowing I've got to move on.'

I'd made my decision while on holiday on the Isle of Mull in Scotland, one of our favourite places to escape to. I'd spent three weeks not caring what I looked like, no make-up, no worries, feeling alive and full of positivity, and I didn't want that feeling to be swamped and buried again on my return home. I went on to say:

In the four weeks I've been away from the Mirror over the summer, and probably for at least a year before that, I've been weighing up the benefits of having a job most people would kill for against the negative effects it has on me and my family. Twelve years ago when I first sat on the sofa alongside Eamonn Holmes I was a single girl just back from America, after completing two years as *GMTV*'s LA correspondent. Being given the top job, even though it meant rising at 4 a.m. five days a week, was like a dream come true. Over the years I've interviewed three Prime Ministers — John Major, Tony Blair and Gordon Brown — and four Tory leaders. I've announced wars, election results and Diana's death to the nation. I've seen the Spice Girls become Spice mums and enjoyed exclusive chats with Victoria Beckham and David. I've chatted to countless people, all who have made an impact on me, but non more so than so-called ordinary folk like Kate and Gerry McCann, Helen Newlove, whose husband Gary was kicked to death by thugs, and Sara Payne, who continues to campaign for Sarah's law following the murder of her beautiful daughter. There are too many names to mention, but they are all firmly etched on my mind. And so much has happened to me personally in the twelve years that I've been perched on the sofa. I've got married, had two children, nursed my mum through a long and tortuous battle with Alzheimer's disease and juggled several jobs and a ton of guilt along with running the house. Now my dad is ill and I have finally discovered that I can't have it all. Even though I scaled back my commitment to *GMTV* to three- and four-day weeks a while ago, I've got to the point where I feel I'm 'dropping balls' all over the place. I rise at 4 a.m. and never go to bed before 11 p.m. having usually not sat down, or eaten properly, in between. No one is standing over me with a whip and forcing me to work, but my parents brought me up with a strict work ethic and consequently I try and give 100 per cent to everything: to being a good mum, a good daughter, a good wife, a good professional, a good, caring citizen. And you know what? It is not possible to be that person and still live life to the full. I've got a lovely husband, beautiful children, a nice house, but I'm too tired to enjoy it all, so what's the point? It was while I was away in Scotland over the summer with my family, feeling care-free, laughing and joking with my husband — a rarity when I'm working — that he said, 'It's lovely to see you relaxed and happy for a change.' And it was lovely being relaxed and happy for a change. Not rushing around like a mad woman, never having time for proper conversations with anyone, dreading the phone ringing at night because I'm too tired to talk, not having a social life, hoping the children won't want me to kick a ball around when I get home because I'm constantly knackered. Those are the things that make life full and enjoyable. Yet they were all enough to tip me over the edge. I love my job. I worked hard for years to get it, I'm lucky to have it, but in the scheme of things it means nothing when life feels as though it's passing me by and I'm not on the journey. The children ask every night: 'Are you working tomorrow?' If I say yes they groan, if I say no they shout 'Yay' and deal out high fives all round. They love my on-air partner Ben Shephard — as do I — but they can't understand why I'd rather go in and chat to him than be with them. 'Why do you have to go and sit on that sofa and just talk to other people when you could be taking us to school?' they ask. They're right. And then there's my husband, who increasingly says: 'You're so busy with the children, your parents, your work. I'm just like the lodger around here. There's no time for me.' Which normally leads to an argument about him not understanding how much I have to do. So instead of ditching the children, the parents, or him, it's the job that had to go. Yes, I'm a fool, I know. But to celebrate the end of a relationship, as girls do, the hair had to go too. I had my long locks lopped off. Free at last! Obviously chucking a brilliant salary away along with the hair might seem pretty reckless. It does to me too. And I'm scared — we've still got to pay the mortgage. But I know it's the right decision. Since the news came out, the phone hasn't stopped ringing, and people have been so supportive. And I'll still work. I'm looking forward to new television and radio opportunities and, of course, I'll still write for the *Mirror*. I never wanted the day to come when I would have to go to bed before my children, and now it won't. I'll miss the viewers, my lovely colleagues, and the people I meet on a daily basis on the *GMTV* sofa, but I won't miss feeling shattered all the time. Getting up at 7 a.m. instead of 4 a.m. will completely change my life, and me, for the better.

Phew! I'm glad I got that all out! It's funny, but reading it back I think I sound a bit self-righteous, a bit 'poor me', but that's not how I meant it to come across. Still, it helped to piece it all together in my head and write it down. And once it was out there in print there was no going back, so it sealed my fate too. In fact the bloody awful photos that accompanied the story might have sealed my fate in more ways than one: my new haircut didn't suit me and I'd done my own make-up — I looked as if I'd been punched in both eyes. Who in their right mind would ever want me presenting anything for them ever again, looking like that? Then the phone started going mad with interview offers — the broadsheets wanting to concentrate on the 'I can't have it all' angle with the tabloids homing in on 'Why I left *GMTV*'. Meanwhile *Grazia* magazine posed the question: 'Can women have it all?'

On the Friday of that memorable and loaded-with-emotion week the telephone rang in the evening. It was Gordon Brown, phoning from his home in Scotland. 'So what's this I hear that you're leaving *GMTV*?' he enquired with a warmth and a mischievousness I'd come to know over many years of talking to him. I honestly can't remember most of what I said or what he said either; I just remember at one point exclaiming, 'You are soooo sweet for taking the time to phone me.' So *sweet*? What *was* I thinking of? Maybe I was losing my marbles like Mum and Dad. Maybe it was because I couldn't believe that I'd actually done it. Maybe Gordon's words had confirmed that it really was true. Otherwise, what the hell possessed me to call the man who ran the country 'sweet'? I didn't read any of the other stuff in the papers or elsewhere because it made it seem too real. Plus I didn't want to be crushed by the usual dumping off of bile and vitriol which I was sure was going to accompany some of the reports on the Internet. I felt very unsure of myself as it was. I could always change my mind, I suppose, I tried to reassure myself. I had four months to go before actually leaving; maybe they'd forget I was going! But I knew inside, with an increasing inevitability, that the die was cast.

On and off in the build-up to my last day I got freezing-cold feet. It was an emotional time for all sorts of reasons, but it was mainly the thought of leaving my colleagues, some of whom I'd worked with since the very beginning of *GMTV* in 1993. I'll never forget walking into the office at the crack of dawn after the story of my resignation had hit the papers. I felt terrible for not telling them first, but I couldn't. It had been decided that we had to control the story — such is the nature of a job in the public domain — so the first that most of my lovely friends heard about it was when the newspapers were dumped off in the middle of the night. They'd found out from Thursday 28 August's headlines and I was due back after my summer break on Monday 1 September. In the car on my way to work that morning I had butterflies in my stomach for the first time in years. The security guards, some of whom I'd also known for fifteen years or more, greeted me as I skulked in, saying, 'I can't believe you're leaving us' as we shared the usual banter that had greeted me at that ridiculous hour of the day for so many years. They were always my introduction to the morning — comforting presences who made me feel the world was all right whatever lay ahead of me in the hours to follow.

The *GMTV* offices had undergone a massive makeover during my time off, so it was like walking into a different company that morning, which was good in a way, as though they'd left me rather than the other way round. I don't know how I absorbed what was on the programme that day because all the talk during the briefing with Abi my senior producer and the guys on the news desk was about me leaving them. The next four months went by in a blur of what amounted to near-hysteria on my part: positive one minute, 'what on earth have I done?' the next; all the while holding on to my co-presenters Ben Shephard and Andrew Castle for support and encouragement. There were tears, there was laughter, uncertainty and a whirl of meetings and prospective job offers. And there was the 'What if I never work again?' question. I'm not a doctor, a nurse, a lawyer; I don't have something useful or sensible to fall back on. What if I'm like some of those actors who leave *Coronation Street*, never to be heard of again? What if I'm not good enough to work outside *GMTV*?

★ ★ ★

It had taken me a long time to summon up the guts to make that decision.

I'd had the children and coped with my early starts despite being riddled with guilt, but it was when an uninvited unknown lurched into my life, a thing I'd never encountered before, an evil presence that started to blow our family apart, that I first started thinking about cutting my ties with breakfast television. I knew I had to ease up and concentrate on what was happening at home. Not in our house in London, but in my parents' home in west Wales, hundreds of miles away. It was there that two lives were slowly, cruelly disintegrating.

My mum, the love of my dad's life, was gradually disappearing before our eyes. Alzheimer's had grabbed her, was throttling her personality and robbing her of her heart-jumping smile — the smile that my dad had first fallen in love with. For years she lived without really living, my short nights often punctuated with phone calls begging: 'Please help me.' There was nothing I could do. It's a bastard is Alzheimer's — there's really nothing anyone can do. Anyway, I left it too late. I agonised and cried and beat myself up that I was getting on with my life while hers was descending into a dark pit. She suffered and cried for years, always saying 'please help me', and me knowing there was nothing I could do. And, feeling an all-consuming despair and guilt and helplessness. Anyone who has lived with a relative or friend with Alzheimer's or just watched from close by will recognise these sentiments, I'm sure. My mum died on her own. Then, almost immediately, just when we thought that Alzheimer's was out of our lives, it found my dad. So I made the decision to change my life.

Now I know that when I eventually look back through the years I will never regret being able to be around my children and my dad a whole lot more; I won't have second thoughts about actually having some time for my husband; and I certainly won't have any misgivings about enjoying a full night's kip instead of dragging myself out of bed in the middle of the night. I only wish my mum was around so that I could spend more time with her.

1

My dad worked in telly. He fixed them. He fixed them during the day and worked in a bakery at night. He fixed it that we had the first colour telly on our road. He fixed it that my mum had something momentously interesting to brag about when the neighbours dropped in to gawp. He fixed it that we had a telly in our infants' school. Once, in 1966, he turned up at my class when I was five to install a colour telly! Can you believe that? I was overcome with pride at the time. My dad was the coolest dad ever. I didn't think he rated me that much but, goodness, I rated him. There, in front of my classmates, delivering a TV and having intimate knowledge of the most amazing thing we'd ever encountered! Was anyone's dad *that* cool? And. Get this. When I was seven, he fixed Dora Bryan's telly. She was actually *on* the telly as well as owning one and my dad got to go inside her flat on the seafront in Brighton. He was so important, my dad. And then, as if Dora wasn't enough to top Mum's bragging list, Dad was called round to fix Wilfred Pickles' set. Dora and Wilfred — two of the best-known comedy faces on television in the 1960s and 70s, and my dad fixed their TVs! Could life be more heady?! Well, maybe, but probably only just. If he'd fixed Tommy Cooper's or Batman and Robin's, for example, I think I'd have died a happy human being before the age of ten.

They were proper celebrities back then. Celebrities who put in the graft for their rewards. They mostly came from 'up north', where real celebrities spewed forth from hard work, raw talent and local recommendation. Anyway, I remember Wilfred Pickles, a Yorkshireman like my dad, not just because he was talked about as the first man on the wireless with a regional accent, a man of the people and the star of the 1970 sitcom *For the Love of Ada*, but because his set broke down just before Christmas. It was my dad's busiest time. 'Bloody Wilfred Pickles' I think were my dad's words, when bloody was a word that would get you sent to your room with a smacked behind. Everyone wanted their TVs fixed so they could watch Christmas telly, which was worth staying in for in those days. So Dad was never home until very late on Christmas Eve. And we grew to hate Wilfred and people like him for robbing us of our dad. But particularly Wilfred. Because we knew his face.

My dad worked on tellies when they were worth nearly as much as a car or house. People didn't own TVs in the 60s; they rented them. Rediffusion and Radio Rentals were the most popular stores on the high street. My dad worked for Rediffusion. We thought it must be very special because he told mum he didn't want to be bothered at work. 'When I'm at work I'm working,' he'd say. 'If you've got something to say to me, you can say it at home.' Of course we had to say it in person then, because only the very well-off had telephones, like the Banks family in *Mary Poppins*. But Mum was mischievous and probably bored rigid with staying at home with two children every day, so we did turn up at the hallowed workshop on occasion. I don't know why because the reception was always frosty. 'I've got work to do; I've told you never to bother me here.' So off we'd go back home to our telly, only I don't think we ever properly owned our own, just a procession of other people's tellies which he tested out on us before installing them in someone else's house.

I knew every control around the back of those sets. And I hated it when they wouldn't obey my dad's commands. As those tellies came on they emitted a hot, heated-up smell, like something on the verge of melting, and like his TVs my dad heated up too. He sighed and grunted, got bad-tempered. He hated them, but he loved them. Tellies were his life. Sometimes I think he loved them more than us. Well, he didn't acknowledge us a lot of the time anyway, and he certainly didn't spend as much time with us as he did with his beloved, hated tellies. He had work to do and we were Mum's job.

His indifference made me crave his attention. I was bursting for him to say proudly, 'That's Fiona, my beautiful little daughter.' But he was too wrapped up in work, too lacking in emotion for that. His love sometimes seemed beyond our reach. Occasionally he'd tell Mum, 'I never loved you.' He'd say it — although I'm sure he never meant it — in front of me and my two brothers. It was something we'd rather not have heard, so to ease the awkwardness it became a bit of an

17

uncomfortable family joke. He told me, sometimes with a chuckle, sometimes with a grumble, 'Never get married. Whatever you do. And never have children.' I wanted to show him that I was worthy of his love, so I convinced myself that I'd never get married and never have children, just to impress him. He was too busy to be impressed though. Too busy working in a bakery at night and fixing tellies during the day. All for us, I guess. The family he sometimes wished he didn't have.

We lived in Canterbury in a little three-bed semi. To us, it was the biggest house in the world. To Mum and Dad, who'd previously lived in digs, owning it was their greatest achievement. In 1965, I think it was, Dad had worked enough double shifts at the bakery and Rediffusion fixing tellies to be able to afford our first house. Independence. That was a buzzword in our family. Independence. Never be obliged to anyone; never be a burden; never be dependent on anyone. Dad's determination to be independent and make his own way in life led to his long absences from home and his complete immersion in work, and because of that he was a bit of a stranger to all of us. Perhaps it was his absence which made me want his love more than anything. Even more than Mum's, who loved me without doubt, more than anyone could, even though she couldn't quite bring herself to say, 'I love you.' It was more a demonstrative kind of enveloping-us-in-love kind of love. Always with us. At home. At the school gate. At the oven. By the sickbed. At Christmas. On birthdays. At

18

school open evenings. In the kitchen. Always there. Always smiling. Because she loved us, even though she couldn't quite say it. She was always at the doctor's too. Dr Miles became a family friend. He comforted Mum and heard her sobs when she was pregnant with me, a honeymoon baby, a baby Dad wasn't ready for.

They were married on 26 March 1960 and I was born on 1 January 1961 — 1.1.61 — so easy to remember, yet a date my dad had trouble coming to terms with. When he found out that Mum was pregnant he wanted her to have a termination. Dr Miles wouldn't hear of it, so he put her on Valium, told her my dad was full of nonsense and to go home and tell him so — and that's why I'm here. Dad wasn't there though, when I was born. He had a bit of previous on that front. Mum often told us, when she'd fallen out with him, how he had failed to turn up for a date the day after they got engaged. Apparently he wouldn't speak to her and appeared a week later offering no explanation at all. Of course, it made her love him more. My dad, the embodiment of 'treat 'em mean, keep 'em keen'. I guess it must have been the same when mum was pregnant with me — maybe, like the engagement, it was all getting too serious, too much of a commitment for him. It took him a while to get his head round having a baby, and when he eventually did, he decided it had to be a boy. But I came out instead. Bloody inconvenient. And on a bank holiday as well.

I loved looking at my christening photos when I was little, spotting my mum's beloved sister

Auntie Mary with her husband Uncle Roy, Grandma (Dad's mum), Grandad (Dad's dad) and Mum, lovingly showing me off, wrapped up in my satin and net christening gown. Oh, and there's 'Narnie', my godmother, Mum and Dad's second mother, the kindly lady whose council house, 'digs', we lived in until mum and dad could afford their own. And there's Dad's brother Uncle Barry with his first wife Sonia, and Uncle Tom, Mum's brother, and his wife Auntie Audrey, but no sign of Dad. He must have been taking the photos, I thought, so proud of his new baby girl, turning the dials on his huge camera and snapping away with pride. The truth is he wasn't in them because he wasn't there. Imagine that! My lovely mum, newly married, having moved from Pembrokeshire in south Wales to Canterbury to marry my dad, entertaining the family at her first baby's christening and the father of the child gone AWOL! I don't know to this day where he went. Or if it was his navy background that made him think he could leave port whenever he liked. All I know is that Dad never quite got used to family life. And he made us think that we, in particular Mum, were a hindrance to what he really wanted to do. Although he never quite knew what that was.

One of his grandest plans was to move to South Africa in the early 1970s; I think he actually got a job there, but then we didn't go. Of course we didn't, because Dad was a dreamer. He always put off life; never really lived it, storing bits away for the future and then getting there and storing them away again. Dad's version was: we didn't go because 'That bloody woman wouldn't go without the dining room table.' So it was Mum's fault we didn't go. Mum and the dining room table's — part of a set that she had saved up for when they got their first house in Canterbury. It was oval, oak, I think, and accompanied by four chairs and a Welsh dresser stacked with china Uncle Barry had given them as a wedding present. It eventually travelled from house to house with them each time they moved but never outside of England or Wales! My brothers David and Andrew still laugh about that table: 'There it is. We could have lived in South Africa if that hadn't stopped us!' That was Dad though, always blaming someone else for his excruciating inability to take life by the scruff and live it to the full.

In September 2008 I moved Dad out of the last home that he and Mum had shared in Pembrokeshire. David and I travelled to Haverfordwest in November 2008, having put off the onerous task of clearing the house and sifting through the memories. The table and dresser and chairs were still there. So was Uncle Barry's wedding china. It was a house. But not a home. As if all the misery of Mum's illness, the guilt, the remorse had cast out the warmth, the love and the laughter. Depressing. Cold. Damp. Squalid. Mouse droppings. Carpet almost ingrained into the floor. Dirty mattress in the middle of the living room. Most of my mum's treasured diaries missing. Her wedding dress missing. Our christening gown missing. Bloody

Dad. He must have dumped them all. Were there just too many memories, too many regrets, of a love he never appreciated, of a life never lived? Bloody, bloody depressing. We threw stuff in a skip with no sentimentality at all. We hurled it in. Just stuff. It meant nothing.

Then, among the wreckage of their lives, of our home, I found piles of notes, some of them scrawled, some neatly typed. Dad had talked about a book he was writing for years, since 1984 in fact, when he first started jotting down his thoughts. 'Phil's writing a book,' Mum would brag, and here it was, scattered among the debris. It was all about a time when life was good, when he was in the navy and single. It was called *Chase the Shouting Wind*, and as with everything Dad took on, it wasn't finished. Reading through the dog-eared pages I realised the deep regret for what he hadn't achieved in life and the deep love he felt for my mum.

2

Dad was born in Sheffield in October 1934. His mum, Edith, was a dominant force in his life. Always was, always will be, even though she's been gone for thirty years. He calls me Mother now. It's the Alzheimer's. He's not far wrong though — I'm a bit like Edith. She was a feisty little woman, a rabid socialist and so disgusted by the fact that Neville Chamberlain, Tory prime minister from 1937 to 1940, bore the same name as her eldest son, she never called my dad by that name again. Instead he became Phil, a shortening of his surname Phillips. Edith brought up three children almost single-handed, my grandfather Reginald, a warrant officer in the army, being away pretty much from 1939 to 1945, performing his duties in the war. They lived in Attercliffe, a working-class mining area of Sheffield, where my grandmother ruled the house with a rod of iron and a carving knife which, so Dad says, she attacked him with when his behaviour became too much for her sharp tongue alone to control. In Dad's notes for *Chase the Shouting Wind* he calls her 'a little woman of Anglo-Welsh descent, who spoke with machine-gun rapidity, frequently airing her political views, always with a socialist bias. On one occasion she told me that Winston Churchill was a warmonger.'

Mum always made excuses for Dad when he didn't show us any affection. 'It's because his mother didn't show him any love,' she'd say. He was a loner too, and a 'devil', according to my grandma. I've got a picture of him with his mum, dad and younger brother and sister, Barry and Germaine, and he's walking in front, apart from all of them as though he has nothing to do with them. That's my dad — detached, independent, very independent. A 'bloody independent bugger' according to Mum. Maybe it was the terrible accident he had as an infant, in which he nearly lost a leg, that made him think he was fighting life alone. He told me about it again recently while I was visiting him. He was dressed in his pyjamas, unshaven, no idea of my name, giggling and talking in incomplete sentences, but he remembered it. Aged four or five, he ran into the road and was hit by a lorry. 'My mother screamed and screamed,' he recalled. There was talk that they'd have to have it removed, that leg that he legged it on so frequently after dishing out a mouthful of cheek to my poor grandma. 'They said I'd never play football on it again, but I did,' he often boasted. No one told my dad what to do: not his mum, not his absent dad, not his withered leg and certainly not the doctor. He was too independent for all that.

The other memories that Dad can still recollect are of his time in the Fleet Air Arm. My God, have we heard about the Fleet Air Arm over the years. When I visit him these days I get the same routine. He tells me how he's looked out of the window and, ''Phillips,' he was calling.' 'Who was calling 'Phillips,' Dad?' 'You know. Him. That bugger. Fleet Air Arm.

'Phillips, you bugger,' he says, 'come and have a bloody drink.'' 'So did you go for a drink, Dad?' 'Yes, of course I did.' He hasn't actually seen 'that bugger' from the Fleet Air Arm for over fifty years.

Dad signed up for the Royal Navy for seven years when he was nearly eighteen. It was an act of defiance. He'd been singled out as 'very bright' at his many schools — being an army kid he'd attended boarding schools all over the place after the war — in Germany, Egypt, Malta, Scotland — and his father wanted him to join up and train as an officer in the army. So he joined the navy as a rating. According to the notes I found when we cleared out the house, he signed up for the Fleet Air Arm in 1951, 'reluctantly' he wrote. 'Mother wanted me out of the nest. It was a blue sky June day around 11.30 a.m. when I approached HMS *Collingwood*. Following a good meal, at 12.30 p.m. we made our way to the wooden huts, after which I thought, 'I can't stay long.' It's all my mother's fault. For good or bad!!' He had his mind set on being a pilot. I have a picture of him sitting in the cockpit of a plane, elbow over the side, looking as cool as only a teenager in the 1950s could.

It was the decade when teenagers claimed a voice, became cool, assertive, movie-idol glamorous. I used to show my friends that picture of my dad — how no one had plucked him from that plane and fast-tracked him onto a film set and certain Hollywood glory I really couldn't fathom. But the navy plucked him from that plane because they didn't think his attitude was right. He has always had a dislike of authority — that'll be what they're talking about. In his notes there are frequent references to the effect that authority and institutions have on a free mind. He wrote of man 'abandoning his humanity as he merges his unique personality into the larger institutional structures' and he reckons that 'an individual's conscience ceases to operate when he or she is responding to the dictates of authority'. As for the royal family, I won't even go there, but as they represent ultimate authority in some people's eyes, let's just say they weren't his favourite people.

That decision not to let him fly a plane crushed my dad. I wasn't there; I wasn't even a twinkle in his eye, but I knew this because he told us so many times when David and I were little. 'I could have been a pilot' was just the first in his long list of 'could have beens, but never wases'. 'I could have been a policeman,' he'd say to us, or, 'I'd have made a good teacher, you know.' He never wanted to be a navy rating or a TV engineer. He was bright, enquiring, a voracious reader. His books are where he got a steady education to make up for being uprooted from school after school after school. His most prized possession when he was a boy was a set of the *Encyclopaedia Britannica* which his mum bought so that her children would be 'educated'.

As the years went by and disillusionment deepened he had obviously jotted down what he could have been in the form of notes for his novel. The central character is a twenty-six-year-old man called Michael Harry Dalton, who was born on 1 January (my birthday — maybe he did think more of me than he let on) 1930. Dad had written profiles of all his main characters and in the margin next to Michael Dalton, he'd written in Biro, '*Me, in my mind.*' This is how he describes himself/Michael Dalton, a chief petty officer who was born in Sheffield and educated at grammar school.

Physical description
   Height: 6 feet [Dad was about 5 foot 10 inches].
   Weight: 12 stone 8 pounds.
   Broad-shouldered, muscular, no excess weight.
   Hair: brown. Eyes: blue. Complexion: fresh.
   Features: handsome — round face, high cheekbones, good skin, Greek nose, full mouth and good teeth.

Personality
   Introverted, intense, aggressive, defensive, tough, cool, shy, self-conscious, emotional, strong moral character, avoids commitment, dislikes obligation, dislikes close proximity of others unless by choice — therefore misfit in Royal Navy — craves excitement. Has little respect for authority.

Dad had summed himself up to a T. I found it very moving when I chanced upon this description of himself as his lead character. This was a man so full of promise, just like Dad, yet in real life the promise was never fulfilled and the book never finished. Not surprisingly, the character description of Michael Dalton was the most detailed of all. He continued with general comments:

Smokes, drinks — to excess at times — plays soccer, rugby, tennis and swims.
Politics: steeped in socialist traditions — from mother's side of family — changed allegiance after 1956. [Cripes! You never told me that, Dad!]

Rejected for pilot training at 18 because of attitude; he was, however, offered training as an observer, which he rejected. Took private flying lessons and holds private pilot's licence.

Everything was Dad except for the last sentence, which is Michael Dalton's life alone. Taking private flying lessons was out of reach financially for Dad, and even if it had been possible would probably have been one of those things he should have done, but didn't. It was fascinating and also a little heartbreaking to see this all typed out: my dad's character in black and white along with the dreams he never realised.

Aircraft flown:
    Tiger Moth — 100 hours.
    Cessna — 28 hours.
    Harvard — 10 hours (during April/May 1956).
Has motor car — Morgan 4/4 1954.

Just a few years ago when we didn't yet realise that Dad was ill — just odder than ever, we thought — I bought him a flying lesson at a charity auction which I hosted at a local Pembrokeshire pub as a favour for a friend of mine. It was to be at Haverfordwest airfield. Of course, he never took it. He's forgotten the book now, even though I reckon he was working on it for around ten years. He still wears his Fleet Air Arm badge though — on his pyjamas, on his jumper, on his jacket. But only when he remembers to change out of his pyjamas. He lives in the present because his memory only has a limited notion of the past. Thank goodness his mind plays happy tricks on him though. Different to Mum. Her Alzheimer's grasped her sunny demeanour and strangled it.

It was Mum's happy-go-lucky approach to life that first attracted Dad. In 1958 he was stationed with the Fleet Air Arm at Brawdy in Pembrokeshire, west Wales; we drove past it many times over the years. When I first took my husband Martin home we went out for one of Mum's favourite Sunday afternoon rides in the car and inevitably ended up at Brawdy, where Dad announced, 'I had some great times there.' I guess in comparison with the drudgery of work and family life the times became greater as the years went on. To us it looked grey and desolate, just ugly old aircraft hangars and no sign of human life. It wasn't far from the then county town of Haverfordwest — known as Harford by the locals. It's a pretty Georgian town watched over by a castle, with a high street that runs up a hill. It was my favourite place as a child, when Mum and I did the yearly Welsh relations tour. Now, when we go back to visit Mum's grave and clear Dad's house, the castle looks diminished, the once-quaint Georgian shopfronts have been painted all sorts of garish colours, the pound shops have moved in and the rest are mostly empty.

Back in the late 1950s though the Masonic Hall was the centre of a nightlife that was very much alive and kicking. I guess it's because youth had been given its voice after the huge losses of the Second World War. And, of course, Elvis helped the cause along too. Anyway, I don't know who was playing when Dad and his mates walked into the Masonic one Friday night in 1958. But I know who was there: a beautiful young woman called Eleanor Amy Monica Morris, generally known as Amy. My mum. She was smiling, probably against the odds, because from what she told me about her very strict mum, my gran, she'd no doubt have gone through the mill to get there in the first place. She was twenty-seven, certainly a respectable age to be at a dance, but my gran thought that only whores got dressed up and went out at night. 'Looking for men, *ach y fi*,' she'd exclaim. You'd better get used to that phrase. *Ach y fi*, pronounced 'uch a vee' ('ch' as in 'loch') means 'disgusting' in Welsh and was used frequently, the Welsh of my mum's generation being as strict in their attitude to sex and high values as the Catholic Irish. '*Ach y fi*, going out dressed like that. People will think you're forward,' was one that was frequently levelled at me as I was growing up. Like mother, like daughter; she'd got it from my gran. My mum got her hair dyed pitch black by a hairdresser friend once, and when she got home my gran heated up a pan of water and tipped it over her head. I think that was the night my Auntie Mary grabbed my gran and threw her on the bed. Unheard of in those days, but I think it was my mum's screams brought on by the scorching hot water over her head that fired Auntie Mary's rage. My gran would probably have gone to prison for that nowadays, but back then her word was law, and my mum had to think up all sorts of ruses to get out of the house and escape her all-pervading displeasure.

So, she was smiling. Always put a happy face on, my mum. No matter what was going on beneath the surface. That night her smile was electric. I know so because my dad told me so. 'It was that smile,' he told us on better days. 'I knew then that she was the one I'd marry. 'I'll have that one,' I said to my mates,' he'd chuckle. As the years went on it became 'That bloody woman stopped me from going to Australia with my Fleet Air Arm mates; if I hadn't met her, I'd be there now.' I hoped that somewhere deep inside he meant to add, 'But I'm glad I stayed, otherwise I wouldn't have had my beautiful children.'

When I found all his notes that day it felt intrusive to read them in a way. All his thoughts — some typed, some jotted down in biro on lined paper, some in exercise books — unearthed and there in black and white, revealing the true depth of the character that he'd never let anyone really get to know. All his frustrations — his being unable to finish anything, to live his life to the full, to fully appreciate my mum — were there in those notes. I found them in a kitchen drawer and in his study — my younger brother Andy's former bedroom — where some things never got started and nothing ever got finished. This was how he described my mum: 'Lovely eyes, high cheekbones, full mouth, beautiful teeth, extrovert, opinionated, assertive,' and how he first met her: 'I saw her at a dance. Her and her dazzling smile. My feelings were spontaneous: 'She's mine,' I thought.' Completely smitten by that smile he was, my independent dad.

He's not independent now. He thinks he is, but he's not. He has Alzheimer's. And he's dependent. Just don't tell him. He often looks at pictures of my mum and says, 'Ah, she was a lovely lady. She died, you know. Bloody Alzheimer's.' He's forgotten her name, but he remembers her presence, her huge smile. He thinks Alzheimer's was her illness. Now it's his.

3

Mum was born near Fishguard in Pembrokeshire, west Wales. Actually in a tiny little place called Dwrbach, just outside Fishguard and not far from Trecwn, headquarters of a bleak Second World War ammunitions depot. That's where she roamed the country roads free as a bird on her daily three-mile trek to Barham School. I took her back there when she was very ill, when she didn't understand what was happening to her, when she knew it was bleak and was terrified that she was losing herself. The school was derelict, with a fading beauty and a dignity that refused to give in to the ivy that was slowly strangling it. A plaque on one of the stone fireplaces read, 'The Bible must be constantly read and taught.' She walked around with the past in her eyes, averted for a while from the terror of the future. I just wanted to take her back to a time that was happy. To the narrow country roads where she wandered and the hedgerows where she'd find wild strawberries, pluck them and thread them on grass to wear around her neck, until the appeal of their seductively juicy aroma became too much. And she ate them.

Mum had seven brothers and sisters: Auntie Cenlais, Auntie Dilys, Auntie Jean, Uncle Norman, Uncle Tom, Auntie Mary and Uncle Lesley. Auntie Dilys, Auntie Jean, Uncle Norman and Mum are gone now, but I'll never forget the times I spent with them in Wales as a little girl, sitting quietly and listening to all the local gossip, and Auntie Dilys with her fierce little West Highland terrier called Minty and her bragging about my impossibly clever cousins Georgina, Dianne and Janet. Mum was number seven of the eight brothers and sisters. The youngest daughter and, apart from Uncle Lesley, who was the youngest and *really* naughty, she was the next naughtiest. But only in the way that she loved life, loved people and didn't see why she had to be in at a certain time when she was having such good fun and doing no harm. She worshipped her father, who she called Daddy Noddfa (pronounced 'Nothva').

Let me explain this Welsh thing: everyone we knew in Wales wasn't known solely by their Christian names or even their surnames, but by where they lived; so Mum's father was Daddy Noddfa because that was the name of the house where they lived. As a child Mum used to take me on her rounds and visit Mrs James the Shop (because she ran the only one in Trecwn, why else?), who always plied us with stale biscuits. We'd go and see Mrs Thomas Bengol, who lived in a house called Bengol and whose skin was always smeared with soot from her fire, which sent its blackness all around the house. Mum and I regularly emerged rubbing our eyes and looking as though we'd spent the day down the mines. My favourite was Mrs Jenkins the Forge. The Forge was a farm where I loved squelching around in the cows' runny, reeking mess and patting their beautiful wet noses. I wanted to live there. Plus Mrs Jenkins the Forge didn't serve stale biscuits, and Forge Farm was not engulfed in a haze of soot. And she had a gorgeous boxer dog called Sandra, who I spent hours playing with.

My mum idolised Daddy Noddfa, and apparently the feeling was mutual. Mum's closest sister, my Auntie Mary, recounts the tale of when her father introduced her to someone, and the new acquaintance said something along the lines of 'She's a lovely-looking girl,' Daddy Noddfa replied, 'Ah, but wait until you see my Amy.' Clearly Auntie Mary has hung on to that rather obvious display of favouritism — not that she was offended by it or anything! Mum used to love hearing her sister tell that story. Over and over again. Unfortunately Daddy Noddfa died in his forties and my mum never got over it. That left my gran, Mam Noddfa, the sole guardian of eight children. Four of her children were by her first husband, who also died an early death, and four were Daddy Noddfa's. The family legend goes that Daddy Noddfa wanted four children because his wife had had four children by her first husband, a horrid symbol of machismo which always left me reeling a little. But apparently he was a very kind, gentle man.

Clearly, with eight children to deal with, Mam Noddfa had to be a little toughie. Like Dad's mother, her fist was often out and shaking as she laid down the law to her offspring. When my mum was fourteen Mam took her out of school and lent her to friends to take care of their children so that she'd bring some money into the house. Mum was always bitter that she was made to finish her education early. 'I'm *twp*,' she'd say, 'because I was dragged out of school to earn money for Mam.' *Twp* is another Welsh word, pronounced 'tup', like the northern English pronunciation of 'cup'. It means thick basically, which she very definitely wasn't. She'd often say she was dull too, which is also used to mean stupid or thick in Wales. She may have missed out on a great, classical education, but my mum was as sharp as a pin when it came to emotional intelligence. She instinctively knew right away if she liked someone or not and sussed out their character immediately. She was always right; she'd still be nice to everybody though — a smile for everyone whether she loved or loathed them.

When Mum met Dad, and he was dazzled by that smile, he couldn't have known that she actually didn't have a tooth in her head. At the age of twenty-one she went to the dentist for a check-up. He put her to sleep with gas and when she woke up her teeth had all gone. Every single one of them. Her mouth had been butchered. I think I must take after Mum where teeth are concerned, because mine aren't a bit like Dad's. But I could never tell if they were like mum's because hers weren't her own. I was heartbroken when Mum told me that story. Imagine being twenty-one and single, with a smile that could have lit up a Welsh coal mine, and waking up with no teeth? She walked around with plugs of cotton wool in her mouth for weeks because the bleeding wouldn't stop. The dentist was bloody

36

drunk — off his head, it turned out. That's why he'd taken every tooth out of hers. When she got home her mum shouted at her. Just think if a dentist did that these days — he'd be sued into a deep dark place, further than his drill could reach. If I could see him now I'd punch his teeth out one by one.

That was one of the big traumas in Mum's life as a young woman. The other happened when she was a teenager, an innocent one at that. There was no talk of sex in Mam Noddfa's house. '*Ach y fi*' was what you'd get if anything of that nature was mentioned. Mum had this brilliant saying which was her way of telling me that I wasn't to get involved with members of the opposite sex. 'I was clean until I married your father,' she often told me with high moral superiority. I didn't understand what she meant when I was younger — what was she getting at? Was my dad filthy? Was his fixing tellies a greasy, smelly job that meant she was transformed into the same when he hugged her? No, clean, as I began to gather by the number of *ach y fi*'s which preceded it, meant untouched, with no carnal knowledge of another human being. I'm really trying not to say the s★★ word here, because I never ever heard my mum say it. That was a word which was sealed firmly inside her lips, which was a miracle because she could talk for Wales, Scotland, England and Ireland. But she never talked of that. *Ach y fi*. She was clean. Except she wasn't, we later found out.

In her mind she still was — until she married my father, of course — but she'd alluded, so

37

many times, to something that happened to her when she was a young girl bouncing around the country lanes, running across fields and climbing gates. She often talked of being 'dragged'. She used to warn me that I'd end up getting dragged if I didn't dress 'tidy'. This is another Welsh usage, which translates as 'respectable', or it did when Mum kept on at me about being 'tidy'. It's also used as an approval of something, so you can have a tidy guitar, which means it's really cool. Anyway, Mum was obsessed with me being tidy, with a hint in her voice that she knew what could happen if you weren't. It turned out that that constant darkness, that menacing pleading with me and warning me that things could happen, without saying what or why or by whom, was because she had indeed been dragged. It was by some filthy pig of a farmer as she romped through his field. He'd thrown her on the ground and assaulted her. It's so hard to write that about my very soft, innocent, naive (even while we were growing up), smiley, loving mum. But it happened. In the 1940s it was shameful, not for the depraved monster who did it, but for my mum, and she never got over it. Its presence lurked in our lives through her words and her deeds.

Mum was engaged before she met Dad — to a 'lovely chap', she used to say as she glanced at my father with a look that said he wasn't. Apparently he really was 'a lovely chap', too lovely by all accounts. He would do anything for Mum: he worshipped her and she walked all over him. The more he did for her the more she

38

wanted nothing to do with him. Some nights he'd come round to my gran's little red and white cottage deep in the Welsh countryside to sit and keep her company, while Mum skipped out of the gate to go and meet her friends and have a high old time! She was naughty but fun, and caring, and so very lovable. What else did she do before she met Dad? Oh yes, she escaped from Mam Noddfa's clutches on another memorable night, with a coat over her head to hide her glamorous make-up and wearing another one over her body to hide a beautiful dress that she'd saved up for, and took part in the Miss Pembrokeshire contest. She was runner-up.

Once mum had grown up a bit Mam Noddfa stopped passing her around as hired help for the locals and their children and she forged some independence by going to work for a draper's store in Fishguard before training as a nurse at the local hospital in Sealyham. It was opened in 1923 by the Welsh National Memorial Association for the treatment of Tuberculosis and was transferred to the West Wales Hospital Management Committee when the National Health Service was formed in 1948. I think it must have become a geriatric hospital around that time because that's what Mum said she did. Pity the poor old dears who were under her care. She told me loads of tales about shaking the tops off thermometers and general bedpan antics during her time there.

She loved company, my mum, and she made some good girl friends during her time at

Sealyham. The hospital was quite a way from where she lived so Mum *phut-phutted* to work on her Lambretta. I say 'on', but, according to Mum, that Lambretta spent a lot of time in the hedgerows of the glorious Pembrokeshire countryside thanks to her unique driving skills. Mum was more interested in waving to everyone she encountered and exchanging pleasantries than keeping her eyes on the road. I'm ashamed to say that my driving skills sometimes bear an uncanny resemblance to hers. I've been known to drive with no hands on the steering wheel while waving at someone I know with one hand and reaching into my handbag with the other! And that's when I'm on my own in the car — imagine the chaos when I've got the children fighting in the back as well. The thing is, Mum probably spent nearly as much time in hospital as a patient as she did tending to them.

Mum's mischievous ways of dealing with her very strict, moral and not often loving upbringing shaped her character, and she remained true to it, no matter how far she travelled. She used to visit me in London as often as she could, and I remember one occasion when we went shopping in Chelsea's Kings Road. We went into a trendy clothes shop, where I looked around for some trousers for Martin, who was then my boyfriend. I could hear her chatting away to the impossibly cool-looking guy behind the counter: 'Yes . . . breakfast TV . . . Eamonn Holmes . . . She's my daughter.' Oh God, she's bragging on about me being on *GMTV* again! Then I heard her saying, 'Oh dear, when did that happen? You poor thing . . . and so

40

handsome too.' Now she's getting his life story! Wincing, I quickly grabbed a pair of trousers and bought them without even checking the size. Anything to bundle her out of there.

I went back to that shop, it must have been two years after that visit with Mum, and the same guy was there. 'How's your mum?' he asked me, 'She is so lovely.' She was ill by then and her character was already disappearing. I choked up, felt ashamed of ever having been embarrassed by my happy-go-lucky mum, and cried.

4

After the small hiccup of Dad not speaking to Mum the day after they got engaged, they eventually got married on 26 March 1960. They saved up for their wedding, the usual tradition of the bride's family coughing up for the nuptials having been scuppered by the fact that Mum's father, the main breadwinner in their family, had died by then. They tied the knot at St Paul's on Church Street in Canterbury opposite the Duke's Head pub, which Dad's parents then ran. Mum had moved to Canterbury to marry Dad and set up home there. Dad had left the navy and Mum gave up her nursing to join him. Apparently Grandma and Grandad were thrilled with Mum. They hadn't thought Dad was the marrying type and often said that if he hadn't met Mum he'd never have got married. 'You look after her, she's a good 'un' was Grandma's advice. Dad was twenty-five and Mum twenty-seven, quite old for a woman to get married then, but she had wanted to make sure she'd made the most of her life before settling down. She bought her own wedding dress, her brother Tom gave her away, and Auntie Mary was maid of honour. Oh, and Dad did turn up and he looked gorgeous. And happy.

Once the church ceremony was over, they retired to a restaurant at the end of Church Street which Mum had booked and paid for. She must have worked so hard to save up for that wedding, but judging by the smile on her face in the photos it was worth every penny. I think they went to Salisbury, for some reason, for their honeymoon, because I seem to remember when I lived there as a student radiographer years later we walked past the Red Lion Hotel, a thirteenth-century coaching inn, and they said that's where they'd spent it. It's a Best Western now, rated three-star and with the ominous boast that 'during recent times many modern facilities have been incorporated within the framework of the traditional style and ambience of the original building'. But back then it must have been delightful.

When they returned from their Red Lion sojourn, Mum and Dad lived at 5 Edward Road in Canterbury, just a five-minute walk from the Duke's Head and not far from the prison. I have a picture of Mum standing outside the Victorian terraced house, looking radiant, in August 1960. A wonderful widow, Mrs Wilson (which is what they and I always knew her as — you didn't call your elders by their Christian names back then) took them in as lodgers. That's when Dad worked his double shifts fixing TVs and working in a bakery. By then Mum was pregnant — she must have been, because I was born just over nine months after they got married. I was probably conceived at the Red Lion and born on 1 January 1961 at the Kent and Canterbury Hospital, not far from Mrs Wilson's little red-brick house, the pub and the prison. It must have been hard living in digs, as Mum and Dad called it, in a strange town, pregnant and hundreds of miles away from home, but with her ready smile and ever-wagging tongue Mum adapted easily to any situation you put her in. She loved Mrs Wilson, who was a great friend to the young couple who were embarking upon a very responsible, grown-up path, unlike anything they'd ever been used to before.

When I was born, I think Mrs Wilson's two-bedroomed terrace became a bit of a tight squeeze, and the three of us were soon off to Mrs Wright's, or Narnie as she lovingly became known to all of us. Narnie lived in a council house but thought she was the Queen of Sheba. She had a blue rinse, strangled vowels and a son called Bernard, whom she called BerNARD, as in 'lard', only he wasn't fat. Her first name was Lydia and she became like a mum to my parents, and a loving if a bit strict, not wanting us to ever show her up, grandma to me and subsequently my naughty brother David, who was born while we were at Narnie's. I can't remember a thing about David's arrival — he's only twenty months younger than me — but he soon made his presence felt.

Narnie was a man's woman. She loved men. She felt her conversation was too intelligent for womenfolk to appreciate and her vowels went into plummy overdrive when she encountered gentlemen. She was the first person I ever knew to use Wheelbarrow butter, which was white, not yellow like the stuff we were used to, and unsalted. Very refined. It tasted delicious with her Robertson's marmalade. You can still buy it.

It's Dutch apparently, and according to their website 'very special', 'one of life's little luxuries' and can be 'found in leading stores such as Harrods and Fortnum and Mason'. Crikey! It's even posher now than it was then. Narnie would be made up.

Life with Narnie — as far as I can remember, because I was very little when we were there — was secure and instructional. Mum credits her with being a real mother to her; she taught her all the basics of baby care and how to cook and run a house. She also encouraged Mum to look glamorous, just like she always did. Narnie was a widow when she took us in and I reckon she must have been in her fifties. She always looked immaculate, as well as her perfectly coiffed blue rinse she wore gorgeous fitted shift dresses, peep-toe heels and, if the occasion called for it — and she always managed to find one that did — wonderfully elegant hats. She was a real lady, as Mum often told us. Despite her pretensions to grandeur though, Narnie got down and dirty when she needed to: my brother David wouldn't be here today if it wasn't for her practicality. And that's a bit of an understatement. Mum went up to check on David in his cot one night and found him rasping and blue in the face. She didn't have a clue what to do and screamed. Up charged Narnie, grabbed David, turned him upside down and whacked him on the back. He cried and a huge great gobbet dislodged itself from his throat and everyone could breathe again. Especially David. My special brother could have been another cot death statistic — only I don't think they called it that then — had it not been for Narnie's wonderful no-nonsense skills.

Narnie was also a big noise in the hospital's League of Friends, a charity which supports hospital services. Once Princess Alexandra came to open something that Narnie had helped raise money for at the hospital and I was chosen to present her with a bouquet of flowers. Mum had borrowed a camera for the big occasion. And it was big. Narnie's backside, that is. There's Princess Alexandra with a royal beam on her face and Narnie's great big behind obscuring even the merest glimpse of me! That snap has been the source of many laughs at family gatherings when Mum would whip out her photos to show off — the Princess Alexandra one often took pride of place, along with pictures of other occasions featuring all sorts of people that she knew or had met, usually minus their heads. We'd laugh till tears rolled down our faces when Mum looked at the image and said things like, 'Oh, this is David the groom; such a handsome chap,' and then passed it on to us. It *was* the groom, only no one would have known because his head was missing. The image was still in Mum's mind, but unfortunately not in the photo.

Mum was the source of so many laughs and loved nothing more than a good laugh herself, but she suffered with depression from a very young age. She used to call it 'trouble with my nerves'. We'd know when she was on edge because she'd snap at us for nothing, when otherwise she was so loving and warm. Some of my earliest memories are of Mum having violent headaches — *pen tost* she'd say in Welsh — and having to close herself in a dark room. I guess they must have been migraines, but we were too little to know that then. She was terribly, terribly sick all day, and we could hear her throwing up. I was only four and I remember hating those days because my mum wasn't in them, and I missed her. It must have been very difficult for Mum living in a strange place, with her husband working most of the day and all night and with someone else's house as home.

Narnie was brilliant to Mum and Dad, better than any blood relative could have been expected to be, but she was also very domineering and often critical. Mum said, when I was old enough to understand, that sometimes she felt she was going mad with the criticism and being put down and told to do things 'this way, not that'. I don't think Mum had ever been told how valued she was by anyone but her dad; certainly Mam Noddfa, with her eight children to think of, only had time to scold. And so she found herself with all her new responsibilities being watched over and constantly criticised. When I was older and we'd moved out of Narnie's, she was still very much part of our family, so we spent a lot of time with her and I can recall how she'd look at me and say negative things too: 'Look at all those ugly bruises on your legs,' she'd say. 'You're more like a boy than a girl.' Simple words and I'm sure she didn't mean them to hurt, but they did. More than the bruises. No wonder Mum sometimes felt worthless. Narnie also disciplined David and me if we misbehaved — not physically, but with her sharp tongue, sort of pushing Mum out of the equation.

One vivid incident concerned my naughty little brother. His modus operandi when he was angry was to destroy as many of my things as he possibly could. One day after we'd fought and nearly killed each other, Narnie stepped in and separated us. It was quiet for a while so I thought it was all over, until I wandered into another room and saw a killing field of my precious dolls and a wooden puppet that I was fiercely proud of, all dismembered, some decapitated, spread around the floor. I hated him but didn't have the heart to turn serial killer on his toys, so I told Narnie. She didn't punish him at all. So I hated her too. Still, she was soon to get her come-uppance. One Christmas Narnie received a box of her favourite liqueur chocolates. She hid them away for private moments of indulgence. Until David found them. The next time Narnie went to her hiding place to get those coveted, delicious choccies she found all the heads of the chocolate bottle replicas bitten off and the much-prized liqueurs drained from inside by a greedy, inquisitive little mouth. The foil wrappers were tightly screwed up and hiding under the chocolates hoping that she wouldn't notice. She brought them down and displayed the ransacked booty in the hope that the guilty party would come clean. I remember feeling quite smug that both of them, Narnie and David, had suffered. That'll pay them back for my massacred dolls and little wooden puppet with strings (but no legs), I thought.

After around three years at Narnie's, Dad's long hours at work started to mean something. He'd grafted enough for us to be able to move into our own house. It was a new-build three-bedroom semi with a red front door. The builders were still working around us in our cul-de-sac when we moved in. Yes! We lived in a cul-de-sac. It was called St Stephen's Close, and we thought we'd arrived among the Princess Alexandras of this world. I was certain she'd soon be showing her relatives, the Queen and Princess Anne, pictures of that memorable day featuring herself and Narnie's bum. Not long after, the new house was set off by a bright red mini parked on our little drive. Our first house and our first car, and all in a cul-de-sac. All at the same time! We thought we were the luckiest family on earth.

I'm not sure if it was then that I began to realise that Dad's love of work was not that at all. It became clearer that he worked because he had to, but because he loved us and wanted to provide for us. It was then, I reckon, that I first began to get a grip on a lesson that has stayed with me ever since: there is absolutely nothing to beat that feeling of achieving through hard work and discipline. My dad had worked his guts out, he was a stranger to us for most of our early years, but he'd denied us and himself for a reason — he wanted the best for us. No one ever gave him or Mum a penny, but the richest person in all the world could never ever have

49

enjoyed anything near the excitement and the pride that we all felt when Dad's hard graft resulted in our new house and a car. In a cul-de-sac.

We loved it in that little close. We lived in the first new house on the left. You had to walk past a whitewashed stone wall with a lovely old-fashioned wooden gate with one of those round, black, knobbled handles that you grasped and turned to raise the latch, to get to our house. But if you paused and turned that handle, that magical gate opened onto a beautiful garden scented with fluttering sweet peas and orange runner bean blossoms climbing up bamboo tripods alongside brightly coloured dahlias and chysanthemums. That was Mr Aslett's garden. Mr Aslett must have been in his seventies and he lived with his sister Marjorie. Mum went round there not long after we moved in, extracted their life stories from them and came away with a basket full of home-grown fruit and vegetables and a bunch of sweet peas. She promptly set to work with her freshly dug and picked groceries and went back to Mr Aslett's with a steaming blackberry and apple pie. She often cooked for them and ran errands, or sent us round to see if they needed anything. She also befriended an elderly lady in the block of flats opposite our house — she had a very grand name Mrs Voisey-Martin and I loved going to her flat with Mum and just sitting there and listening to them chatting about family, the neighbours and anything else that cropped up. I still have a little white cotton lace-edged handkerchief that she gave me one Christmas — although on receiving it at the time, I remember feeling distinctly disappointed that it wasn't a toy or something sweet to munch on.

There weren't many scandals on that little close really, and Mum got to know everyone. If they needed help or one of her apple pies, she delivered herself faster than an email to assist. It was an idyllic childhood — Mum besotted with us and smothering us with love, our new house, the freedom to roam around without fear and our friendly neighbours. It was a tight-knit community that little close. Next door lived Joy and Frank and their daughter Gillian, whom David and I loved to play with. One day David was playing with Gillian and they were being very unkind to me; I was helping Mum wipe up the dishes and complaining that David and Gillian weren't letting me play with them, when David grabbed a carving knife that I was just about to wrap my tea towel around and told me to stop telling on him. I tried to grab the knife, ended up with the blade in my grasp and nearly whipped my little finger off. Fortunately it remained resolutely attached to the rest of my hand, but it produced an enormous amount of blood, which made David's face drain of his. Good! I'll make the most of this, I thought, and hopefully they'll feel sorry for me and play with me. And they did.

Gillian had a grey rabbit called Dusty and a guinea pig named Buttons. David and I loved playing with them and helping Gillian fill their food and water bowls and change the straw in their hutch. We didn't have the heart to tell her that veterinary science wasn't one of our specialities, having dispatched two goldfish — Emma and I can't remember the other one because it was David's — with rotten fin disease just weeks after going to the pet shop and carefully transporting them home in plastic bags to their new round bowl next to the stereo unit. The stereo unit? It was the thing to have then and no one else on the close had one. Another reason why Dad's job had its advantages. He bought us a single to play on it, 'That Man Batman' by Mike and Bernie Winters, with a version of 'Incy Wincy Spider' on the B-side. I still know every word to both songs. It's probably one of the most special gifts I ever had. If only I hadn't had to share it with my brother.

That's another lesson I'll always take with me through life, I think, and one that I bear in mind for my own children: the more you have, the more you really don't appreciate the wonderful little things in life. I never want my boys to have everything they want because it robs them of the excitement and sense of achievement that saving up pocket money or, later in life, working hard to achieve their goals brings. Because we were showered with love rather than things, we appreciated every little gift we got as though it was the best of its kind in the whole world.

Anyway, gifts were the reason Mum managed to fall out a little with Dusty, Buttons and Gillian, but only because she cared. Gillian's mum and dad were Jehovah's Witnesses, so she wasn't allowed presents at Christmas. Jehovah's

Witnesses must abstain from any of the celebration surrounding the birth of Jesus, as well as everything else associated with the festive season. They are taught that it is part of the false religious system and consider the death of Jesus to be the more important commemorative event. So into this scenario waded Mum with gifts galore for Gillian, because she felt sorry for her being the only child on the close not to receive anything from Father Christmas. She went round, knocked on their door and returned with her tail between her legs and a very frosty, even for that time of year, cooling of relations between us and our next-door neighbours.

So we played more with our friend Gary then. He lived at the top of the round bit of the close and was about the same age as us. Mum was good friends with his mum Pam, who was very 1960s glamorous: big, teased-out blonde hair, short skirts, knee-high boots. As usual I loved listening to the adults talk, and as they were both young mums I heard plenty of stuff that stuck with me while playing on the floor with my Sindy doll and pretending I wasn't taking any notice. They'd talk about breastfeeding and how Pam had had a curry and the baby hadn't slept all night because it was too spicy. No wonder. It was one of those Vesta packet prawn curries; the height of sophistication, it being the first taste of Indian cuisine that anyone had had in the early 1960s. Just add water to reconstitute the chunks of 'meat' and powdered veg and spices. Yum! And they talked of 'Young Wives', a club for happily-marrieds that they belonged to. Oooh, I used to get all my information for facing the world from those young wives chats, while David and Gary played in the garden or with their Meccano sets. One of Gary's more memorable characteristics was that he called poo 'tigers', as in 'Mum, I need a tiger,' or 'Mum, I've done a tiger in my pants.' Don't ask me why, but I still remember Gary vividly to this day — what he looked like, his brown jelly sandals, his grey shorts and his tigers.

Often David, Gary and I would take off down to the bottom of the close, laden with buckets, jam jars and our fishing nets. We'd cross the main road and head towards our little bit of the River Stour, which winds its way through Canterbury before unloading itself into the English Channel near Ashford. We spent hours by the river, just messing around on the banks, swinging from the weeping willow trees and catching all sorts in our nets. We'd have eels in our buckets and a plethora of tiny unknowns flapping around in our jam jars. Then we'd proudly take them home, hope they'd last the night in our bedrooms, before tipping them back into the river the next day. There was an island across one part of the river which my adventurous brother managed to get to, before getting lost on it one memorable day. I was too scared to cross the river in my plastic sandals, so I didn't accompany him on his island adventures. You can't blame me though because, one day as I sat on the riverbank, I leaned back and the earth underneath my back moved. Out scuttled a huge, damp rat, hair greased down on its horrible hump of a back and its vile slimy worm of a tail whipping along behind it. I had to give up my fishing that day and go home snivelling to Mum. I've never quite managed to resurrect my enthusiasm for tales of the riverbank since.

Our best friends Julie and Jane lived outside the close, a walk away on the main road at the end of our little cul-de-sac where the River Stour flowed along the bottom of their garden. We knew them so well because Mum and Auntie Brenda (we called all of Mum's friends Auntie) had been at the Kent and Canterbury Hospital at the same time having me and Julie and they remained firm friends right up until Mum's ability to communicate was whipped away by her Alzheimer's. Julie and Jane had a swing in their garden and loads more toys than us, so we always loved going to theirs and marvelling at all their stuff. They had brilliant birthday parties with pass the parcel, musical chairs and musical statues, and because Auntie Brenda worked at Pedigree, the toy manufacturers which produced Sindy dolls, they always had the latest and best Sindy gear of anyone I knew.

Some Saturday mornings we'd all set off for the Odeon cinema, where before the B-film came on there was a talent contest. I sat there for weeks watching girls the same age as me doing ballet and tap, day-dreaming of the day I'd have ballet lessons too. That day never came because Mum and Dad couldn't afford it, but my Saturdays watching other girls showing off made me determined to get up there myself.

Eventually I summoned up the courage, but only because Julie and another friend, Stephanie, agreed to do it too. We got up and, er . . . sang Mary Hopkins' 'Those Were the Days'. It was a memorable performance: three seven-year-olds, unknowingly tone-deaf and completely out of time with each other and the backing track, having the time of their lives and feeling mightily affronted when the judges made the very rash decision that they were not good enough to win. Still, the cowboys-and-Indians B-movie, then the interval filled with sweets and ice cream, followed by the main film *Oliver!* made our defeat a distant memory in just over two hours. After, we'd often go back to Julie and Jane's so Mum and Auntie Brenda could let out all the gossip they'd had to stifle in the cinema, while we related our experiences to Nan Todd, Julie and Jane's brilliant grandma. She was great fun, with a naughty glint in her eye and always on our side versus the adults. She was warm and funny and interested, a huge contrast to Dad's mum, Grandma.

Yes, our Grandma has a lot to answer for. I loved her and remember mostly her squeals of delight when we did something funny or not too naughty. She'd put her hands up in the air, whoop and laugh, then lower her hands to her knees and look at us with pleasure. But other times Mum would get us all dressed up in our 'best' clothes — the ones we usually wore to the doctor's or church — to walk to the pub and knock at the door before opening time. Sometimes she'd open the door, peep around the edge and say, 'I'm too busy to see you today; I'm doing the doings.' She did the doings a lot. They took up a lot of her time because she was immensely house-proud; in the 'best room', the sofa, armchairs and carpet were covered in thick transparent polythene so that no one could dirty them. The outside loo was spotless with its brilliantly white-painted bumpy stone walls and a toilet seat you could have sat the Queen on without having to line it with toilet paper first. It was also the pub WC, but you could still see your face in that loo seat, no matter how many drunken locals had lurched over it to do their own doings.

Her kitchen was the same — Grandma's cuddly pear-shaped figure was the only clue that cooking actually took place there. She never sat down. One minute she'd be talking with her back to you scrubbing away at something, the next she'd be across the room dusting and then standing on a chair to swat imaginary cobwebs away. I think now they'd call it OCD — obsessive-compulsive disorder. Even when she was ill in hospital, dying of cancer she'd look at the rubber plant in her room and say, 'Can you get Phil to dust the plants please; I haven't had time to do the doings?' I loved Grandma best in her woollen two-piece suits that Mum had knitted her; she had two of them, and we knew that if she had either one of them on she'd spend a little time talking to us — they were too good for dusting in. While David was off exploring for mischief I'd sit and listen to Grandma and all the gossip that she had about the locals and her bingo friends, who she always seemed to be in the middle of some spat with. She dressed up in her black astrakhan-fur-collared coat for bingo, so it was a serious one-upmanship fashion event, as well as a competition. If her friends Queenie or June won, she wasn't best pleased, and I took great delight in hearing her put-down stories of how they'd cooked up some plot which had enabled them to snaffle the winnings.

Most times when we went to the pub we'd be hived away in the lounge bar, which was a small room at the back with dark-patterned wallpaper that looked as though someone had designed it with the aid of a Spirograph set. We sat at a round table, also dark, and I think there was a dark green or red carpet. It was dark and snug. Maybe it *was* the snug; maybe they didn't have lounge bars then. I don't know; all I know is that if we went in the snug lounge bar, it meant that Grandma would sit and talk with us for a while rather than doing the doings.

Sometimes we'd pop into the pub on the off chance and sit in the front bar, where all the locals gathered, mainly men, who eyed Mum up and down. Mum would have a Babycham, depending on what day or what time of the day it was, or a snowball if she was feeling adventurous. I was known as 'Mrs Guinness' because I liked to sip the velvety liquor and show off my foamy moustache. Meanwhile Grandma would be feeding tokens into the fruit machine, pulling down on the big metal lever on the side and whooping with delight as she heard it spitting out cascades of tokens when three lemons came up. I loved going to that pub, with my grandad pulling pints and serving White Horse whisky behind the bar, and my favourite Babycham Bambis looking at me as they lined up on the top shelf in front of the liqueurs. I had a collection of them at home, all different sizes, with one very special giant Bambi which Grandad had got from the suppliers as a huge surprise for me. Grandad was very different to Grandma: warmer for a start — he called everyone 'mate'. He was a gentle man and very popular. He was called Reginald, but, like Dad, most people called him Phil.

One day Grandad made a rare excursion out from behind the bar and came knocking at our door; he'd bought a nurse's outfit for me and a cowboy suit for David. 'Don't tell your mother I've been,' he conspired with Mum. It was a reference to Grandma who'd have been livid that he'd been out and spent money on us, on top of the half a crown they gave us each week to put in our red post box money tins. 'Yer daft ha'p'th,' she would have scolded him in her Yorkshire accent, 'what did you do that for?' I'll never forget that visit; it summed up Grandad's gentle character, his warmth and generosity, which marked his life right until the very end, when his care home staff told me how much they'd enjoyed looking after him because he was such a gentleman. Anyway, that day Grandad's thoughtfulness meant we couldn't have been happier: David as a wounded cowboy — Trampus from our favourite cowboys and Indians TV programme *The Virginian* — and me in my blue and white pinstripe nurse's dress, white apron with a bold red cross on the front and a blue cloak and white cap, tending to his injuries. That was for all of about ten minutes, before we inevitably fell out over something and injured each other.

Grandad had a passion for cars, in particular the old British make Armstrong Siddeley; he had two of them, first a maroon one when we were little and then, years later, a tan and cream one. They were his absolute pride and joy, and we felt we were on a royal visit every time we were allowed, very carefully, to clamber inside and sit upon those immaculate leather seats and gaze at the wood surrounds. Grandma never entered it without wearing her fur-collared astrakhan 'best' bingo coat set off with a hat, like a grand duchess sat there smelling of mothballs with her mouth full of gold teeth. She must have wished the people from her home town of Sheffield could have seen her sitting there, better than royalty, because she'd worked for it. It was like another grandchild in the family that beautiful car, only they made more time for it than they did for us. I watched a repeat episode of *Keeping Up Appearances* while I was cooking one Sunday lunchtime quite recently, with the inimitable Patricia Routledge as the monstrous but lovable snob Hyacinth Bouquet and Clive Swift as the wonderfully put-upon Richard. After the usual series of odd coincidences they'd ended up test-driving a Rolls-Royce, and Hyacinth's face as she sat there looking around to see if anyone had noticed that a Rolls-Royce was passing with her in it, reminded me of my grandma, only she was much too grounded in her Yorkshire mining upbringing to ever be a snob. The cars are long gone now; Grandad sold the cream and tan one when his health started going downhill after he and Grandma gave up life at the pub. The building is still there though, opposite St Paul's church, where Mum and Dad got married, packed full of wonderful memories. It's not called the Duke's Head any more; it's a Moroccan restaurant called Azouma now — at least it was last time I was there.

Mum kept us busy all the time in those pre-school years. We walked everywhere, me beside the pushchair and David in it. David was a gorgeous baby, with big chubby, cuddly bits in all the right places. Outings with Mum always took twice as long as they should have because she talked to everybody: even if it was 'What a lovely day' to a complete stranger, she couldn't pass anyone without saying something. We dreaded bumping into someone she knew because we'd be standing around for minutes on end while she discussed the lives of what seemed like every resident in Canterbury. One time I was in my usual position, tagging alongside Mum with David in the pushchair, and I remember, even though I can't have been more than four, feeling very hurt when she met someone, and the lady, looking at David, said, 'What a beautiful baby.' 'Yes,' Mum replied. 'Little boys are so much more lovable than little girls.' As you can see, that's stuck with me. I often think of it when I'm about to say something that I know might be

61

hurtful to the children. It's amazing how a throwaway comment that seemingly means nothing can stick with a child for ever. Another remark that's lodged in my head was when Mum had dressed me up, sculpted my hair, as she loved to do (sometimes I went to bed with my hair wound around bundles of torn-up white cotton rags, which resulted in a whole head of ringlets in the morning), and was so excited about me that she went to the front door and called Dad, who was on his way out to work, so that she could show me off. 'What *does* she look like?' was Dad's withering response. Not brutal, not callous, probably not meant either, but because he never said anything that was remotely loving to me it's one of the remarks I've gathered up and kept.

It was on one of these trips into town that Mum took me to the optician. She'd noticed that when I was watching *The Woodentops*, *Camberwick Green* or *Crackerjack* I sat very close to the television. Not long before, I'd had measles very badly, with so many spots joined up all over my body, it looked more like a pink padding than a rash; I was almost delirious with it, according to Mum. At one point they were going to hospitalise me, but didn't because Mum said I'd be better off at home with her home-made food. I don't remember much about it, but I spent three weeks lying in my bedroom with the kidney-shaped dressing table and thin, unlined curtains which let the light in. The combination of the light and the measles had damaged my eyes, according to the very sensitive optician, who told me, 'You'll be walking around with a white stick before long if you don't get some glasses.' Nice. So I got my first pair of glasses, a charming flesh-pink set of frames with lenses like milk-bottle bottoms. 'But at least they're not National Health frames, so count yourself lucky,' warned Mum. And so began her battle to try and make me wear them — a habit which to this day I've fought against with a passion, although I have to confess that I do wear them when there's no one around to see me.

One of our regular outings was to head out of town along Stodmarsh Road, where it all became a bit more countrified. Mum used to tell the story of me and my new shoes and how I insisted on wearing them on a long walk even though I hadn't worn them before. 'You'll get terrible blisters,' she said. 'But I want to wear them,' I cried. So I did. And I got really terrible blisters, so much so that Mum had to call in on the local garden centre and ask if they could give us a lift home. They loaded Mum, me and David in his pram, onto the back of a truck and unloaded us all off when we arrived home, which was still Narnie's house at that time. That story was used to illustrate the fact that 'You've always been a little madam' on countless occasions.

Mind you, it's a wonder David and I are here to tell the tale at all. Mum used to take us to another venue up Stodmarsh Road, to a lovely place where there were acres of smooth grassy land and lots of sandpits to play in. One evening when Dad came in from one of his shifts Mum told him how she was going to take us to 'this beautiful place I've found on Stodmarsh Road'. 'Where's that then?' Dad must have enquired. 'I don't know what it's called, but it's great for the children: they can take their buckets and spades to play in the sand, and there's loads of trees and lovely grass for them to play on.' Dad racked his brains to try and think where she'd been taking us on a regular basis for months. Then it clicked. 'You fool,' he said, 'that's the golf course!' Yes, that's right: our mum had been taking us, armed with our buckets and spades, to play in the bunkers of Canterbury Golf Club! 'I wondered why there were so many little white balls about the place,' she said sheepishly. It was a shame because we looked forward to our outings there. Mum, courtesy of her very innocent, unwordly, Welsh country upbringing, hadn't even heard of a golf course, let alone that you weren't supposed to take children to play on them. How we ever made it to our school days is a mystery to David and me.

5

My most frequently recurring dream, apart from losing all my teeth, is of standing in a school cloakroom dressed only in a pink (and I really hate pink) brushed-nylon nightdress while everyone gathers round and laughs at me. The cloakroom I'm standing in is the one I remember from my first school, Kingsmead School in Canterbury. I don't know why I imagine myself in that cloakroom, because I loved that school and did well there. Kingsmead was built in the nineteenth century to 'give instruction to children of the poor without religious belief'. It was designed by an architect whose previous work included the Canterbury Lunatic Asylum; I think some of the dinner ladies must have been former inmates, such delight did they take in upsetting us and baiting us with triple helpings of gloopy, lumpy semolina and bogey-like balls of vomit-inducing tapioca, especially if you said you didn't want any at all. I was five when I went to school, having been at home with Mum all that time. There weren't that many nurseries around then, if any, and anyway Mum wanted us at home for as long as she could. I already loved reading more than anything by the time I went to school, thanks to Mum putting piles of *Woman* and *Woman's Own* magazines in front of me when she dragged me around to friends' and relatives' houses. I can't remember whether

Mum taught me to read or whether I somehow picked it up by myself, but I'd just sit there for hours (and hours knowing how Mum could talk) thumbing through those magazines. 'As good as gold, you were,' she told me.

As soon as I could speak, Dad bought me Ladybird Peter and Jane books. 'Jane likes Peter.' 'Peter likes Jane.' 'They both like Pat the dog.' I loved reading absolutely anything: it could be the side of a cereal box, instructions for something or other or devouring my treasured books. However happy or sad I was about things going on around me, I could escape it all by transporting myself to another world through the pages of my books. I read anything and everything and I credit Dad with that; for making me realise that there was a whole lot more to life than knitting, crochet and the recipes between those much-fingered pages of *Woman* and *Woman's Own*. He told me often — still does, when he remembers — about his mum buying him a set of the *Encyclopaedia Britannica* when he was little and how he found out everything he could ever want to know from those precious books. They made a huge impact on him, and our shelves were always stacked full of Dad's passions, from Dickens' *David Copperfield* and *Oliver Twist* to Churchill's *A History of the English-Speaking People* and *The Rise and Fall of the Third Reich* by William L. Shirer, the first and most successful large-scale history of Nazi Germany. I read bits of that book when I was very young and I couldn't believe it was true, but I loved leafing through them all and smelling their pages, and later, as I got older, hungrily reading every page.

The downside was that Dad saw every reading opportunity as an educational opening, so while my six- and seven-year-old friends were reading *Bunty* and *Judy* comics, with free gifts and tales of 'The Four Marys' and 'Sandra and the Secret Ballet', I was presented with *Look and Learn*. Luckily, Mam Noddfa sent me *Diana* every week from Wales, featuring heroines such as 'Paula With the White Mask'; it was the highlight of the week waiting for that to drop through the letter box first thing in the morning (remember when that used to happen?!) Still, *Look and Learn* taught me handy things like how ice rinks are maintained, all about the Alsatian dog and a heritage of all the Princes of Wales that there ever were. Dad belonged to book clubs for as long as I can remember; there was always some lengthy tome that he'd ordered arriving at the door. I couldn't have known it then, but it turns out that my love of reading was about the only reason I received a decent education. My secondary schooling was appalling; my dad's constant reminder that 'If you read you can learn anything' was the only reason I managed to pull myself out of a substandard education relatively unscathed. Well, him and maybe a little bit of credit's due to Mum's marathon *Woman* and *Woman's Own* coffee sessions too!

All that early reading helped my English at school no end. At Kingsmead I won a national poetry competition run by Brooke Bond Tea, and received a book, *Ebeldum E. Elephant*. I was regularly paraded around the school to read out my stories and poetry to other classes, with the procession ending in the headmaster Mr Dibble's office, where I'd receive high praise. Another time I won a schools art contest and was awarded a book based on the Bible, *Tales of Jesus*. What a little goody two-shoes I was, although even then I had a 'silly streak', as the teachers put it, and liked nothing more than chasing around with a set of twins in my class called Guy and Austin. By the age of six I had a reading age of eleven, so Mr Dibble told me. I wanted to be a doctor from very early on, yet English was my best subject. One teacher, Miss Clark, once said to me, 'Remember me when you're a famous writer, won't you, Fiona?'

I think the only bad experience I had at Kingsmead was when a visiting drama group came in to perform *King Arthur and the Knights of the Round Table* and I wet myself. We were all sitting cross-legged on the floor watching the performance, when I don't know what happened — probably my phobia of using the school toilets — but I couldn't stop it coming and found myself in the middle of a pool of wee. I was mortified and blamed it on Merlin, who had a tin bucket, which I told everyone 'really had water in it'. That incident has stuck in my mind because it was mortifyingly embarrassing, as was the bleak day that I came over hysterical and didn't want to leave my mum. She took me to school every single day and met me with her big beaming smile and warm cuddles. I didn't want to go to school that day and at lunchtime I was still crying, so much so that I had ropes of snot hanging down from my nose. I went to the playground dinner lady and she looked at me and said, 'Stop snivelling.' I tried to hold her hand as I sobbed uncontrollably and she just brushed me away. I felt completely worthless and longed for my mum to come and take me home.

Around that time I started to notice tensions between Mum and Dad. At that age it seemed like a big thing, but looking back as a parent myself now, I can see it was the pressure of Dad's long hours at work and Mum's life as a full-time mum, along with keeping two children fed, clothed and entertained. They'd often argue. I remember us all being around the Welsh oak dining table one day and he lost his temper a bit and rapped her with a spoon. I loved my dad, but he could go from zero to 100 miles of temper in about ten seconds flat. With the hours he worked, it was no wonder really. We didn't often have people round when Dad was around — his life was work and us, he wasn't bothered with socialising at all and I think Mum felt that she couldn't have friends round when he was there. The house was buzzing during the day though, with friends popping round for coffee, tradesmen having a cuppa and any excuse for 'some company and a chat', as Mum would say. Mum was a bit of a soft touch with us, but Dad, with being tired after work, had a much shorter fuse.

One incident which set him off involved my slippers. I've always hated slippers, don't ask me why, but to this day I've never worn them.

Martin and I made a pact before we got married that if either of us ever resorted to wearing comfy slippers we'd shoot one another. But as a child we were made to wear slippers around the house. One night — I must have been about six, I think — I was in my Ladybird dressing gown ready for bed, but without my slippers. 'Where are your slippers?' enquired Dad. 'I don't know,' I lied. 'Get them on,' Dad demanded. I didn't move. 'I said go and get your slippers.' I walked towards the kitchen. 'Hurry up and get your slippers on.' And I still can't believe I said this, but something came over me and I found the words 'Bloody shut up' escaping from my mouth. 'Bloody' was a proper swear word then, as I found out when Dad got me by the scruff of the neck and rendered slippers redundant by lifting me so high my feet couldn't touch the ground.

But life was generally happy at home, buoyed by Mum's unrelenting sunny disposition — most of the time anyway. Even then though Mum had problems and we'd go to see Dr Miles a lot. Sometimes she'd cry in his surgery and I didn't know why. As a child I just knew that something was wrong with my mum but looking back, I've often wondered whether she was homesick for Wales, whether she had clinical depression, or was just bored rigid with the coffee mornings and looking after two toddlers full time. She was on her own now, no Narnie to boss her about and help out. It was around this time that I started noticing her headaches. They were sometimes so violent that she simply couldn't do anything apart from be sick. I don't know what we did — I was too young to remember then — but they were like a monster in the house when they came, those headaches and she simply couldn't deal with them and with looking after us at the same time. I know Mum took Librium and Valium, probably at the same time because I found out on one of my eavesdropping sessions when she had friends round and they were discussing it. It seemed, from their conversation, that most of them were on it, even though at the time I was too young to really understand what it was for. Librium is used to treat anxiety disorders, so maybe that was Mum's problem.

It had been a huge lifestyle change: meeting Dad, giving up nursing and moving to England to get married, followed by two children and all without the familiarity of her brothers and sisters and her mother around her. Dad's parents were busy with the pub, and Grandma was, as you know, very often too busy to even answer the door to us, let alone to help Mum out. So maybe, with Dad working all the hours he could, and with caring for us full-time and it not being Wales, maybe she *was* anxious. We certainly noticed her saying, 'I've got trouble with my nerves,' quite frequently then. Valium (or diazepam as it's now known) was first licensed for use in 1963, so it was a pretty new drug when it was prescribed for Mum. It's also used to treat the symptoms of anxiety and was known as 'mother's little helper' in the 1960s, when it was prescribed in vast quantities by GPs. It became well known for tranquilising a whole generation of 60s housewives and doctors were accused of

71

handing it out like 'sweeties' when all the patient probably needed was a good old chat and a bit of counselling instead of a chemical cosh. I don't know if it helped Mum to cope with life as a stressed out housewife, but I know it didn't stop her headaches which made for very dark days when she had them.

Mum found a lot of comfort in the church. As soon as I was old enough she signed me up to Sunday school, and whether it was her belief, or more likely because it reminded her of her upbringing in Wales, she made sure we attended the occasional Sunday service. She'd put on her 'best' outfit, dress me up, sculpt my hair and off we'd go. I was overawed by the solemnity and grandeur of the church, rapt by the vicar's sing-song voice, even though I didn't have a clue what he was saying, and hypnotised by Mum's gentle singing when we stood for the hymns. Mum took the prayer cushion and knelt down and prayed when we first entered the church and I wondered what she wished for. I still do. Those visits were special — just me and Mum and the privacy of our prayers.

Despite her obvious difficulties Mum always looked out for ways to keep us entertained without spending Dad's hard-earned money or, more importantly her housekeeping allowance, with which she bought all the food and our clothes. Or that's what she was supposed to do, but Mum always had an agenda on the side that we weren't meant to know anything about. She used some of the cash for food and clothing but hived the rest away for a rainy day. So she kept her eye on how much we were eating and made a joint of meat take on so many different guises, it would often last for up to a week. She'd shop around for bargains and we'd get dragged from shop to shop, market stall to market stall, talking to everyone along the way, to make doubly, triply sure that she got value for money. A joint of lamb would appear on Sunday with all the trimmings, including home-made mint sauce from Mr Aslett's garden; then there'd be a few sandwiches with dripping and wafer-thin slices of lamb for tea on the Monday; lamb salad on Tuesday; on Wednesday the carcass was stuffed in a pot along with swede, onions, potatoes and carrots to make cawl, a Welsh hearty stew-like soup with pools of fat from the lamb-remains floating on top, and if there was enough, it would last until the end of the week. All this thrift and ingenious recreation of a cheap joint of lamb several times over meant that Mum could secretly store money away in her savings account. I think she did this to maintain a semblance of independence, so that she didn't have to ask Dad for extra money for her own clothes or little luxuries like furniture.

She took great pride in a brand new teak dressing table which she saved up for and surprised Dad with when he came home from work one night. And I seem to remember a big fuss being made over a rectangular teak coffee table too. She made that housekeeping stretch by her cost-cutting in the kitchen and on the money she spent on our clothes. She loved knitting, and our evenings spent watching the only colour telly in the close were all set off by the gentle *click-click-clicking* of her knitting needles in the background. She knitted everything: jumpers, skirts, suits for Grandma, gloves, scarves, hats, stuffed toys and little matinee coats for friends' newborn babies. And what she couldn't knit, she sewed — tablecloths, cushion covers, dresses for me and my dolls; she was a one-woman industry with her vast range of knitting needles and a Singer sewing machine. One of the most precious items she made me was a suit for my toy panda 'La Da' (because I couldn't say panda when I first had him) after he'd got lost in an orchard during one of Mum's apple-picking summers.

Never one to waste an opportunity to make extra cash, Mum utilised us during our school summer holidays in Kent's apple orchards. We'd be picked up early every morning in a green Land Rover which smelled of oilskin and ripe, moist earth. We bundled in with our bags full of food which Mum had prepared for lunch and sat on the narrow, slippery bench-like humps lining the sides of the back of the old Land Rover and held on for dear life as we were transported into the countryside. Dad was disgusted, as though we were acting like low-bred peasants in our old clothes with bags of food in the back of a rickety, mud-spattered jeep. One summer we spent the whole of the school holidays in the orchards, and when I returned after the vacation our teacher asked us all to describe what we had done during the summer. I wrote about my wonderful adventures apple-picking with my mum and brother, our packed lunch, the portable toilet and the crispy toilet paper. When my parents found out they were beside themselves, convinced that my teacher might think we were a family of itinerant travellers drifting from one seasonal job to another.

But if we were like peasants, we didn't care; we loved those days in the orchards, David and I, getting dirty, playing with caterpillars as they basked in the sun and occasionally helping Mum pick the apples and grade them in metal gauges which measured their circumference. We made dens, we ate the apples with bird pecks in and we played *Dr Who* games in the orchard's only convenience, an old corrugated toilet cubicle which, to us anyway, looked uncannily like a prototype Tardis. The only unpleasant memory I recall is the Izal toilet paper, which smelt of TCP and was so hard it scratched your bum when you used it.

My panda La Da accompanied me to the orchards on many occasions until one fateful day when, in a *Doctor Who*-like incident, he disappeared without trace. I was inconsolable. He'd been with me since birth, and no amount of 'We'll buy you a new toy' could make up for the loss of my La Da. Now we have to fast-forward what seemed like ten years to me, but which in fact was probably more like six months, and a knock at the door one evening. It was the orchard owner. But he wasn't alone. In his hand was a bald, soiled creature with orangey-brown what-looked-like-rust stains all over him. It was La Da! He'd been through the mill since I last saw him; maybe that toilet really was a Tardis and my precious panda had been off on adventures that he wasn't allowed to talk about.

That knock at the door and the return of battered, reeking old La Da, I have to say, was one of the standout moments of my life — not even meeting Donny Osmond for the first time on the *GMTV* sofa matches up to the moment when La Da was returned safely home, if a little bald and smelly, which Donny Osmond definitely was not. That's when Mum came to the rescue, this time with scissors and a needle and thread, and fashioned him a little jumpsuit in mustard yellow. The happy ending didn't last too long though because Dad threw him out, not long after, in one of his getting-rid-of-anything-that-he-didn't-think-we-needed binges, before we moved to Brighton.

6

To a five-year-old and a seven-year-old, Brighton was the most magical place in late 1969, especially the seafront, which then had two piers and was festooned with lights, some in the shape of fountains with tiny lights pouring down their fronds like water and others assuming the shape of dolphins and clowns. Dad had been promoted by Rediffusion and was awarded a brand new company car, a white Ford Anglia estate (so he could transport broken tellies), which went toffee-coloured inside before long with the tar from his ciggies. He'd often pile us all in, get behind the wheel and drive down to the seafront, David and I in total wonderment at the cascading lights, the Royal Pavilion, the sound of the amusement arcades, the smell of candyfloss and toffee apples, Punch and Judy, the aquarium and Louis Tussaud's.

Louis was the great-grandson of Madame Tussaud, whose waxworks of the famous and infamous still draw huge queues in London. Her relative's effort in Brighton wasn't quite up to his great-grandma's exacting standards but David and I loved it. We never actually went inside, mind you, because Mum said it was 'a waste of money, when you can see the real thing on telly', but just peering at the window with its waxwork scene from the 1961 horror film *The Pit and the Pendulum*, featuring a man strapped to a table and a huge scythe moving back and forth, getting lower and lower until it only just missed carving him in two, before starting all over again, was enough to fuel our imaginations for at least the duration of the journey home. Dad, of course, didn't need to peer at waxworks of contemporary icons because this is where he entered the real world of showbiz by attending to Dora Bryan and Wilfred Pickles' TVs. Oh! Hollywood had nothing on it!

We lived in Peacehaven, a flat, unattractive post-First-World-War encampment, devoid of trees, with uninspiring architecture and a bakery with a proper green and gold Hovis sign. Our three-bed semi was set on the corner of Seaview Road and the main south coast road, about seven miles east of Brighton. We could walk to the South Downs and our sea view in five minutes flat, passing the working men's club, where we experienced the joy of our first bottles of Coca-Cola with a straw, on our way down. David and I explored every inch of those cliffs, even sitting on the edge with our feet dangling over if it took our fancy. With the number of arguments and fights the two of us had in those days it's a wonder one of us didn't push the other right over.

We often ask ourselves, 'Where was Mum?' while we were practising our suicidal tendencies overlooking the might of the English Channel. Was she having one of her 'head days' or were our childhood memories so self-centred that they revolved only around us? I think there's a certain element of the latter, but I do know that we definitely wandered off on our own quite frequently. I knew that Mum was always there for us, but I get the impression that, like most stay-at-home mums, she also had a yearning to be independent. She was such a happy soul in the company of her friends. She loved people and cared for them and made friends everywhere she went. She put Dad on a pedestal. The way she talked about him we thought he was King of the World. In fact, such was his stature, we had a sneaking suspicion that he might also be running the country in his spare time.

'Your dad works so hard,' she used to tell us. 'He's such an intelligent man,' and he was and he did love us. He just had a hard time showing it. Dad was respected and loved by his colleagues. 'He's a good bloke, your dad,' they'd tell us, 'a great boss, always on our side.' That was Dad's Yorkshire, socialist upbringing, courtesy of Grandma — he always veered on the side of the underdog, except when it came to matters at home! Mum would sometimes brave the indignation of his wrath and take us to see him at work despite the fact we'd been strictly forbidden to do so. I think she missed him and wanted him to see us all dressed up and looking cute. She loved us so much and wanted Dad to feel the same. I think he probably did, but we don't remember him being a sunny presence in our childhood at all because he seemed to be at work all the time, and when he got home he was too tired for us.

We invariably received a frosty reception when we turned up at Rediffusion, even though to us

Mum was as glamorous as a young Elizabeth Taylor with her miniskirts and knee-high white boots. I was in awe of Dad's workshops: nearly all male apart from a secretary; with broken tellies lined up on huge shelves and that hot smell of soldering irons and electricity firing up the huge inner tubes. Dad was an honourable, very decent man. He wasn't the sort of man who'd go to the pub with his mates; it was work and home, and that was pretty much it. If it hadn't been for Mum he wouldn't have had a social life at all, and he wouldn't have been bothered about it either.

Mum wore a gold heart-shaped locket around her neck with two pictures of Dad inside and a lock of his hair. Most mums would have had their children in the locket, I guess, but because Dad's love wasn't as readily available as ours she wore him close to her heart. I have that locket now, complete with little teeth marks bitten into it after one of David's revenge missions. It wasn't just my toys that got it if he felt unfairly treated, but Mum's jewellery too. Another notable casualty was a double-string cultured-pearl choker with a diamante clasp. It was a treasured gift from Dad, kept lovingly in a grey, satin-lined box with a gold lock. I don't know what sparked his ire on that occasion, but Mum opened up that special box one day and found the string of pearls unstrung. David had pinched a pair of scissors from her knitting bag and snipped the prized baubles asunder. In fact I think those pearls were a gift from Dad when David was born. He was pleased to have a son and bought

Mum two gorgeous skirt suits too.

Being a boy, of course David received certain privileges, for instance there was a definite disparity, in my eyes, between the amount of time I spent in the kitchen wiping up compared to the number of minutes per week that David brandished a tea towel. The ratio was thus: me two and a half hours a week, David two minutes per week. It was a 'girl's job', you see, as was shopping. When we lived in Canterbury Dad took David to dig bait on the beach for fishing trips. Meanwhile, I'd be dragged around town, listening to Mum's ten conversations every ten paving stones, while gathering the weekly shop. Once I got lost in David Greggs, where Mum got her ham and bacon; she was talking as usual and I wandered off, dreaming of unearthing worms at Whitstable or Herne Bay. Sometimes, for a treat, we'd go to the posh department store, bizarrely called LeFevres, and I'd have one scoop of strawberry ice cream in a stainless-steel dish. I ate it as though it was caviar, all the time with a vision of David in my head, thinking how jealous he'd be and how it served him right for not wiping up or shopping.

Mum and I always did our chores on Saturday, and when we got home we'd have crumpets while watching the wrestling on telly with Dad and David. Grandma was a wrestling addict. If we visited the pub while the wrestling was on, we'd hear a commotion coming from the 'best room', where she was shaking her fists and shouting at the referee or egging on Jackie Pallo or Mick McManus. Even more remarkably, she'd taken the plastic wrapping off the telly and the settee so that she could sit down and enjoy it in peace. We didn't ever stay too long when the wrestling was on because the worry that we might dirty the 'best room' spoiled her enjoyment of the fighting. I loved Saturdays. Dad was home at the weekends, and on Sundays we'd always go somewhere in the car, Mum singing beautiful Welsh hymns like 'Calon Lan' or 'Yesityrion' to us in the front and David and I fighting in the back, with Dad's hands jabbing back from the driving seat in an attempt to hit us into submission.

During the week we didn't see Dad at all in Brighton — he gave 100 per cent to every job he did, so much so that every job he started at home never got finished. Our house in Brighton didn't have a stair carpet all the time we were there, and there were incomplete decorating jobs all over the house. Soon Dad became so run-down that he had huge boils on his legs. One, a carbuncle in his thigh, was like a crater, and after weeks of pain but not one minute off work Mum finally persuaded him to see a doctor. He was diagnosed with viral pneumonia, which by then was so severe he was immediately rushed off to an isolation hospital just outside Brighton, which Mum could only get to with the help of several buses and a journey which took over an hour. At first, when Dad was really ill, we weren't allowed anywhere near the hospital. Being children we thought it was quite an adventure — at home in the house, just Mum and us. Until one night when I was upstairs in bed and I heard the phone ring. It was our first phone, so I was always excited to hear it ring and to find out who it was on the other end of the line.

'Peacehaven 4583,' said Mum in a very subdued not even pretend-posh voice. 'Oh, thank God you phoned,' I heard her say, her voice breaking with relief. 'They said you should come,' she went on. And then she broke down in tears. 'How long will it take you to get here?' Then silence and some muffled sounds. 'You need to be quick.' It was only then that I realised that Dad wasn't expected to recover from his pneumonia. When Mum had finished on the phone I crept downstairs and asked, 'Is Daddy dying?' She tried to smile and reassure me, but her emotions wouldn't let her and she cried. After a while she'd composed herself enough to give me some hope, so I went back upstairs to bed and lay in my own little insecurity zone, full of the fear of never seeing my dad again. I felt as though I'd betrayed a confidence, hearing Mum break down on the phone to Grandma, so I felt wretched about that too. 'You need to be quick, you need to be quick, you need to be quick . . . ' over and over it went in my brain, and for once I wished I hadn't overheard one of Mum's conversations.

My childhood memory is a bit fuzzy after that, but I know that Grandma and Grandad got the Armstrong Siddeley out of its salubrious quarters, fired it up and drove along the south coast to Brighton. I don't know who looked after the pub, if anyone did, but I don't think it was a priority. Dad, of course, didn't die, 'the stubborn bugger,' as Grandma sensitively put it, 'no one tells 'im what to do.' Dad told me in later years that when his parents arrived at his bedside, fearing he was breathing his last breaths, he'd told them, 'I'm not going anywhere; I'm not ready yet.' He also told us that he'd had the whole peaceful, almost euphoric, beautiful-white-tunnel-to-heaven experience, without reaching the end to see what was there. He firmly believes that he did momentarily die, and for a man who's not a believer, that's some statement, so I believe him.

Once he'd recovered enough to smile and wave at us, Mum got us all dressed up to go and peer at him through a hospital window. We still weren't allowed anywhere near him; only Mum was permitted that particular honour. I was so proud to see him I almost burst as Mum lifted me up at the window and I could see him in his room, in his pyjamas and dressing gown, smiling and waving. I wished he could see me properly as Mum had bought me a new dress from C & A especially for the occasion. Everyone in the Brighton store knew the ins and outs of Dad's body and his prognosis and anything else they wanted to know, by the time Mum and I had chosen my outfit. I'll never forget that dress: it was a sort of faux-skirt-and-blouse-with-waistcoat affair. I can still remember every detail: white nylon blouse with a ruffle right down the middle joined to a white skirt with red lines forming checks all over it, and with a particularly cool fake belt which had a shiny red ring as a pretend buckle. The whole ensemble was nattily finished off by a waistcoat, which was actually part of the dress. I loved that dress so much that when we got off the bus I almost skipped to the hospital to see my critically-ill father.

7

Life in Brighton was generally good, except I hated school. I went to Telscombe Cliffs Junior School and because I was new I was shunned by most of the girls in the class. There was one girl who was particularly cold to me and I spent most of my time dreading being anywhere near her. She didn't actually physically bully me, just made me feel really stupid, inadequate and really not welcome.

I took to inventing illnesses — Mum and I spent a lot of time at the doctor's with him feeling my stomach and me wincing in what I thought were all the right places when he pressed my tummy. I could see him exchanging knowing glances with Mum, but I figured that if I said I was ill and he thought I wasn't, then my view must form the strongest case, me actually *knowing* I was ill rather than him merely *thinking* I wasn't. Anyway, it got me a day off school, away from those girls who made me feel I wasn't wanted and at home with Mum, who made me feel so wanted. When I feigned tonsillitis, she made me the most comforting, warming concoction of mashed potato, carrot and swede with glorious thick brown home-made gravy, all washed down with Lucozade, which she told me 'cost an arm and a leg'. After a series of visits to the doctor though, Mum got wise to me and my school-avoidance ploys, so I decided I'd better recruit a different professional to my cause. That's when I started faking toothache.

Unfortunately, dentists then were still pretty rubbish: dressed in a scary white coat, they were more like oral master butchers than masters of oral precision work. Mine was based in a beautiful Regency crescent along Brighton's seafront, where, once you entered the heavy panelled door, the stuff of nightmares took place — I should know, I still have dreams about my times there! I had so many black fillings, all mostly in my milk teeth, that when I opened my mouth it looked like a piano keyboard. I had a suffocating rubber mask placed over my nose and mouth and was put under powerful halothane gas — which knocked you out the minute it hit your system — that many times, I almost found it odd going to sleep naturally at night. When he'd finished and I was coming round from the effects of the gas, the sounds and images flooding my head were like a horror film. Finally I was left with a pounding headache and waves of nausea. He was a maniac who, once he'd finished filling nearly all my teeth, decided he'd start taking some out too. As a result, and in a spooky near-repetition of what had happened to Mum, I've been left with only twenty-three teeth, when the average is thirty-two. Nice. But not as bad as a day at school with those girls who made me feel so unworthy.

Eventually though, as I had no more teeth left to fill or take out, I had to face my classmates. Back in the classroom a thaw took place. It happened one day, when the girl who made me feel like I was useless picked me for her general-knowledge quiz team. That nearly made me have a panic attack, 'but I'm useless. I can't. What if I let everyone down?' I repeated over and over in my head. Before, when they were all sniggering and nasty to me, if I was asked by a teacher to answer a question, my guts would hit the floor, my mind would empty and I'd tell myself I couldn't answer, when in fact I pretty much always knew what the correct response was. I did all right though and I ended up being best friends with the girl I once feared the most. We'd cycle back and forth to each other's houses and I learned more from my visits to her home than I could ever pick up from school. She had an older brother, he must have been about fourteen or fifteen, but let's just say that I think his hormones had kicked in — big time.

During the school holidays, or sometimes after school, if we were allowed, I'd grab my new bike — my first ever bike, which I'd had for my eighth birthday, I think — and pedal like fury along the flat Peacehaven back streets to my new best friend's house. We played doctors and nurses, quite innocently at first. She had a brilliant toy medical kit, and we split up her nurse's outfit between us, taking turns to wear the hat. We tended to a whole line-up of dolls who'd all find themselves in emergency situations courtesy of a big red felt-tipped pen, which we'd craft horrific injuries with. We spent hours looking after our patients and there was always a sense of urgency and excitement about our medical activities.

Clearly our emergency surgeries were so dramatic that one day her brother asked if he could join in. Being a boy, he took charge of us. We were the nurses and he was the boss boy doctor. He quickly lost interest in the dolls though and asked us to be his patients. That was fine at first, until he told us to undress so he could examine us. When he looked at us we soon found out that something happened to him. We found out because he showed us his frighteningly huge erect penis. At eight years old and never having seen a willy in that state before, I didn't think too much of it when he asked us to touch it. We laughed and giggled and shrieked with amusement while he went all weird. We figured it was because he was our boss and we were questioning his authority so to us it was pure, innocent fun. I'll never forget how it felt though — like one of those eels I used to catch in the river in Canterbury, only with rigor mortis.

It wasn't long after this that I was fully enlightened about the birds and the bees. Just near our house on Seaview Road was a detached bungalow with a white-painted fence. My friend Lesley lived there with her mum, dad and brothers. She was older than me — I'd say she was ten years old to my eight. You can learn a lot in two years, but I wish she hadn't shared it with me, because I was horrified when she told me how babies were born. She didn't concentrate too much on the conception bits, but the giving-birth story nearly made me want to grab her brother's Chopper bike and ride it over the cliff. 'Girls have to have babies in their tummies and it comes out of their bottoms? Are you sure?' I kept asking with a tinge of horror in my voice.

Mum and Dad had a new baby when we moved to Brighton, but thank goodness it had four legs, otherwise I don't think I could ever have looked the two of them in the eye again. His name was Rufus, a naughty thorough-bred beagle, with a pedigree 'as long as your arm', as Mum used to tell anyone who'd listen. With Dad at work all day, Mum being as soft as a marshmallow and Rufus being a beagle, it was never going to be a cuddly, happily-ever-after story. Rufus was a hound and he had houndish tendencies. He wanted to wander, no matter how many walks he had; never mind if he'd just returned from a gander, he was always ready for the off. Training could have got him in hand before he got out of hand, but that didn't happen. Mum let him out in the garden, where he'd rampage over her vegetable patch and dig and dig frantically under the brick wall which surrounded the garden. He wasn't big enough to jump over, so we thought he was safe in the garden. We should have called him Steve McQueen because he eventually dug deep enough, without anyone noticing his work in progress, to enable him to perform the great escape. He wandered around the neighbourhood wreaking havoc, while we were sent on fruitless searches for our little black, white and tan rogue of a dog. We eventually discovered that he often turned up at his brother Dax's house, a few roads away, from where the two of them would run for miles along the cliff tops, before arriving

90

home at their respective houses looking for food, drink and affection.

We managed to contain him after a while by constantly blocking his tunnels up, but one passer-by who regularly walked past our house really riled him. He barked at people who walked past — nothing out of the ordinary for a male dog on his own territory — but this one guy, a grumpy old git in his fifties, lobbed lighted cigarette butts at him. When he was small he barked furiously, but one day he was so angry at this guy that he summoned up all the energy he could, took a run at the wall and sailed over it. He chased the man all the way down the street, barking at him, but not touching him. The relationship between the two continued until it really became a problem; they hated each other. One day Rufus came back with a huge hole in the middle of his back. It emerged that the grumpy old git had attacked him with a pitchfork and embedded it in his back. Dad confronted him the next time he walked by and he replied, 'You're lucky I didn't kill him.'

In fact, we're lucky Rufus didn't kill anyone, because after the fork incident he became really aggressive. From incidents with the fire brigade, when they were called out to rescue him from the sea after the tide came in and left him stranded, to the day when Mum and I noticed there was a bit of a traffic hold-up on the main road only to find out that the cause was Rufus in the middle of it barking at the cars and refusing to budge, he was an ASBO dog. One day I was in the kitchen with him; Mum and Dad were there, and I bent down to give him a kiss. He went for me, but not just a warning, like he used to, his nose wrinkled up like a walnut and a grumbling sound from his mouth — this time he *really* went for me. He hung on to my mouth and sank his teeth in, making a horrible noise. My dad picked him up and threw him against the back door. The window smashed and Rufus slunk into the corner, ears back, tail between his legs and shivered. I cried with shock, but more because Dad had thrown Rufus across the room. 'It's not his fault,' I whimpered as my mouth swelled and swelled and bled into the tissues that my sobbing mum was plying me with. I looked in the mirror and was shocked; I really thought I'd never have a proper top lip again. It was severed in two just below the middle of my left nostril, and it was so pumped up I looked like the Elephant Man. I was rushed to the doctor and administered with a tetanus injection, antibiotics and goodness knows what else. 'I don't think she needs stitches,' the doctor told Mum, to my immense relief. I spent the rest of that night cuddling Rufus and apologising to him.

When new neighbours moved in, Mum, as usual, wanted to make them feel welcome. She baked them some things and asked them to come round one afternoon for a cup of tea. They were a young couple with a little girl who must have been about two or three. Rufus was in his basket in the sun, chomping on a bone. Unfortunately, while our backs were turned the toddler went over to him and tried to take his bone. He went for her just as ferociously as he had for me and all hell broke loose. That little girl must be in her forties now, but I bet she still has the scar across her mouth. The family were so decent, insisting that Dad 'wasn't to worry' when he intimated that we may have to put Rufus to sleep because he was becoming a problem. So he was let off. For a while.

A lot of our time in Brighton was spent in a haze on reflection, thanks to Mum's visits to our dearly loved neighbour Ann, who lived two doors away. Ann must have been in her sixties then — you can't judge age when you're little, can you? She lived with her brother Fred, and like everyone who met Mum, they absolutely adored her. We often nipped round to Ann and Fred's on a weekend afternoon, Mum, David and me. I can't remember what Mum drank, but David and I were wide-eyed everytime we were invited around and were offered some sort of exotic fizzy pop, the like of which we'd certainly never seen on our Corona lorry — which made weekly deliveries laden with drinks like cream soda, dandelion and burdock, and ginger beer. This drink was the same golden-brown colour as fizzy apple, but with a kick to it. We'd have a couple of glasses and start giggling hysterically, slurring our words and stumbling around in a woozy haze. Mum and Ann gossiped on and on while we drank more and more. David and I, at six- and eight-years-old respectively, were necking cider on a regular basis we eventually discovered. Dad, increasingly puzzled at our strange behaviour every time we returned from Auntie Ann's, started asking questions. One night, as he tried to manhandle our wobbly, bendy yet heavy with drunkenness little limbs up the stairs, while shouting, 'And don't forget to clean your teeth,' he cottoned on. 'That's not fizzy apple they've been drinking, it's bloody cider!' he exclaimed. It was a golf-course moment: Mum, never having heard of cider, couldn't possibly have known that she'd been illegally plying her children with alcohol.

8

Sometimes Mum got fed up with us all, and I don't blame her, but I don't think she meant to intentionally lose my brother. David had a really good friend called Gordon, the son of Mum's friend Joan, who lived down the road. We had sleep-overs at Auntie Joan's if Mum and Dad went out in their Ford Anglia to a works do, which wasn't that often. So when David said he was going to call for Gordon one day and then didn't come back, Mum assumed that he was at Joan's house. I don't know which way round it happened, but clearly one of them phoned the other to find out where one or other of the boys was, and when they both came up with a negative answer, all hell let loose.

They'd been out since about ten in the morning, and it was tea time and they'd not even returned for food. I remember feeling Mum's frantic vibes as she flew down towards the cliffs and started madly searching along the gorse- and bramble-dotted hills and falls furthest away from the cliff's edge. We'd turned left at the bottom of the road, but they could easily have gone right and walked along to the steep steps leading down to the rocky beach and the incoming tide. We didn't dare look over the cliff edge in case we saw what we didn't want to see. It was getting dark and we returned home, and then I knew it was really serious because Mum phoned Dad at work.

I'm not sure if she got the usual earful about 'I've told you not to phone me at work' or not, but Dad arrived home in a black mood, obviously livid that Mum had managed to lose a son. They called the police and they sent out a search party. They turned left too and must have looked away from the cliff edge as well, among the snaggy blackberry bushes where Mum and I spent hours picking bowls full of the juicy black jewels towards the end of summer and the beginning of autumn for her delicious blackberry and apple crumbles. But we didn't feel hungry that evening; we'd lost our appetites altogether with the worry and the visions of the cliff's edge and two little six-year-olds out on their own all day. Even though I fought with my brother, even though he still mounted evil battles against my toys, and even though I knew he'd been smoking cigarettes and hiding some in his bedroom for a big twelve-year-old boy called Tony whom he was trying to impress, I didn't want him to be found all broken and limp, like one of my toys, washed up on the beach. After what seemed like an eternity the police phoned, said they'd found the two of them camping out in an old air-raid shelter, where they'd stockpiled blackberries, clearly intending to spend the night in their new home, oblivious to the hell they'd put their families through.

The police got us all together and gave the naughty renegades a grim talking-to and that was the end of that. I think I was about the only member of the family who didn't go missing. What with Dad at work all day, Rufus rounding up cars on the south coast road and David squatting in abandoned Second World War refuges, I half expected Mum to take flight one day too. And then she did.

It must have been in the Christmas school holidays as it was on or near my birthday. I was either celebrating my eight or ninth and David and I were having one of our fights. It was a big one, which involved most of the utensils for the coal fire. The deciding blow came from the iron poker, which David whacked me around the head with; I almost passed out and so did Mum. Right out the door. I think Mum had phoned Dad to say she'd had enough of us and she'd been told not to bother him at work, so she'd had enough of the lot of us. She went, with a bag, so we knew it was serious. We ran after her to the bus stop just two minutes up the road from our house, screaming for her to come back. I had a lump the size of an egg thumping away on my forehead from where David had whacked me with the poker, but the pain of Mum's imminent departure was tearing my heart apart. When the green-and-cream-liveried Southdown bus braked into the stop she hopped aboard and sailed off down the south coast road towards Brighton. We couldn't believe our eyes. Maybe she'd had one of her 'tight in the head' days when she wasn't vomiting but was just deeply depressed, and had decided she needed to get away from it all. David and I always look back on that day and feel it was a pivotal event, the day when warm, sunny Mum on whom we relied for everything, especially our happiness, snapped, and we felt that all was not right with the world.

I can't recall her returning, only the leaving, but when Mum came back she told Dad she had to have a bit of a life. So she applied for a job at the Butlin's Ocean Hotel in Saltdean. Housed in a 1930s art deco building, this wasn't your common-or-garden Butlin's holiday camp; this was the Ocean *hotel*! It was popular with honeymooners, and Billy Butlin himself said it was one of the best investments he'd ever made. Mum, dressed in her knee-high boots, with back-combed hair and a minidress, had acquired a job as a barmaid there. She worked in the evenings when Dad got home from work. She loved it, and I adored hearing her stories of the other workers, the guests, the exotic tipples and food, and the customers who bought her drinks or left big tips. To me it sounded like she was going to Hollywood of an evening.

There was friction between Mum and Dad over the Butlin's job. I wonder if he was jealous that she took such pride in her appearance before going out. Or if he thought he should be the sole provider. I just picked up on the fact that he didn't exactly endorse her surge for independence. Maybe she was receiving male attention and enjoying it after years of dad's work and two children. Who could blame her? Even more exciting for a nine-year-old's ears was the fact that Mum came home talking about the new international language, Esperanto, which some of her colleagues were learning at the time. Maybe it was Butlin's policy — who knows? But I was fascinated to hear of this exotic-sounding invented language designed to foster world communication and understanding. I truly thought that Mum was becoming a very important figure on a world stage. And then she gave the job up.

I don't know whether Dad put a stop to it or whether she decided that working at night wasn't compatible with family life, but that was that, and the glamour went out of our little lives as quickly as it had come in, and a little piece of my imagination which had conjured up an unreachable, glamorous world all contained within those Ocean Hotel walls, died along with it. Not long after, Mum got a job at the Peacehaven Hotel. This time she worked during the day, and if we were at home when she was working I loved nothing more than riding my bike down Seaview Road towards the cliffs and then cycling along the downs to visit Mum during a break. I loved the sound of the sea lashing below and the wind in my hair and the prospect of seeing Mum smiling behind the bar and bringing happiness to all who encountered her. Sometimes I'd get a Coke in a glass bottle with a stripy straw, and if she'd done a bit of over-time that week, I'd get crisps too. It was magical, being ushered behind the bar, sipping and crunching, and being introduced to all the locals. I was so proud of Mum, you'd think she owned the place. She needed that recognition outside of us and Dad and the house and she loved earning her independence money.

Mum wrote regular letters to Mam Noddfa and all her relations back in Wales to keep them up to date with her news, although none of them ever ventured as far as Brighton. Canterbury wasn't that far along the coast from Brighton though, and one day we received a royal visit in the shape of Grandma and her sister, my dad's Auntie Flo. When the Armstrong Siddeley rumbled up outside, Grandma perched high up on the leather seats and Auntie Flo in the back, with Grandad behind the wheel like Parker to Grandma's Lady Penelope, it was an event worthy of our shrieks of excitement tinged with embarrassment at the showiness of it all. When Grandma's astrakhan coat eased into view as she climbed out of the car, we knew it was a special event. From her humble hard-working background as the daughter of a Yorkshire coal miner who was killed in a pit accident, to the army wife often left alone to raise three children, to the leather passenger seat in the Armstrong Siddeley was quite a journey.

I loved Grandma and I mostly remember her smiling and laughing, but Mum and Dad talked about her in terms of her coldness and how she 'never showed any love'. I don't know, maybe she didn't show affection, so we didn't expect it, but she was my gran and I adored her. She was difficult though, and I began to see what Mum and Dad meant when she came to stay. Mum had dug up half her vegetable patch for The Visit. She'd chopped and baked, and crafted them into pies, bakes, soups and roasts. She'd whipped up eggs and flour and butter and sugar to make butterfly cakes, rock cakes and Welsh cakes. The kitchen resembled a royal pantry and

David and I were in our element.

We took lots of strolls to walk off all that food, so one day while Dad was at work and David was somewhere he probably shouldn't have been, we set off for the cliff tops. Mum and Auntie Flo, arm-in-arm, chatted and smiled and greeted passers-by with a cheery 'Nice weather . . . ' while I skipped along beside them. Grandma wasn't quite as carefree. 'Saying hello to strangers all the time, what's wrong with you?' she chivvied as we all meandered along. Mum was dog-mad and so, it turned out, was Auntie Flo, so every five minutes they'd stop and pat some dog or other and chat to the owner. Grandma spluttered and sighed and walked on in disgust. By the time we got home I sensed they'd all fallen out. Or rather, Grandma had fallen out with Mum and Auntie Flo because they'd enjoyed exchanging pleasantries with strangers and their dogs. So Grandma went back home to Canterbury, and in 1971 it turns out we left Brighton too and moved along the coast to Southampton.

9

Dad was champing at the bit for another job and promotion, and both came in the form of Telefusion, a very successful TV rental and retail company in the 70s. It was a new-kid-on-the-block rival to Radio Rentals, Rediffusion and Granada, and all Dad's hard work paid off when he secured a job as area service manager. A manager! My mum was puffed up like a pincushion. 'Of course now that Phil's in management . . . ' formed the beginning of nearly every sentence she uttered. We moved into a tiny new-build three-bed semi with an integral garage to the right of the front door. It was £7,000. There were four new semis and a detached house built on the end of an already established close. Another close! Only this one was called a court! Rylands Court, a fitting place for the Armstrong Siddeley and its royal occupants to park up, I thought. We had to name the house as the other houses were already numbered, so Mum and Dad chose Newgale after the beautiful Pembrokeshire beach where they had done a lot of their courting twelve years previously. Annoyingly, it was often called Newgate by various postal correspondents and chirpy postmen, who clearly thought it was hilarious that we'd apparently named our abode after the famous London prison where felons were held before being executed at Tyburn.

So it was time for another new school and to break into a group of strangers who'd already made their best mates and didn't particularly want to accommodate the 'new girl'. Aldermoor Middle School was situated about half a mile's walk away from our house, in the middle of a large council estate. There was a green uniform, and Mum had knitted me a bottle-green woollen skirt. All the other girls had cloth ones, pleated or straight, but I had a woollen skirt! God bless Mum, those knitting needles had been clicking away like mating crickets in order to produce that skirt. But being the *new girl* in a *knitted skirt* made me stand out like, well, the new girl in class in a skirt made of wool. I loved my teacher, Mr Gardener, a slim, gentle man with dark hair cut in that sort of fringy, bowl-cut, Beatles style and a neatly trimmed beard. I was bright, and he really encouraged and looked after me, but in the playground it was misery, with girls ganging up on me and alternately recruiting me then breaking friends with me, and teasing and bullying. I sought refuge with the boys — so much more straightforward — and played football with them.

David was suffering too and he became very upset, hated school and often feigned illness so he could miss it. We were both the subjects of fights in the playground and, more chillingly, after-school. It would start off by one of the pack leaders in the class being vile to me; then I'd answer back and she'd say, 'Right, there's a fight after school.' My guts hit the floor and I couldn't think of anything else for the rest of the day. When the bell rang for the end of school I'd hope they'd forgotten and file out as usual, hoping for the best. But they never forgot. It was their chance to be the centre of attention, to be the hero, to wreak revenge on someone else for the rough treatment meted out to them at home. I regularly arrived at the back door with bleeding knees, cut elbows and scratches, but was always too ashamed to tell Mum that I'd been beaten up.

Once they found my glasses in my basket, which was the fashionable thing to sling over your arm for school then, and ridiculed me. I always carried them to school so that Mum would think I was wearing them, but I never did. I didn't have the guts to. It was bad enough being new and not liked without suddenly appearing a freak in glasses too. I didn't want to worry Mum with my troubles. She'd say, 'As long as you're happy, I'm happy,' so I didn't tell her when I wasn't. Eventually though just like my experience at Telscombe Cliffs School in Brighton, I managed to fit in, and the bullying stopped. The awful thing is that when another new girl joined a while later, I turned from bullied to bully so that my new 'friends' wouldn't reject me again. I'm ashamed to say we made that girl's life a misery, just as they had once done to me, although I couldn't bring myself to hit anyone.

Soon I was in the netball team, the rounders team, the athletics team, and I played the treble recorder and the trombone. I loved that trombone — the pleasure I got from moving that slide up and down to form recognisable tunes was immeasurable. A group of us formed a dance troupe and performed our routines at the school disco — I remember a particularly spectacular effort to the sound of Sweet's 'Wig Wam Bam'. I loved sport, mainly because it was a way to earn the respect of my toughie mates. I wasn't brilliant, but I was good and stayed late at school most nights to practise something or other, particularly if Mr Glue was around. Mr Glue was everything a teacher should be — patient, kind and encouraging, he turned me into a confident high jumper despite my knack of telling myself, 'I can't do it.' At school open evenings Mum and Dad were told that I definitely had the ability to fulfil my dream of becoming a doctor. 'She can achieve anything she wants to,' my teacher said, 'as long as she guards against a certain silly element that's crept into her behaviour.'

In the classroom my behaviour was causing concern. Not that I was a delinquent or anything, far from it — I'd have had Mum and Dad to answer to for that — but because I was 'easily led', as my teachers put it. They knew I was bright, they knew that my parents were decent and honourable, so they were worried that I seemed to be going off the rails a bit. What I had done was adapt my behaviour to fit in, to stop the bullying. What was I supposed to do? But suddenly I found myself being called into the head's office for the cane, which he rapped across my hand with a creepy delight. It was a pointless punishment because it elevated me in the eyes of my mates. I'd think of Mum, swallow the tears and go back to class, all bravado, to enjoy the attention of an audience for my stinging hand. I was growing up that's all, and, like Mum and Dad, had a fiercely independent streak.

I really got into fashion, which had started in Brighton with hot pants and Marks and Spencer £2.99 flared crimplene trousers, and gradually gained momentum so that by the age of eleven Ben Sherman shirts, cheesecloth tops, Oxford bag trousers, loons (jeans with really huge flares) and platform shoes had become part of my 70s fashion repertoire — the very best of the very worst decade of fashion that ever there was. And then in the summer of 1972, there was Donny Osmond, the first boy I ever loved. The lyrics of 'Puppy Love' perfectly summed up that awakening of sexuality and of seeing boys in a different light: 'And they called it Puppy Love, Oh I guess they'll never know.' Oh! The heartache. The pain.

Since my horrific conversation with my friend Lesley in Brighton, when she'd told me how babies were made, I'd not heard a word about the dreadful 'facts of life', as it was very delicately called then. I'd already put 'it' on hold as something I wouldn't need to worry about until I was an adult, and as I'd listened to Dad's advice about not getting married, I didn't want children anyway, so I'd put 'it' on hold pretty much indefinitely. Mum hadn't thought of broaching the subject with me; it was too *ach y fi* for utterance in a respectable house like hers. I

106

don't know what my friends had seen and heard in their homes, but I was as naive as a spring lamb, a ten-year-old gambolling around thinking that life was one big, soft, sunny day. Nothing could prick that rose-tinted view, not even the day when I heard Mum offering my services by saying. 'You need the dogs walked? I'll go and get Fiona.'

So she did and I reluctantly took them, two Jack Russells, a boy and a girl, who after a bit of back-climbing and general interference from the male dog got stuck together halfway down the road. I didn't have a clue what was going on, but I suspected it wasn't altogether above board when I dragged them round to our front door, still joined together, showed them to Mum, and she exclaimed, 'Ach y fi. Dirty mochyns,' before throwing a bucket of water over them. She didn't explain what had gone on, but I had a feeling that it was something I should know about, but didn't like to ask.

Maybe the world wasn't as rosy as I thought — as I was about to find out when, in my last year at middle school, I was constantly subjected to the perverted pleasures of a male teacher who delighted in calling me up to his desk in front of the class, where he'd tell me to bend over, no matter what I was wearing, and hit me on the backside with a black plimsoll or a ruler. I can see his clammy red face now and the look of menace laced with enjoyment that lingered upon it. I despised him and his teacher's authority which gave him licence to do what he liked. It was decided that I was going off the rails, and that for my own good I was to be moved into another class, where, I was told, there was a 'better class of person'. I didn't know what they meant by that then, but it was a gentler environment and I had so much more in common with the girls in my new class.

I settled in and became firm friends with a group of three girls, one of whom was to become my best friend for life. Her name was Debbie and she lived in my road. I hadn't encountered her before because I was so busy trying to impress the girls who bullied me that I couldn't see beyond it. It was like breathing in fresh air where before there'd been smog. Mum was made up that I'd got someone from a 'respectable family' as a friend, and the only low point was when Debs and I went to call on a boy from our year that we liked. His name was Bobby and we dared each other to go and knock on his door. Unfortunately his mum answered, told us he wasn't in and sent us packing with our tails between our legs. We thought that was the end of it, until Mum bumped into Bobby's mother, who delighted in relating our post-tea-time misdemeanours to disapproving ears. 'How dare you be so forward', she scolded me when I came home from school. '*Ach y fi*, calling for boys at your age!' Let's just say it put me off Bobby.

Anyway, I was too busy for all that now I was a working girl. My fashion longings and Mum's saving-for-a-rainy-day mentality didn't fit. I wanted clothes because they were trendy, not because they were a necessity. Much to my consternation though, Mum's sewing machine and knitting needles were always poised, ready to save on 'ridiculous' shop prices. One of her proudest accomplishments was a white crimplene confirmation dress with little daises sewn around the collar, sleeves and hem, which I duly wore for my official introduction into the Church of England. It was a pair of yellow sling-back platforms with a green apple on the side though, that signalled my breakaway from Mum's measly fashion budget. 'If you want all these clothes, then you'd better get out and earn some money to buy them with,' she chided. Then, in a repeat of Mam Noddfa's employment scheme for her, she went and hired out my services without telling me. 'I've got you a paper round at the local newsagent's,' she announced, 'every day after school for seventy-five pence a week and early Sunday mornings if you want to earn extra. You start next week.'

And so began my road to financial independence. I learned, aged eleven, that if I want something I know the only way to get it is to work for it. It's a lesson which has stood me in good stead for life in general and for everything it's chucked at me. I took on that paper round with a vengeance, delivering the *Southampton Evening Echo* every evening, getting up at 6 a.m. every Sunday and then progressing to delivering the daily newspapers in the morning too. The sense of earning my own keep was addictive, but more important was the pride I took in doing a good job. I was becoming a mini-Dad, always at work, probably illegally, and defining myself by how good I was at my job. I loved gossiping with the customers and hearing of local scandals and rivalries, and I took great pride in delivering their papers on time. Mum was delighted, not least because I bought a lot of my clothes from her Brian Mills or Great Universal catalogues. I spread my payments over forty-eight weeks if it was a big item, and Mum delighted in receiving the cash after I'd got my wage from the newsagent's. What a curious change of attitude — my mum, encouraging me to spend money? I puzzled over that one for ages until I found out she got commission on her orders. I eventually squeezed a Littlewoods Pools round into my schedule too, so I could pay for haircuts and stuff I didn't want to ask Mum for. It was just one night a week, so it was a good fit and if I couldn't do it Mum would stand in and keep my pay for herself, of course!

She took pride in the fact that she didn't 'ask your father for a penny', which wasn't strictly true as he paid the mortgage and all the bills and gave her housekeeping, which she eked out to the max so there'd be some left over to stash away in her savings account. She bought her clothes with her own money though, which she earned from doing part-time work that fitted in with our school day. To my complete horror she worked as a dinner lady at my school for a while, but thankfully she was in the infants' playground so I could pretend I didn't know her, which was hard at times when she specifically sought me out to give me a hug. Luckily she found a more lucrative post on the tills at Sainsbury's before long, and I could relax back into my deteriorating behaviour.

★ ★ ★

Mum had a very good friend called Joan, whom she'd known when they were both growing up in Wales. Joan was now living in Hampshire too, so they regularly met up and shopped and talked and shopped and talked and talked. I often went with them on their shopping/talking trips, taking great delight in their reminiscences and their professional combing of every inch of Southampton's department stores. One particular outing was different though — they were acting conspiratorially, whispering things to each other, and then we ended up in Mothercare, where Auntie Joan guided Mum around the baby things. What? I thought to myself. No, she can't be. Auntie Joan had grownup children and a little girl who was born years later, surely she wasn't having another baby — not at her age; she must be at least thirty-eight!

It slowly dawned on me that this trip wasn't about Auntie Joan at all. My mum was pregnant! And she was forty! Ugh! Ugh! Ugh! Ugh! How was I going to tell my friends? How bloody embarrassing. How disgusting. How dare they! My stomach churned and I hated Mum and Dad for obviously being fed up with David and me and for wanting a baby to replace us in their affections. But I really resented Mum for telling Auntie Joan and for not telling me. Did she think I was stupid or something? How could she

111

possibly drag me around Mothercare, giggling with her friend and treating me like a stranger by not telling me? Maybe she hasn't let me know because she isn't pregnant, I prayed as we went to the till, and Mum and Joan hatched a plan which involved Joan paying so that I wouldn't twig. I felt worthless, being excluded from Mum's big secret. I went quiet and she must have known, but she didn't say.

At home, my fears were confirmed by Mum's new pill-popping habit. 'Have you got a headache?' I asked when I saw her taking them, praying that she had, even though it would be a horrid day for all of us. 'They're iron tablets,' she replied, 'because I'm anaemic.' I knew that pregnant women took iron supplements and my heart sank to my stomach. It was an almighty blow, which would have been easier to bear if Mum had taken me into her confidence. Instead I accused her with a hostile tone: 'You're pregnant, aren't you?' I could have hit her when she smirked and said, 'How do you know?'

I ran off to my room and she took it all the wrong way, not realising that I was hurt that she hadn't told me, more than that I was upset that she was pregnant. I felt discarded, thrown off, unwanted and I reacted by treating her with disgust. How was I going to tell my friends? People will think it's mine. Oh God, what if it's a girl and it's a really girly girl like Mum wants, not a boyish girl like me? I wanted to run away. I don't remember Mum and Dad ever gathering David and me together and telling us we were to have a new brother or sister, and I couldn't help recalling that conversation with Lesley and the images it conjured up in my mind, and what should have been a joyful family occasion was not, because of Mum's screwed up notion of 'the facts of life'.

I still hang my head in shame at one episode in particular during that ground-shaking episode. One day towards the end of school I looked out of the window and saw Mum waiting at the gate with Rufus, our naughty dog. 'Oh my God,' I muttered to myself as I eyed her bulging stomach, 'how can she come and meet me looking like that?' The bell went and I did my best to disappear into the bundle of children heading for the gate. 'Toots,' I heard her cry — it was her pet name for me. 'God, why's she calling me that bloody name too?' I looked to one side and saw her beautiful, smiling face, so thrilled to see me. And I walked on, pretending I hadn't seen or heard her.

Thankfully, as the months passed, David and I got used to the fact that the little family unit we'd grown up in for eleven years (in my case, nine in his) was to undergo an irrevocable change. We weren't exactly ecstatic about it, but there was nothing we could do but accept it. I was worried about Rufus too: how was he going to feel, having his nose pushed out by a baby? We were all to find out on 28 December 1972, when my lovely little brother Andrew was born.

I was working at the newsagent's — they'd offered me work in the shop because I'd done so well on my numerous paper rounds — and I nipped out to use the phone box at lunch time to

113

see if there was any news. I phoned Southampton General Hospital and they told me Mum had had a baby boy. I phoned Dad, who was at work as usual, and then went back to the shop, told them, went shopping for some flowers and a baby hairbrush and got the bus to the hospital. Mum cried when she saw me, 'like a little woman you are,' she sobbed as I stared at my gorgeous brother, who, weighing in at over nine pounds, wasn't the scrawny baby I'd expected at all.

We loved him, but that didn't stop David and I doing everything we could to end our baby brother's life before it had begun. In the first year we regularly bundled him into the Ali Baba laundry basket before rolling him downstairs in it; we chucked him over the back of the sofa, where he landed on his head and emerged with a bump the size of a large free-range egg on his forehead; and I once pinned his willy to his towelling nappy after offering to change him and wondered why we couldn't stop him screaming. As ineptly as they'd handled telling us about the pregnancy, Mum and Dad managed to perform a masterclass in how not to introduce a dog to a new baby. When they arrived home with Andrew, Rufus jumped up to greet them and Mum pushed him off, while Dad took him into the kitchen. He'd been their baby and now he was being rejected; I knew how he felt and went to cuddle him.

Sadly that very small action had an almighty consequence. Mum's constant pushing Rufus away whenever he approached the baby led to

Rufus hating that child. He couldn't be left alone with him and became more and more aggressive towards everyone apart from me. Mum and Dad said they were going to have to 'let him go' and they advertised for a 'good home'. I decided to run away with Rufus, so off we went on the bus and into town. We walked around and we sat in a park, where I cried all over him and vowed I wouldn't let him go anywhere. And then it got dark, the trees looked scary, and I didn't have much money despite all my jobs, so we both went whimpering home. When a farmer came to the door, having answered our advert, Rufus ran to the door and bit him. 'That animal needs bloody putting down,' he yelled.

One day after finishing my paper round, I arrived home and asked, 'Where's Rufus?' Mum was crying. 'He's gone,' she sobbed. 'Gone where?' I asked, even though I knew. 'He's gone to sleep. Dad took him this afternoon.' Yet another momentous occasion they'd neglected to include David and me in. When Dad came in his eyes were tear-filled; I'd never seen him express real emotion before — anger yes, occasional laughter, but never tears. It was like losing part of the family, losing Rufus, and it was their fault and I didn't even have a chance to say goodbye to him.

10

I left Aldermoor Middle school with a brilliant report, A's for everything, and the promise of a bright future. They obviously hadn't heard that I was destined for Millbrook School. For a girl whose parents hadn't ever enlightened her on how she'd got here in the first place, Millbrook was an education. The first time I heard about blow jobs I thought it was a technique artisans used to make little glass animals. I used to collect them, so I knew what I was talking about. I didn't have a clue. I thought I was hard and worldly because I smoked Sovereign ciggies (twenty-three pence for a pack of ten); I hated them, but it impressed my friends so I smoked them until I became addicted and sported attractive nicotine-stained fingers. Surely no one could be more worldy than that? 'I started smoking when I was eleven,' I boasted in an effort to be the coolest thing anyone had ever encountered. But my new contemporaries had 'done' smoking and they'd done a lot of things I'd never even heard of.

You're dealing with a girl here who had to borrow her first bra from a friend and wash it in secret, because her mum was too embarrassed to talk about anything to do with bodies and what you did with them. Yet I found myself dealing with twelve-year-olds who'd seen and done and talked about things I didn't even know the name of. Boys came on to me and I didn't know what to do with them. Sometimes a gang of them would 'bundle' me on the way home and I'd feel their fingers everywhere. One guy walked me home, pressed me against a wall, then moaned and moaned until I felt a wet patch on my skirt. I didn't know what had happened; I certainly hadn't participated. It was traumatic, but it seemed to be what happened, whatever 'it' was. Girls in the fifth year were pregnant, boys were in borstal, and the whole school seemed like a hotbed of carnal curiosity and knowledge. One boy had the horrific habit of getting hold of cats then holding them by their hind legs and thrashing them against brick walls until their heads smashed. It was overwhelming. If only I could have gone home and talked to Mum and asked what they were all talking about, and doing and threatening to do. But she wouldn't have known about some of it either, and even if she had she wouldn't have talked about it because her experience in a field in Wales when she was an innocent girl had sullied her dealings in anything to do with 'that'.

Amid this deluge of learning, the actual learning took a back seat. I was in the top set for everything, but that didn't mean much in a school which struggled so much with discipline and lack of ambition. We were supposedly the elite of the school, yet our maths classes consisted of walking in, being given an exercise book and told which pages to work on, before the teacher walked out and returned at the end of the lesson to go through the answers, when she hadn't explained how to tackle the questions in the first place. I gave up my trombone lessons because I was called a geek; I gave up sports because I was embarrassed by my body and didn't like changing in front of everyone else; I just gave up really. There wasn't much point in trying to learn when most of the pupils were set against it and their parents didn't care.

Mine did, and the teachers knew it, so if I misbehaved they'd call Mum into school. 'Not my Fiona, she wouldn't do that,' Mum would say, her voice breaking with emotion and disappointment. 'Tell your mother what you've done,' the deputy head would say. I'd hang my head in shame, afraid to meet my mum's broken gaze and say, 'I did do it, but I know it was wrong.' The teachers leapt on me because they knew I would have to answer to my very decent mum and dad. It's what dragged me through that school still able to achieve despite the lack of education; in the end I had to answer to them and to myself and I always kept a bit of me back to use when I left that school.

Thank goodness my best friend Debs was there with me. We'd call for each other every morning and walk home from school for lunch in the middle of the day. It was a refuge being at home for a little piece of the day with Mum and her 'dinners'. She loved cooking, but we didn't have a recipe book in the house — she experimented and always came up with inventive dishes. One of my favourites was a fish casserole which she made with condensed mushroom soup, cheese, leeks and fish, served up with buttery mash and peas, which I loved to help pod. 'Why would anyone buy frozen peas when you can get fresh ones for a quarter of the price?' Mum was one of the first people I knew to serve up spaghetti Bolognese or chilli con carne; we were already used to her curries on Mondays containing the leftovers from the Sunday roast, and all of it such good value! And then the freezer moved in.

What an occasion that was. Mum had saved up the bits of housekeeping money left over from her thrifty shopping habits and selected a sparkling new fridge-freezer which now dominated our tiny orange kitchen. Freezer sales increased dramatically in the 70s and they were right up Mum's street with their sales push of being an economical way of storing home-made food. She was in her element and that freezer took over our lives. Before long we'd get used to Mum arranging her day around the freezer, organising deliveries and devising recipes. Often a whole sheep or half a pig, all chopped up and complete with nostrils, ear, head and trotters, would turn up and Mum would get down on her knees and lovingly arrange and re-arrange those poor dead animals according to their species and body parts. Nothing went to waste; we'd have joints of pork or lamb from the freezer on a Sunday, but if Mum had really splashed out and bought a piece of 'best' beef, it would often make a reappearance the following weekend too, what was left of the joint having been thrust back into the freezer, despite already being cooked. But nothing surpassed the day she studiously spent in the kitchen cooking up a speciality the like of which we'd never seen before, nor ever wanted to see again. She was determined to find a use for the pig's head and was totally foxed until she realised its brain was still in there. She bunged the head, the trotters, a tail and some vegetables and herbs in a pot, boiled it all up and produced the most disgusting dish we'd ever encountered: brawn, or jellied pig's head. She loved it, and, as she was the only one who did, the rest of it went back in the freezer.

Mum's storing habits were rule-free but miraculously we never got food poisoning, although I did once get worms, a shameful episode in my life which no one has ever known about — until now! I felt so disgusting and dirty I was beside myself as to what to do, being too ashamed to tell Mum. Eventually I wrote a note to the local chemist as though it was from her. I can still remember what I wrote: 'To whom it may concern. I think my son has worms. Is there anything you could provide my daughter with to sort this out? She has plenty of money. Thank you. Yours faithfully . . . ' and scribbled my mum's signature. I stood there and blushed, shuffling from foot to foot, convinced he knew that the patient was me. When he eventually handed the packet over, cloaked in a white paper bag, it was like being given a magic potion, an elixir which meant my life could carry on as it once was — worm free.

Mum was at home most of the time now because of Andrew, so her money-making abilities were curtailed somewhat. At night though, as soon as Dad came home from work, she'd be out of the door, armed with her case of Sarah Coventry jewellery, and off to someone's house to host a jewellery party. She got commission on all that she sold, and spent hours poring over the paperwork, totting up her earnings. It wasn't regular income though, which is maybe why she started charging David and I for Angel Delight, our favourite pudding, especially butterscotch flavour, and even better if accompanied by a tin of fruit cocktail. Mum decided that because it required a pint of milk to make the Angel Delight, as well as the mix itself, it was a luxury too far, especially as David had taken to stealing packets and making up a whole four-portion pack for himself, which he hid under his bed. So if we wanted Angel Delight we had to pay ten pence for it. I spent most of my spare time before and after school working in the newsagent's to earn money to fund my Angel Delight and clothes habits.

My bosses and colleagues were like a second family to me and I took great pride in performing my duties to the best of my ability. They trusted me so much in the end that I actually opened up the shop at 6 a.m. on Sunday as well as working Monday to Friday after school, all day Saturday and the school holidays. Strangely, Tuesday was the busiest day in the shop. It was Family Allowance day — it's called Child Benefit now — and a queue formed outside the post office as soon as the school run was over with mums eager to get their hands on their cash. As soon as they'd had their Family

Allowance book stamped and they'd got the money in their hands they'd come next door to us and stock up with cigarettes, and tobacco for their husband's roll-ups. 'Four hundred Number 6, please,' or 'Four ounces of Old Holborn and four packs of Rizla papers, please,' were requests that I became very familiar with on a Tuesday. It was one Friday though, that I was completely stumped, when a man who often told me, 'I only come in here to see your smile,' came in to see me smile and then said, 'You haven't got any French letters have you?'

My older colleagues burst out laughing as I dutifully scampered over to the stationery section and helpfully offered, 'We've got Basildon Bond, blue paper, white paper, lined and plain.' They were corpsing behind the counter, but I couldn't understand why. The French letter man came over, completely invaded my space, rubbed himself against me and then walked out with a lascivious smirk on his horrible face. I was none the wiser when my colleagues told me that French letters were in fact condoms, and they convulsed all over again at my naivety.

I learned a lot in that shop, and I earned quite a bit too with all the hours I put in — so much that I didn't have to ask Mum and Dad for anything and I pretty much became self-sufficient, buying my own stuff. One awful day though, my independence was nearly taken away from me when David and some mates robbed crates of fizzy drinks from the back of the newsagent's. As I worked there and had inside knowledge, they suspected I had something to do with it too. I cried and cried, angry at David for putting me in that position and equally angry with them for thinking that I would do such a thing. They believed me in the end, and because it was my brother involved they didn't call the police. Still, David and I were soon to get involved with them of our own accord. The rest of our mates had, so why should we be any different?

I think I must have been about thirteen when I began shoplifting regularly. I'm not blaming Mum, but she'd always made a habit of pulling off the outer leaves of cabbages and the like in supermarkets or even at market stalls, because she said, 'Why should I pay for something that I'm only going to chuck in the bin when I get home anyway?' She had a point, and she did it right in front of people, so assured was she of her penny-saving mission. I took it further. It started off with trifles from Marks & Spencer of all things, probably because we never had luxuries like that at home. Food was my thing then, especially sweet stuff, which wasn't freely available in Mum's cupboards. I'd go off shopping with Debs, armed with a teaspoon from the kitchen drawer, and nick delicious treats, which we devoured on a bench in the middle of the shopping centre or in the nearby park.

One Saturday it all went wrong when Debs and I bumped into a group of girls from school. They were in a lower set than us and were considered to be very cool, hard and fearless. So

I wanted to impress them. We headed for Boots, where I pinched false nails, even though I hadn't a clue what they were; I pocketed eyelashes, green nail varnish and all manner of things that would have prompted Mum to lock me in my room for a month for fear I was turning into a whore. Off I skipped with my booty from Boots, swelling with pride inside because I knew I'd impressed the rest of them. Then a hand on my shoulder and the chilling words, 'May I see inside your bag, please?'

We were escorted back into the shop and taken to a room at the back of the store, where we were all asked to explain ourselves. Debs and I sat there snivelling and bleating, 'They made us do it.' To be fair, Debs hadn't stolen a thing, her parents being even stricter than mine, and I pleaded pathetically, 'I've got money — please let me pay for everything,' so that she wouldn't be in trouble. The others said it was our fault, so the store detective decided that, 'If you can't tell the truth between you, I'm going to have to call the police.' And she did. We were bundled into two white Ford Escort police cars — Debs and me in one and the rest in the other — and driven, like wretched, snivelling felons, to the police station at Southampton Civic Centre, where they split us up.

Mum was at home with the baby when the phone went. She couldn't cope with what she was hearing and phoned Dad at work. They arrived together, Mum clutching Andrew to her chest and all the while crying that familiar refrain: 'Not my Fiona, she wouldn't do that.'

'I'm afraid she has, Mrs Phillips,' replied the police officer. I was then given a humiliating lecture about my potential for becoming a serious criminal while Mum sobbed, the baby cried and Dad let out huge sighs of disapproval and looked at me as though I was dirt. 'Don't worry, officer, she won't do it again — I'll make sure of that,' he gravely uttered. I was let off with a caution, the officer telling me, 'You obviously come from a very decent, caring family, but if you offend again, you'll have a criminal record.'

Bloody hell! I shrivelled in the back of Dad's car as though making myself smaller would stop what I knew was coming. 'But I didn't do it; they made me,' I whined pitifully. 'Of course you didn't,' Mum added hopefully. 'Of course you bloody did, stop snivelling,' barked Dad, gripping the steering wheel and driving like fury. Mum's sympathy soon turned into a grim realisation of the truth when we got home: 'Bringing shame on this family — how dare you!' she scolded. I was sent to my room, banned from contact with Debs and grounded from my paper round for a week. When I went into school on the Monday, news of my weekend encounter with Hampshire Constabulary spread like wildfire. Was I held up as a bad example, a person to steer clear of? Of course not. I was treated like a hero with a big badge of honour.

It was OK for Mum and Dad to moan about us going off the rails, but it was their fault for putting us in that school, David and I figured. How were we supposed to be model children when all around us was aggression, sexual activity, petty crime and bullying? It was all very well Mum moaning about David 'looking like a thug in those Dr Whites' (they were actually Dr Martens boots, but Mum, as ever, had her own take on things and unknowingly re-christened them after a well-known brand of sanitary towel!), but those Dr Whites, sorry, Martens, were part of a uniform that all the cool guys wore, and if you didn't fit in, life was miserable. School was chaotic, verbally abusing teachers, locking them in cupboards, throwing one particularly annoying one over a hedge, nothing seemed to be out of bounds. I lived one life at home and in the newsagent's and a completely different one at school. I didn't do a scrap of homework and the school didn't seem to care. Dad was still working all hours, and Mum was consumed with Andrew as well as everything else she had to do, so David and I pretty much got away with a string of concocted stories to cover our wayward tracks. Anyway, Mum was still under the impression that we were a pair of angels who'd never stray from our holy mission, so it was easy to run riot.

Around that time I started drinking, pretty heavily, enough to make me sick or pass out. I'd buy barley wine from the off-licence and crack it open on the kerbs in the back streets, then off we'd head to the youth club, a den of iniquity, where the air was thick with hormones. Often there'd be parties at friends' houses, where we'd get so legless we'd throw up for most of the night before blacking out. God knows where their parents were, or if they even cared, but I couldn't ever imagine Mum and Dad reigning over adult parties for children barely out of middle school. One weekend Dad got a call to go and fetch David — he must have been about thirteen at the time — from a party. He was lying in a hedge, completely unconscious, with most of his clothes missing. Dad picked him up, threw him over his shoulder, dumped him in the back of the car, raced home and dropped him on the kitchen floor, with disgust. Mum cried; I was scared; and David stayed on the floor until the next morning, with Mum making frequent sorties downstairs 'in case he swallows his tongue'. Dad was livid: 'I've never got myself into a state like that, not even in my navy days.'

Never mind the navy. 'Yo ho ho and a bottle of rum' didn't even sum up some of the antics that went on at that school. At the end of it all, I'd received one hell of an education. But not many qualifications: I took eight O levels and got one, English Language, which I took a year early because I was 'bright'. My School Leaving Report said, 'Fiona is a pupil of more than average ability.' All in all it was 'a criminal waste of intelligence', according to Dad.

11

As Millbrook School could barely cope with educating pupils as far as their O levels and CSEs, there was no chance that they'd offer sixth-form education — thankfully. So Debs and I went off to Hill College for Girls to try and repair the damage done to our education between the ages of twelve and sixteen.

I still had it in mind that I wanted to be a doctor, the only obstacle being that I didn't really want to lock myself away in my bedroom for two years studying to get three grade-A science A levels. Actually that wasn't the only obstacle — nor was it the biggest — there was the small matter of retaking all my failed O levels before I could even consider ascending to the dizzy heights of tackling my As. So I did that in year one while also embarking on A level English, and then took on two more A levels in year two. I was really good at English, so I had that covered, and I had a knack for picking up languages quickly too, so I decided to do Chemistry and Biology. Duh! In fairness, I wanted to keep my options open for some sort of medical career and I did enjoy a challenge, but in reality I should have played to my strengths, which very definitely didn't include anything to do with the periodic table or photosynthesis. I loved Hill College, not least because the absence of boys meant there was no pressure, apart from the academic sort. I made some brilliant friends from a world so far removed from the one that I'd been used to that I might as well have been in a different country. Debs and I ventured off to big, posh houses into which we could have fitted both of our family homes with room to spare. We went from not wanting friends to see our houses because they were private not council, to not wanting our new friends to visit our homes because they were like dolls' houses compared to theirs. After what we'd been used to, it was a revelation to us that our new friends had parents who cared where they went, who they went with and what time they came in — just like ours did. Although I've yet to meet another parent who'd be waiting outside the front door armed with a thin, wooden-handled dish mop, like Mum was when I dared to arrive home late. She'd attack me with it on sight, while yelling, 'It's only because I love you and care about you, you little madam,' as she struck stinging blows with the mop across my upper arms.

Unfortunately, on the scholarly front nothing changed. I didn't manage to shed my frustrating tendency of leaving everything until the last minute — a family trait which has crippled most of what Dad ever wanted to do in his life. In the notes I found in his house, he'd jotted down all sorts of lines for his book which referred to his debilitating habit of deferring everything he didn't want to deal with. One quote, 'Procrastination is the thief of time,' made me giggle because he had written in the margin next to it, '*I should know!*' Another reads, 'Intelligence is

129

wasted without concentration and application,' and once more in the margin he had written, '*I know!*' So do I.

My exam results were all marred by the fact that most of my revision had been done the night before rather than steadily across the preceding three months. Dad's failure to grasp life and live it, aligned with his catalogue of regrets, have been a valuable lesson for me though — I was determined that I was going to make the most of my life, if not my revision time! Plus there was the small matter of being a seventeen-year-old and, at the time, going out with a twenty-eight-year-old man. Mum thought he was a 'gentleman'. He called her 'Mrs Phillips' as he picked me up in his car, and whisked me off to places my contemporaries could only dream about. It didn't last long because I took offence at a pair of shoes he was wearing one night — they were very twenty-eight, not eighteen, and I suddenly saw him in a different light — a bit old-fashioned and past it. So despite the fact that he lived in a big house and had posh parents (who, Mum had convinced herself, must have been 'high-up' the pecking order of society), I decided he had to go. Only I didn't have the guts to hurt him. So one night when I knew he was due to come round and pick me up I told Mum I was going to Debbie's, and when he arrived could she pack him in for me.

'Bless him, he's a gentleman. You can't do that to him,' she said. 'I'm going to Debs',' I replied haughtily, and dashed out before my conscience got the better of me. Debs' house was just up the road from mine, and as it was a close, nay a court, whoever drove into it had to go up the end to turn round and drive back out again. Either way, we'd be well placed to view the victim just after he'd received Mum's news. Debs and I crouched down below her front-room window and waited for the injured party to drive by. Sure enough, just a few minutes after he was due at my house — which, as he was irritatingly punctual, meant he'd already received the news — his car crawled past at a deathly pace. Debs and I ducked down and were gripped by a tide of mirth. 'What's he doing now?' I gasped hysterically as I urged Debs to pop her head above the windowsill again to spot the wounded prey. 'He looks really sad,' she howled as she plunged down again when he drove back down the road.

We rolled on the floor laughing like two hyenas. Two very cruel hyenas. My conscience did sort of prick, and I did think, 'isn't it awful how, after spending weeks being treated with the utmost care and respect by this lovely man, I could treat him like a piece of dirt?' But that's what happens at the end of relationships, as I was to find out myself some years on. In the meantime I had Mum, the Relationship Assassin, to deal with. Debs and I piled down the road, still spewing mirth and laughing so much that we could hardly stand up straight. We bundled in through the back door like two crazed lunatics, our voices rendered so high-pitched by hysteria that Mum must have wondered what the hell had breezed in. 'I don't know what you find so funny,' she said, glaring at us as we held on to each other. '*Ach y fi*. Doing that to such a gentleman. Bless his heart; he was all dressed up . . . ' At that Debs and I collapsed on the floor, gasping for air, at the comedy of it all. 'All dressed up,' we screamed as we rolled around on the parquet flooring. 'What did you tell him?' I spluttered. 'I told him you'd gone out.' 'But you were supposed to pack him in.' 'I'm not doing your dirty work. Bless his heart. I could have cried with him.' 'Ugh, he cried?' I exclaimed. 'He had tears in his eyes. You horrible pair,' she said, trying to look cross, but with a hint of a smirk at our histrionics. We were gripped by a renewed wave of hysteria and spent the night rolling around and going over and over it in detail.

Mum had previous form when it came to dumping my potential suitors, so it wasn't her first outing as the Relationship Assassin. The year before she'd been dispatched to the Co-op to deliver a killer blow to someone I'd taken against because he'd had the temerity to turn up in light-grey shoes last time I met him. Apparently, when he encountered Mum he was wearing 'beautiful black leather gloves and a gorgeous scarf. Bless his heart.' Phew! What a lucky escape.

Meanwhile, Dad had had enough of authority, 'petty bloody managers' and 'being treated like some bloody idiot'. Many times over the years, we'd hear all about the 'incompetent, puffed-up farts' that he had to answer to. The observations would become even more colourful on his return from annual management meetings in Lytham St

132

Annes, near Blackpool. 'Bloody waste of my time, spending hours on end listening to some self-important berk telling me stuff I could have told him years ago,' he'd reflect so he decided not to waste his time any longer. For a while Dad had been going on about 'the bloody rat race' and how he wanted out of it and, unknown to David and I, Mum and Dad had been discussing the idea of moving to Wales. Dad got a job there running the service department of a small TV and hi-fi business in St Clears — 'Gateway to the West Wales Coastline' — in Carmarthenshire.

David and I were still at school and sixth-form college respectively, so Mum stayed behind with Andy and us while Dad fulfilled his dreams of a solitary existence and shacked up in a caravan just outside the medieval seaside town of Tenby. As we didn't remember Dad being around very much, I don't remember much of him not being around either, especially as it coincided with me meeting and falling head over heels with my first love. Before that it had pretty much been Donny Osmond, a boy in the fifth year at my comprehensive who I went out with just to show off, and Micky Channon the Southampton FC and England striker.

Years of being dumped in goal and being called Gordon Banks or Ray Clemence by my brother David and his friends had rubbed off. I loved football and would much rather have played that than netball, if the school had let me. I remember the brilliant glory years of Don Revie's Leeds United and Arsenal winning the double in 1971, and of all the people I've met over the years, the legendary football commentator John Motson is right up there at the top of the tree. The two of us talked and drank so much that at one point I turned round to speak to him and his head was in his dinner! Motty was commentating in the mid-1970s, when I followed Southampton everywhere, my newsagent's job permitting. I once lied to Mum and Dad and told them I was going on a sleepover when in fact I was in Belgium, having saved up, and got the coach and the ferry over there to watch Saints play against Anderlecht in the European Cup Winners' Cup.

So when my best mate Debs got a job in Mike Channon Sports, I thought she'd died and gone to heaven, only she wasn't a football nut like me; she was more interested in the money. So I died and went to heaven instead. I went to meet her from work one day during the summer holidays and nearly perished on the spot when Mick Channon himself wandered in. I was so overcome I couldn't speak; in fact I felt like crying, just like a small child when she comes face to face with Father Christmas for the first time. I had to go outside the shop for some fresh air and wait there until he'd gone. Not long after, when Channon moved to Manchester City (which nearly resulted in me applying for a job at the Trafford Centre and leaving home), the store became the Saints Sports Shop.

I'd often meet Debs from work or pop in for a chat; we were absolutely inseparable, always in each other's houses, ceaselessly talking and collapsing in waves of hysterics. Debs' dad called us 'Mutt and Jeff' after two American comic-strip characters, one of whom was tall, dim-witted and motivated by greed, while the other was a half-pint, former lunatic asylum inmate. I'm not sure who was who, but just like Mutt and his mate, Debs and I were never knowingly apart. Debs was a much-loved fixture in the sports shop at the weekends, during the holidays and after college some nights too. Often the Southampton FC apprentices would come in after training and all their other duties (such as cleaning the professional players' boots) to have a laugh with the shop staff. Most of them were around the same age as us, seventeen or eighteen, and lived in digs paid for by the club while they were going through their apprentice-ships. We ended up becoming really good friends with them and often met them up the Top Rank on a Saturday night, along with some of our college mates.

Debs and I, having worked all day, would meet at either my house or hers to get ready. It took anywhere between two and four hours and involved several changes of clothes, hairstyles and shoes. Deb's dad would call up the stairs, 'Is it this Saturday you've got to be ready for, or next?' But as he usually drove us there, we forgave his witty interjections. We drank Pernod and blackcurrant, a classy concoction, and danced all night to Chaka Khan's 'I'm Every Woman', Sylvester's 'You Make Me Feel (Mighty Real)' and 'Get Down' by Gene Chandler.

Oh! I'm going to have to leave my writing and dance around my handbag. Hang on a minute . . .

12

Phew! Sorry about that. Where were we? Ah yes, the Top Rank in Southampton, where First Love hit me like a Micky Channon strike.

It was like picking a puppy from a new litter really: you know, when the others jump all over you and lick you and you go for the enigmatic one that doesn't look bothered? Not the best-looking of the bunch, but with a certain something that sets him apart? That was my first love. I'm going to call him Joe. It's not his real name but he has a wife and children and a life in the present and future, not the past. He was a big guy with a huge heart, a brilliant sense of humour and riddled with decency. He was about six feet something, stacked up with muscle and possessed of huge, steady hands. You had to be if you were a goalkeeper. He asked me if I'd like to go out with him one night as we sat and talked and talked while the others danced. I met him for our first 'official' date outside a cinema in the centre of Southampton; he was late and so apologetic and eaten up with it that I fell completely head over heels in love with him.

I can't remember what we did, what I wore, what he wore, except I remember he had a scarf, so it must have been cold. I don't think we ate, because I wouldn't have been physically able to, my heart being in my mouth and thumping away and making its presence felt everywhere else too.

Over time I calmed down enough for us to actually be able to swallow food when we went out. For a student who worked in a newsagent's and an apprentice footballer who lived in digs we didn't do too badly, always managing to cobble together enough pennies to hit Southampton's hot spots. One memorable meal at a Berni Inn, a steakhouse chain which was the height of provincial sophistication then, I stuffed enough down my neck for Joe to totally fall in love with me as 'a girl that actually eats'. And eats. I started with a prawn cocktail, followed by the house special, steak with chips, peas and a bread roll, followed by Black Forest gateau and cream. It was such a dizzying evening — we were only eighteen and Mum and Joe's landlady had it marked out as a special occasion, when we'd have a 'little drink' (didn't she remember my crazy barley wine days?) — that I had to finish it off with a Tia Maria float. And that was it. For the next four and a bit years he was the love of my life.

Fortunately Mum adored him too. He was such a great guy, you couldn't fail to. He teased Mum and called her Meg, after Meg Richardson in *Crossroads*, only she didn't have a silver tray with whisky and sherry decanters on it, nor a maid called Amy Turtle. Joe quickly tuned into Mum's stately-home-trapped-in-a-three-bed-semi ways and knew how to wind her up. She treated him like a son and couldn't have wished for me to have picked a better boyfriend if I'd ordered him from her Great Universal catalogue. The only thing missing was the commission.

At college my stomach would turn over and over, unfortunately not in time with the cogs of my brain, which ceased pondering the intricacies of cell exchange and plasma membranes to concentrate on the biggest event in my life so far. My friends called it the 'love affair of the century' and teased me as I bounced around the corridors in a permanent mental swoon. I couldn't wait until the end of the day, when I'd skip to the gates, where Joe would be waiting in his yellow Mark 3 Ford Cortina, having finished training. We'd go home to Mum's for tea or, if we didn't have too much on the next day maybe drive somewhere for a drink accompanied by Elvis Costello's *Armed Forces* in the cassette recorder. Before long he wanted to introduce me to his parents, so one weekend, after his match, we drove up to the east Midlands for the big occasion.

I was so nervous all weekend that I couldn't eat — during that first meal, just after we arrived, a mixture of anxiety and nerves completely blocked my throat and I was incapable of swallowing. I was starving and the food was delicious, but I couldn't get it down. The few mouthfuls I did force through performed against such opposition from my own throat that I made the most peculiar noises as it passed through. It was an absolute agony of embarrassment and wind. As for going to the loo, I didn't dare. What if someone heard me? What if . . . Oh it was too awful to comprehend. So I spent the weekend starving, yet full to bursting, relieved to fall asleep in the spare room, where I wasn't on show. His parents and his two older brothers were lovely, but they had the most peculiar way of carrying on: they were allowed to go in the fridge and stuff their faces with whatever they wanted without being told off. The fridge was crammed full of delights the like of which we'd never seen in our house. We weren't allowed near ours unless Mum, the food monitor, was around to deal sops out. If there were any treats lurking in there, yoghurts for example, she'd be on patrol for most of the evening.

Oh how I missed her though, when in 1980 she moved to Wales with Dad and Andy, thus releasing Dad from his caravan, where, he often teased us, he'd 'never been happier'. He had settled nicely into his new job in St Clears so it was time for Mum and Andy to move away from us and join him in their brand new home in Carmarthen. Mum was returning to Wales twenty years after she'd left to marry Dad, this time to a four-bedroom bungalow. By the way she prepared for the move you'd have thought she was upgrading to a grand country mansion. I spent days shopping in Southampton with her, poring over curtain fabrics and carpet colours and sifting through bed linen. The Welsh oak dresser, table and chairs, plus Uncle Barry's dinner set were on the move again, this time joined by a grandmother clock, a new purchase that Mum and I couldn't resist, and which was destined to tick away in the hall of their new home for years to come.

Now it was time for David and me, aged

nineteen and seventeen, to experience living on our own. We couldn't wait: it had been a tight fit with three children, Mum, a peripatetic dad and all our arguments squeezed into that tiny little semi. Mum sorted me out with a room in a lovely lady's house — the mother of one of her friends, a widow who still worked and wanted some company. David went to live with a mad but wonderfully kind ex-RE teacher from our former school and we still saw each other as often as we could. In February of that year Joe had signed for a club in the Midlands, which left me inconsolable and longing for the weekends when he'd drive to Southampton from wherever he'd been playing. The absence of Joe and of Mum's cooking meant that I initially lost a lot of weight, so along with a new life I had a new body — which fitted into a size 10 instead of a 12 or 14.

When Joe came to stay he'd put his head down on the sofa in the front room, before sneaking into my rented room, where he'd stay the night. I was drunk on the adventure of it all, I was so grown-up, so unlike my college friends, who were still fettered by their parents' rules. I was in the last term of my last year at sixth-form college, which was very different to the previous two years, because boys had finally been let in. I think I started to get a bit beyond myself with all the freedom I had because soon I resented having to hang around until the weekend waiting for Joe. I was out and about every night with my old mates and my new male college friends, until I wanted my life during the week to continue at the weekends, without changing down a gear for Joe. I started resenting his arrival and the fact that spending time with him detached me from my friends. I had a new life now and he felt like part of the old one, despite the fact that I loved him. One weekend I was so cold and awful to him that he twigged and made it easy for me to finish with him. He was devastated, and after a week of teary phone calls, the following Friday when I walked out of college he was there in his car, begging me to change my mind. He gave me a cuddly rabbit with 'I Love You' on it. I hate cuddly toys for grown-ups, and of course I considered myself to be very grown-up then, but it melted my frostiness and by the end of the weekend we were back on track again.

After college I decided to train as a radiographer, having decided that being a doctor was not worth sacrificing my social life for. I was based in Southampton for lectures and at Salisbury General Infirmary for the practical side of my training. I spent my whole time travelling between Southampton, where I still had my rented room, Salisbury, where I also had a room in the nurses' home, the Midlands, where Joe was, and Wales, where I travelled home to Mum and Dad as often as I could.

Radiography, I soon twigged, wasn't really my bag. For one, I had a chip on my shoulder that I wasn't a doctor when if I'd pulled my finger out instead of going out, I'm sure I could have been, and two, I'd chosen the diagnostic side of radiography, which was ultimately unfulfilling for me. My fellow trainees and I could see when

141

X-rays showed tumours or other devastating conditions, but we weren't allowed to get involved with the patients because our job was positioning him or her, before taking and processing pictures. We processed them in a darkroom back then, where all sorts of incidents which had nothing to do with X-rays took place! The consultant radiologist was a cold man who would flick disinterestedly through *Country Life* magazine while we helped carry out the procedures. He only ever showed any emotion when he had to shake hands with the private patients, who'd jumped the queue and paid for the privilege of a meaningless handshake from a man who cared more about listed country properties than their insides. The final straw came when I was sent up to intensive care to perform a mobile chest X-ray on a patient whose whole family had been killed following his daughter's eighteenth birthday party. It was a car accident and he had been at the wheel. He didn't want to live and my heart broke for him. I chatted away, trying to get him to smile, to have hope, to want to see the future. I was told off for getting 'too involved'. I guess my job satisfaction should have come from the fact that I was helping sick people on the road to recovery, but it wasn't enough for me, and towards the end of my first year's training I decided to leave. I got on the train and travelled to Wales, where Dad met me at Swansea station with the encouraging words: 'You're now one of the three million unemployed.'

13

Thanks to Margaret Thatcher's strict monetarist policies, which resulted in raised taxes, higher interest rates and government spending cuts, Britain was plunged into recession, and there were indeed three million unemployed. I was determined not to be one of them for long and anyway I'd been further stung by the National Health Service demanding I pay my grant back because I'd jacked in my course. I couldn't blame them but I could have killed them. I ended up selling everything just to keep myself afloat — my precious music centre, which Mum and Dad had bought me for my eighteenth birthday, clothes, records, books — anything to get some money in. I was still living in my room in Southampton, still going out with Joe, my lifeline, and still being reassured by my lovely mum, who often shared my bed in that grotty old room when she came to stay. One day we were walking arm in arm along the street, heading for that depressing room, and she said, with her customary optimism, a huge smile on her face, 'It won't always be like this, you know, Toots.' I often think back to that day and those words. She was right, but at the time she had more confidence in me than I did.

And then an exceedingly horrible episode began. I went to a job agency and got a position at Mr Kipling's cake factory. It began miserably, with the shock that I'd have to get up at 4.30 a.m. to be in time for the minibus which transported us to the 'Goolag'. That's what it was to me: a penal system featuring tons of goo, used to make Mr Kipling's 'exceedingly good' Fondant Fancies. My job was to sort the faulty fancies from the faultless ones. The faultless ones were reserved for Marks & Spencer. I spent hours watching that conveyor belt go past, laden with an outbreak of fancies. I didn't fancy it much. But it was the petty politics that really got to me, the seriousness with which a Fondant Fancy was pored over, discussed and dissected drove me near crazy. I didn't wish for my workmates' lives and I felt guilty that I felt like that. It wasn't that I thought I was better; it was that I thought they were better and they didn't seem to know. One day I went for lunch and bolted for the door never to fondle a fancy again. I was unemployed once more with barely any money and not a clue what to do. I strode urgently towards the bus stop, with visions of Mr Kipling's exceedingly vicious army hot on my tail and even scarier thoughts of what I was going to tell Dad.

I knew I had to start looking towards a proper career, one that would take me through my working life, and I realised that my 'criminal waste of intelligence' at school, as Dad had put it, couldn't turn into a serial habit. I decided that I would study for a degree. It had been in my mind when I gave up radiography and it had percolated during the time in between. I spent hours at a time in the public library in

Southampton looking at prospectuses and applying for courses. Once I'd sent them all off, I didn't see the point of hanging around in Southampton. My friends had planned better than me and had already gone off to university or were in jobs, so I moved up to the Midlands to be near Joe. I found a bedsit, decorated in gloomy bottle-green gloss paint, in a tiny terraced house. The shower was in the kitchen and shared with the occupants of the other two bedsits. I lived on pot noodles and salad because I couldn't face using anything in the kitchen other than the kettle, and anyway I didn't have the money. But Joe was there, albeit living far more salubriously in his digs than I was.

The pride of watching him play at the weekends, hearing the crowd and thinking 'he's mine' was enough to keep me going all week. Plus we'd often spend wonderful weekends at his parents', where we were fed to last us all year, never mind seven days. Back in my bedsit I spent hours on my own looking for jobs and waiting for Joe to pick me up after training and rescue me from my depressing reality. I signed up to be an Avon lady and then didn't answer the door when it went *ding dong*. It was Avon calling all right, with my case full of products which I had to stump up some money for. I weighed up whether I should spend the money on something I didn't exactly feel enthusiastic about or whether I should keep it for bus fares to attend interviews for jobs, with a guaranteed income, that I actually wanted to do. So I didn't answer the door.

Mum came to visit me as soon as she possibly could. I went to meet her off the coach where she'd had a bit of a hellish journey, owing to Andrew, who was seven by then, being sick most of the way. They stayed in my grim old bedsit; Mum made friends with and found out the history of most of my co-residents and Joe took us out and about after training. One day Mum took Andy for a bus ride into town while I got on with something or other. They were gone for ages and I started to get worried. When they hadn't shown up by tea time I went outside and started pacing the streets close to the nearest bus stop. After a while I heard that familiar cheery voice: 'Toots, it's us; we got lost.' No wonder. Mum had been chatting away on the bus, got off at the wrong stop and then tried to find her way back to mine by asking where 'Rupert Street' was. I lived in Newport Street.

Eventually, after a few months of spending most of the day on my own in a place where I didn't really know anyone and without a job — probably because I foolishly told everyone that I was going to do a degree at the end of the year anyway — I decided to base myself at Mum and Dad's in Wales, where I got a job in a local wine bar, worked all hours and saw Joe when he travelled down after his game on a Saturday night and applied to get on a degree course. In the end I got a place at Birmingham, where I opted to read English, playing to my strengths at last and, more importantly, not committing myself to any career in particular, although I was definitely toying with the idea of journalism.

Following my abysmal school record, the three years I'd had to spend at sixth-form to make up for it, and my aborted attempt at training as a radiographer, I was well into my twentieth year by the time I commenced studying for my degree, far too mature and worldly, I thought, to live with stupid eighteen-year-olds in halls of residence. So I found another bedsit on the Hagley Road in Edgbaston, a leafy part of Birmingham just down the road from the BBC Pebble Mill studios. It was an elderly woman's house, and there was another student there, who was just about to study her teaching certificate after completing a music degree. Like me, she'd recently arrived in Birmingham and knew nothing about it. Mum, Dad and Andy bade me tearful goodbyes as they left for the journey back to Wales. 'You will look after her, won't you?' Mum implored my new friend, who was no older or more experienced than I was. I bustled her out of the door before she could say anything else more damaging and off they went, leaving me feeling empty, full of trepidation and not at all convinced that I liked Birmingham or knew what the hell I wanted to do.

Thank God for Joe. During those first few weeks of meeting new people, living out of college and feeling like I couldn't face the three years ahead of me, his visits were the one thing I looked forward to, the light that I longed for all the time he wasn't there. He was doing really well at his club by now, and I continued to spend all my weekends with him, mostly at his parents' because I'd have had to sneak him into my room in Birmingham and it wasn't worth the hassle. Not that we were allowed to sleep in the same room at his parents' house either, mind you — you had to be married to do that. The very thought of Mum finding out and the torrent of *ach y fis* that would gush from her mouth was enough to make me feel satisfied with my single bed status for life. In my second term, feeling a little bit excluded because of my living arrangements, and as I spent most weekends away, I decided to move into the halls of residence after all. Having smoked since the age of eleven and drunk myself silly thereafter, as well as living away from home for the past two years, I still felt like a bit of an outsider though, and didn't have much truck with my fellow students' infantile relish at being on their own for the first time in their lives.

It was during that first term in halls that something else happened which made me feel even more grown-up — my grandma died. She had cervical cancer, but before that she'd apparently been behaving oddly. I recall one time, when I went to visit them in the little Canterbury city-centre flat that they'd moved into after retiring from the pub, that Grandma had lined up her photos of Dad, Uncle Barry and Auntie Germaine as children and put piles of sweets in front of them 'in case they get hungry'. She entreated us to 'look at the children enjoying their sweets' and laughed and clapped her hands in delight. She bought toys for 'the children' and generally busy-bodied around them, making sure they were happy.

At the time I found it highly amusing, not realising the significance of Grandma's behaviour and, coming from a family where nothing personal was ever discussed, Grandad didn't mention a thing either. Dad too was indifferent. On reflection though, I realise that it was probably the first time dementia entered our lives. I often wonder whether it was Grandma's cancer that caused the dementia or the dementia that prevented Grandma from getting the cancer treated before it was too late. She'd never been one for visiting the doctor — too personal, intrusive, undignified — but I wonder if she knew she had cancer and it caused her mind to go. Whatever the truth of the sequence of events, when she died I went to find Grandad crying in his flat surrounded by dozens of packets of disposable nappies. He'd obviously gone out and bought them for Grandma, for the bleeding. 'Thank God you've come,' he whispered to me as he hugged me close when I turned up after she'd gone. The flat was dirty and they'd been washing laundry in the bath. There were no plastic covers over the furniture. Illness had robbed Grandma of the thing she held most dear — her cleanliness.

At the funeral Dad and Uncle Barry recalled memories of Grandma and laughed at intervals. I thought this insensitive and very strange, but casting my mind back to visiting Grandma in hospital I could see why they did. Close to death, having suffered for goodness knows how long without telling a soul, she lay in her bed and instructed us, 'Get someone to do the doings; it's filthy in here.'

14

In the summer of 1982, in the football close season Joe was signed to a First Division side — today's Premiership. With his transfer money he bought a two-bedroom new-build house which, because he was a footballer, was carpeted throughout for free by a local company. He was on £1,500 per week, not bad for a twenty-one-year-old. He really wanted me to move in with him, but if I had that would have been it for life in my mind — not to mention Mum's — and I was too young to commit myself to the first real boyfriend I'd ever had, even though I loved him with a passion. So I phoned him from the halls of residence payphones most nights and stayed with him at weekends, glad to get away from student life. One memorable Saturday I travelled to Old Trafford, where Joe's team were playing Manchester United. It was his debut for the first team, and his parents and I were beside ourselves with a mixture of nerves, excitement and pride. He played a blinder and, with a score of 9 out of 10, was man of the match in all the Sunday papers. I can't remember whether they won or lost now, but I do know that he was an absolute hero and couldn't believe that he wanted to be with me. We went out to celebrate that night and everywhere we went people wanted to buy him a drink.

So Joe lived in his new house, I lived in my

My mum in Newgale, South Wales in 1956. She would have been twenty-four when this was taken. According to my Auntie Mary, she was vivacious and full of life, with a smile that captivated everyone who met her.

My dad's great dream was to be a pilot. I think he certainly looked the part of the dashing matinee hero. This was the closest he came – sitting in the cockpit hoping that his dreams would soar.

Mum worshipped her father, Daddy Noddfa, pronounced 'Nothva', named after the house they lived in – a Welsh thing!

26 March 1960, Mum and Dad's wedding day. Eleven months later on 1 January 1961 I was born

Grandma and Grandad at my christening. My father didn't turn up!

Dad – with some rare time to spare – and me, aged eighteen months.

My naughty brother David – in front – and me in 1963. I was just two years old.

With Dad constantly working, Mum was always there to wrap us up in love. She never stopped talking and laughing.

Me and David with his toys. He broke most of mine!

Grandma and Grandad behind the bar at The Duke's Head pub they ran on Church Street, Canterbury. It's now a Moroccan restaurant called Azouma.

My grandmother 'Mam Noddfa' and me, aged around five. In her day she was frighteningly strict, but I loved visiting her in Wales during the school holidays.

Mum and Dad in Brighton in the 70s, looking like they've just walked off the set on *The Sweeney*!

Mum in 1974 with my little brother Andy and our hoodlum beagle Rufus. By then we had moved to Brighton and Rufus found great sport rounding up cars on the South Coast Road.

A rare picture of me as a podgy, surly teenager with Mum and Andy on holiday in the Norfolk Broads in 1975.

With my brothers and Mum on her 60th birthday in 1992. She was already behaving erratically, but we didn't twig that she was ill.

Broadcasting from the NBC studios at Burbank in Los Angeles in 1994. One of the best times of my working life.

The first time I took, now husband, Martin home in 1996. I'm looking exasperated because Mum wouldn't stop clicking away with her camera!

In Vegas for our wedding in May 1997. No fuss, no guests and the limo driver took the pictures.

Martin, my son Nat and my lovely Mum at David's pub in 2000. She was very ill by then, but as always, tried to mask it with her smile. She died just six years later.

My treasured boys! Nat and Mackenzie, aged ten and seven when this picture was taken by Martin, on a weekend away in Dorset. Nat never likes his picture being taken. Mackenzie loves it! Mum would have adored them!

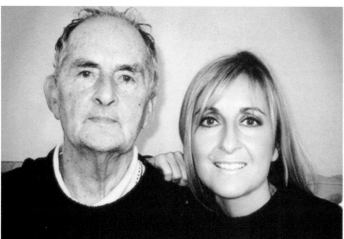

Just the two of us! Now Alzheimer's is taking Dad from me as well. This was a promotional shot for my Channel 4 documentary *Mum, Dad, Alzheimer's and me.*

Leaving GMTV in December 2008. Goodbye early mornings. Hello life!

horrible room in halls, returning to Wales in the holidays to be with Mum and Dad, with Joe travelling down every weekend. I worked in the wine bar/restaurant in Carmarthen town centre — a real 1980s affair, where Carmarthen's elite gathered in their finery, and dirty old men with florid, thread-veined cheeks and dressed in pinstriped suits pinched my bottom as I squeezed past the tables holding aloft huge steaks as they swam in chasseur sauce. My colleagues were brilliant fun, and when the kitchen closed we'd go out carousing around town until the early hours. One weekend Joe was coming down as usual, but instead of going home after work, I stayed out with my wine bar mates. He arrived at Mum and Dad's, as always looking immaculate in his match-day suit, and I wasn't there. He told them he was going to pick me up from work, but Mum knew what I was up to, that I was 'being a little madam', as she called it, and saved him from humiliation. I treated him really badly — why, I don't know, because I adored him — and a couple of similar incidents later Joe finished with me.

I was devastated — what a stupid, cocky, foolish, arrogant 'little madam' I'd been. Nothing meant anything any more. I felt as though a limb was missing, that I was totally on my own, that I wanted to die, that I didn't want to go to bed at night because I dreamt of him and didn't want to get up again in the morning because I thought of him all day. After what seemed like decades of pain and suffering I was in the kitchen one evening when I heard the

151

phone ring. Mum answered. 'It serves her right,' I heard her say. 'Bless your heart, you did everything for her.' I didn't think much of it — Mum knew everyone's business and was always willing to lend an ear — it was probably one of her friends ringing up for advice. Then she called me and, with a disapproving look which suggested, 'You really don't deserve this,' she said, 'There's someone on the phone for you.'

I think she hovered behind a door to listen after that. It was Joe. And what she'll have heard was me almost whimpering, grovelling, apologising and saying 'I promise I will'. He'd finished his match and realised, he said, that he 'couldn't live without me', but . . . it would only work if I went and lived with him. I'd have gone and lived with the Yorkshire Ripper if he'd asked me to right then. I nearly burst with happiness. He got in his car and drove to Wales to see me. A brave move. How were we going to tell Mum and Dad that we were going to 'live in sin'? It turned out to be quite a to-do, with Dad refusing to speak to either of us after Joe took him into the garage to tell him of our plans and Mum saying, '*Ach y fi*, it's all about the sex.' God bless her; she really thought it was. It culminated in a meeting of his parents and mine along with Joe and me, the guilty pair, in the new house. We didn't say a lot, but his mum and my mum muttered things like, 'The trouble is, the more we tell them not to do it, the more they'll want to.' 'Yes, we're just going to have to let them find out for themselves,' Mum agreed, presumably alluding to the horrors of sex.

So we did find out for ourselves, and I commenced the last year of my degree by commuting to and from Birmingham. It wasn't ideal being a student during the day and a WAG at night, and I railed against the conventionality of it all. I didn't like having a clean fridge that I didn't have to share with several others, or spanking new, pristine carpets and curtains, and I didn't particularly want to spend my weekends gardening. In reflective moments I knew I was growing apart from my first love. I began to stay overnight in Birmingham with my student mates, who didn't seem as hemmed in as me. Their futures were still ahead of them, while mine seemed to have been decided by the commitment to move into that house. At twenty-two, I was too young. I just didn't see myself as a little-wife kind of girl and I didn't like playing house.

I started withdrawing emotionally; I loved him, but that love couldn't weather my doubts and my fear of being trapped before I'd really lived. His mum always said I was headstrong. In the end my recalcitrance killed us — he found someone else, got married and wrote to me on his wedding day saying he'd never forget me. I spent months howling to the Style Council's 'Long Hot Summer', stuffed myself full of Thorntons Continentals to take away the pain and thought I'd never be happy ever again. Mum cried and cried with me, said lots about 'plenty of fish in the sea' without meaning it and told me I had my 'whole life ahead of me', something that, despite once yearning for it, I really didn't want to contemplate. I locked myself away in my bedroom in Wales, where I fled as often as I could for comfort and where Mum would gently knock on the door to administer warm drinks and advice. Dad meanwhile, just six weeks after the death of my relationship, popped his head around the door and offered, 'Good God, you're not still snivelling over him, are you?'

15

With all that heartbreak and torment it's a wonder I actually managed to secure myself a degree, but I did and couldn't wait to leave Birmingham. I was twenty-three by then and had decided amid the tumult of my broken love life that I really wanted to be a journalist. I knew I had to get a move on and had spotted a postgraduate radio journalism course run by the Independent Broadcasting Authority in London. I didn't have a clue how I was going to fund a move to London as well as the fees for the course, so I packed up some measly belongings, got on a coach to London, hopped on a train for what seemed like days, before spotting the smiling face of my brother David, who'd come to meet me from the station at Saint-Raphaël in the south of France.

It wasn't a career move which exactly justified years of learning, but selling doughnuts on a nudist beach at Saint-Aygulf in the blazing sun was a hundred times better than sitting in a bedsit in Birmingham wondering where I was going to get the money to kick-start my future. David and I lived on a grotty campsite, from where we were bussed daily to various beaches to pick up our wares with the aim of selling as many as we could, and thereby earning a percentage of the takings. '*Beignet pomme, boissons fraiche,*' I'd gently chide as, fully clothed, I mentally aimed my ring doughnuts at unwilling bits of flaccid anatomy. When we weren't working, we drank cheap beer and ate frugally, so by the time my stint on the Côte d'Azur had finished I'd managed to save up a bit of money — more than I would have if I'd stayed at home anyway.

With a little part of my future secured I returned to Birmingham, got myself a job as a croupier in a casino just down the road from my bedsit, played lots of the Smiths and Echo and the Bunnymen, went on fund-raising missions for the miners involved in the strike of 1984, dreamed of working in radio, and at the end of that summer went back home to Mum and Dad. As soon as I got back to Wales, I went back to work in the wine bar. The fees for my postgraduate course were prohibitive, no matter how much I saved on rent or earned working as a waitress, and I needed to get on with my career after all the diversions I'd taken thus far. It was suggested that I contact the Catherine and Lady Grace James Foundation in Aberystwyth — that they might well help me fund my dream. I'd never heard of them and certainly wondered how anyone not related to me would ever want to help me get on the path to realising my ambitions. I mean, why would they? I hadn't bargained on the foundation's dedication to benefiting the people of Wales and in particular to helping 'meet the funding of postgraduate studies'. It was set up by a philanthropic businessman, D. J. James, who named the charitable organisation after his mother and wife. I never met him; he died only six years after I was born, but were it not for this kindly Welsh stranger my path through life may have veered towards an entirely different bend. I applied for the course, went to London to be grilled to see if I had what it took to be a broadcast journalist and danced around the living room with Mum when a letter confirmed that they thought I had.

With my place on the ride to my future career secured, I went back to France again, this time to gather in the October grape harvest for a randy farmer who plied us with wine every lunch time in the hope we wouldn't notice his leering and drooling accompanied by wandering hands. There were eight of us: three girls and five boys in a four-berth caravan. We rose at dawn, all bent over like a collection of arthritic pensioners owing to the strain the grape-picking had put on our backs and legs, and returned at dusk, stained with grape juice and sweat, and ready to cook up a lowly feast bought with our daily whip-round.

One night after dinner I gathered together a pile of change and went to call Mum from the phone box near our caravan. It was an uncharacteristically frosty Mum who picked up the receiver. 'At last. I've been terribly ill — nearly died — and you haven't even bothered to phone to ask how I am,' was the opening gambit. Stupid cocky me, full of the joys of wine and France, replied coldly, 'Oh great. I'm in the south of France, in a phone box, and all you can do is tell me off.' It wasn't a good conversation for either of us, with all the emotion on one side cancelling out all of that on the other and resulting in a proud, cold impasse. Mum had had a hysterectomy. It's supposedly a straightforward, routine operation, which most of my friends' mums had already had in the 1970s, when it was almost de rigueur to have one. She hadn't told me, or maybe she had and I didn't remember because I was having such a good time — selfishness rules when you're young and carefree. Unfortunately, because it was considered so commonplace, Mum's operation was conducted by a trainee surgeon, who sewed her up so cavalierly that she had a massive internal haemorrhage which very nearly took her away from us.

I am reminded of that telephone conversation, in which she clearly thought I didn't care, in my darker moments, when I reflect on how much she cared for all of us. There she was, having been at death's door and no one caring for her. Yes, Dad was there, but he had work and his beloved dog. And they came first. And anyway, having stared death in the face three times himself — following his episodes with the childhood lorry accident, a burst appendix which resulted in peritonitis in his teens, and his pneumonia — Dad didn't do illness in anyone else. I think Mum's operation and the subsequent trauma surrounding it was the first dip in her downward road. She was put on hormone replacement therapy and was never really the same again, her sunny disposition now more often veiled by cloud.

After Christmas 1984 I made the longed-for move to London. It wasn't a bright-lights-big-city kind of move really, as I ended up sleeping on my brother David's floor in Islington. He'd moved to London a while before to attend the Arts Educational School to study drama. I'm not quite sure how we afforded any of it looking back, but determination and belief must have had a lot to do with it. We certainly weren't offered any comfort in the horror of the reality laid bare in our monthly bank statements. Eventually I found a room in a shared house in Stoke Newington, where the thumping bass from the landlord's love of reggae made sure I led a round-the-clock existence. My course was based at the National Broadcasting School in Greek Street, Soho, right in the centre of London's partially cleaned-up red-light district. I couldn't have wished for a better introduction to the capital and my hoped-for career — journalism is all about curiosity and there was plenty that was curious and plenty to be curious about. The whole area was throbbing with energy from dawn until dusk, and I was in my element.

After three months of intensive learning, including journalistic law, running our own newsroom, producing our own individual radio documentaries and drinking in most of Soho's all-night hostelries, I felt equipped to take on the world. Only no one else seemed to think so, and I ended up at Two Counties Radio in Bournemouth, where I worked for nothing, covered the local Lollipop Lady of the Year competition and crashed the radio car before leaving because, frankly, I was bored stiff and I couldn't survive on an invisible wage. Back in London, in my jumping-to-the-reggae-beat room,

I signed on the dole and claimed housing benefit to be able to afford to remain there and look for work. As I queued to sign on every fortnight, and made to feel worthless by some smug pen-pushing robot with a superiority complex, I remembered Mum's words: 'It won't always be like this, Toots.'

'No, Mum, it won't,' I reassured her when she came to visit and we shared one of my God-awful cheap as chips concoctions composed of potatoes, peas, carrots, creamed coconut and curry powder, accompanied by Bob Marley. Mum loved coming to London, where she mucked in with my housemates, talked to complete strangers on the Tube — which no one ever does in London — and cried when she saw buskers with coins in their hats. 'Oh bless them, they're just like my David,' she'd choke, referring to my brother's method of supporting his student lifestyle. Funnily though, the emotion didn't stretch as far as her purse. They may have been strumming soulful tunes 'just like my David' in order to eke a living, but the 'bless hims' instantly disappeared at the thought of the dent in her savings.

16

Life on the dole in Hackney, despite Mum's morale-boosting visits, wasn't exactly a bunch of daffodils, so in the summer of 1985 I scampered off to the south of France again, this time hitchhiking all the way to Saint-Raphaël with a mate of mine called Andy, before returning to joblessness once more. After countless media job rejections, during which I had to field Mum's enquiries as to why I didn't 'get a nice management trainee job at Marks & Spencer; they look after you there', I took whatever work I could get, which happened to be at Smiffys fish and chip restaurant on Old Compton Street in Soho, where businessmen in pin-striped suits thought it was OK to grope me with their grubby, fat hands because after all I was only a waitress. Adopting a Mum sort of air, I'd casually drop the fact that I had a degree and was going to be a journalist into the conversation whenever they tried to treat me like a Soho whore.

Smelling of chip fat and surviving on chips and mushy peas, which I got free at the restaurant, I began to feel as though the door to my future was being blocked by a huge great block of solidified fat, and that no matter how hard I tried to slip through the grease, I kept slip-sliding back again. And then, after scores of job rejections for not having enough experience,

I broke through! I can't remember how it happened or even exactly when, but I applied for a job and got it. It was at a company called Broadsystem, based in Camden, North London just down the road from the famous breakfast television station TVAM. It was some time in 1986, when premium-rate telephone services, often on 0898 numbers, first started up. After proving a huge success in America, the information lines, which provided anything from weather forecasts to restaurant recommendations at the end of your telephone line, finally arrived here and proved to be a similar hit.

I was responsible for writing the William Hill Racing Line, in which I'd give the runners-and-riders' form guide as well as my betting tips. My previous horse-racing experience amounted to picking a number in Grand National sweepstakes at various workplaces, so it was a steep learning curve which involved a religious adherence to *Sporting Life* and the *Racing Post*. Before long I was writing and voicing a pop gossip service as well as my racing guide, and in the coup to end all coups, or so I thought at the time, I secured an interview with Ian Botham, the legendary, headline-grabbing cricketer. Adverts for the 'exclusive' interview were placed in the tabloids and featured my name. Mum nearly had a seizure with the excitement, although I don't think she ever phoned up to listen owing to the conflict between her pride in me and the thought of the money she'd have to spend on the call. Needless to say, the pride was bowled out for an LBW, which in Mum's case meant Love (well)

162

Behind Wallet. Talking of which, my wallet was looking good for the first time in years. With a proper wage coming in and a decent flat-share in north London I felt as though I'd joined civilisation at last.

And then I received news that floored me again: Grandad had died — lovely, gentle Grandad, who called everyone 'mate' and who was everyone's mate. David and I travelled down to the funeral in Canterbury together. He picked me up late and drove at breakneck speed all the way, at one point nearly going through a roundabout without stopping, which resulted in me being flung into the footwell. We laughed that sort of hysterical laughter tinged by sadness as we screeched into the crematorium and entered the chapel. It was packed and we couldn't see Mum, Dad, Andy or anyone we knew. We were at the back, because of our lateness, so that was why we couldn't spot familiar faces, we told ourselves. It was only when the chapel emptied, and Mum, Dad, Andy, Uncle Barry and everyone else we knew remained elusive that we twigged: we were at someone else's funeral! We clambered into the car and left a dust trail worthy of Ben Hur's chariot as we skidded out of the crematorium and on to the care home where Grandad had lived since Grandma passed away. The whole family was there, having sifted through Grandad's little pile of belongings, and they assuaged our guilty consciences by reassuring us that Grandad would have found the whole affair highly amusing. And I knew that he would have.

He would also have found the fact that I was dispensing racing tips rather hilarious too, but I'd decided it was time to move on by then anyway, so at a canter I trotted off to AA Roadwatch in Stanmore, north London. I loved local radio, and nearly every station I listened to featured traffic reports from AA Roadwatch. I was beside myself with excitement when one of my first broadcasts involved chatting to the iconic Tony Blackburn on Radio London. We broadcast to radio stations all over London and the South East, and I was in my element swapping banter with the various presenters and gathering vital traffic information from police operations centres. I always got a huge buzz when a big news story meant our involvement was more important too — we worked without surfacing during the hurricane of 1987 and after the tragedy of the Hungerford Massacre in the same year.

I hoped, by getting my name around, that AA Roadwatch would eventually lead to work as a reporter in a radio newsroom. Guess what? It did. Unusually I had a plan, and even more unusually it worked! I secured some freelance news shifts at County Sound radio based in Guildford, Surrey, which led to regular work running the newsroom at weekends. I did this alongside my work in the week for Roadwatch, as well as shifts at other stations all over the south and east. At one stage, having been offered the prestigious *Breakfast Show* news shift on Hereward Radio in Peterborough, I would set my alarm for 2 a.m. each morning, drive up to

Hereward, do the show, then drive back down to County Sound for the drive-time stint there. If I didn't have to do County Sound I'd drive across to Cambridge and stay the night at my Auntie Mary's, where we'd catch up on all the family gossip and giggle over Mum's funny ways.

I was never at home and, as there were no mobiles then, my home answerphone soon filled up with unanswered messages. My car was essential — some weeks I clocked up 1,500 miles or more — and it was my pride and joy. I'd passed my driving test at the second attempt — having hit a lorry on the first — aged seventeen. I was twenty-six before I could muster up the money for a deposit and a loan to buy my own car, so when I finally got the keys to that little black Peugeot 205 I was too scared to drive it off the forecourt and David was drafted in for the honour. My driving was very rusty at first so that when it came to going to work I was more nervous about the journey than what awaited me once I got there. Mum was on tenterhooks back in Wales, knowing I was rampaging around the country and too busy to phone her every day. As it turns out, she had every reason to be worried.

The night before my first TV job I wrote my car off after another car pulled out of a turning onto the dual carriageway that I was travelling home on after an AA Roadwatch shift. The police came, my car was loaded onto a truck, and then everyone drove away and left me there, battered, bruised and traumatised, at the roadside. My legs were cut and bruised, my neck had locked with the force of the impact and it was growing dark. But, more importantly, I was due in Norwich the next day for my TV debut!

I'd been for a screen test a few months before, having heard about it on the off chance via AA Roadwatch. A new BBC2 regional programme called Weekend was looking for a presenter for its live Friday-night show. I turned up for the screen test, sat in a room, shiftily eyeing up the other contenders as they shiftily did the same to me, and concluded that I didn't have a hope in hell's chance of securing the job. I did my best in the screen test, felt surprisingly comfortable in front of the camera, but knew there were much better-looking candidates than me. And that's what telly's all about, isn't it? I went home and didn't think much more of it. The longer time went on, the longer the odds on me receiving a promising phone call. I nearly jumped out of my skin when the 'rring-rring' punctuated the silence.

'Hello, it's Peter from BBC Weekend,' chirped the voice on the other end. 'Thank you for attending the screen test, but I'm afraid to tell you that . . . you got the job!' I screamed. And then blurted something inane back, which included 'thank you' about a thousand times, and put the phone down, screamed again and danced around the room. I've got to phone Mum, got to phone Mum, got to phone Mum. So I phoned Mum. 'What's that, Toots? Hang on, let me get my notepad . . . You've what?! Let me write that down so I can tell Dad . . . When does it start? . . . On BBC2 . . . Which night? . . . When can we see it? . . . Oh, only in the

166

south and east . . . Never mind.' Arrrgh! Trust Mum to turn my most exciting career moment ever into a 'never mind' affair.

I made my TV debut on a Friday night in August 1988, having taken the train to the BBC Studios in Norwich, while my beloved, crocked car remained critically ill in a garage somewhere in north-west London. I slapped make-up all over my legs to hide the injuries and sat on the sofa alongside Guy Michelmore, looking directly ahead, even when he spoke to me, because I couldn't move my neck.

Mum, meanwhile, still managed to claim bragging rights to my appearance, even though she couldn't watch the show in Wales. She must have got Auntie Mary to video it or something, because I found a photo of myself sitting on that *Weekend* sofa at Dad's recently. She'd put the video in, paused it and taken a photo of me on 'the BBC' to share with all those who had the misfortune not to witness my endeavours. I found another one recently, taken later in my career. She'd taken a photo of a teletext page on which were the results of a poll to find Britain's most popular female television presenter. I was second, narrowly behind Jill Dando. On the back of the photo, taken in 1998, Mum had written, '*Fiona on Teletext. Dident she do well.*' The spelling is how it was on the photo. If only I'd realised back then that those signs were pointing to something more serious than I'd ever dared contemplate.

17

It's hard to know when we first noticed that something was not right with Mum. For years she'd had her violent headaches, her depressive episodes, her 'problems with my nerves', and she'd taken to using a new phrase which, naturally, David, Andy and I made fun of. 'I feel odd, not right, really tight in the head,' she'd tell us. Mum's enduring naivety, her refusal to accept that anyone could be horrible or nasty (except for us!), her often inappropriate childlike habit of saying what she thought and her constant mixing-up of words and concepts set her apart as a memorable, eccentric character, the innocent source of many family belly laughs. Or sometimes an embarrassing one because she was our mum. 'Oh Mum!' was an oft-used phrase in our house and down the phone if she said something inapt, as she was often liable to do.

A hilarious example of Mum's utter out-of-kilter-with-the-real-world ways came when I was in the last year of my degree in Birmingham. I was supposed to be studying Jonathan Swift's *Gulliver's Travels* and I didn't want to spend any of my dwindling money pot on a book that I was being forced to read, so I got on the phone to Mum. 'Mum, you know Dad's *Gulliver's Travels*?' I asked. 'I need it for my course.' 'Gullivers?' she replied, not very convincingly.

'Yes, it's in Dad's study.' 'Really? OK, I'll look.' 'Make sure you send it,' I urged. 'I really need to read it soon.' After a couple of days I phoned again to enquire if it was in the post. 'No, I'll get them wrapped up today. I only just found them; they were in the airing cupboard.' Them? The airing cupboard? What was Mum on about?

Right, I have to explain this to you now: Mum had a pair of shoes that David, Andy and I found highly amusing. They were flat and brown with a buckle across, very unflattering and very un-Mum. She'd bought them, she said, to wear while she was riding her bike. Mum was a tall lady, about five foot eight, and she had size 8 feet, or as she liked to put it, 'Size 7, 8 for comfort.' Those shoes looked huge because they were long and flat, and we teased her mercilessly about them and nicknamed them 'Gullivers', after the literary character's adventures as a giant in the land of Lilliput. You must know what's coming next. Yes, that's right, Mum was about to wrap up her famous shoes, her Gullivers, and send them to me. Jonathan Swift himself couldn't have written a more amusing episode. My brothers and I made sure that she was never allowed to live that one down.

I suppose I began to worry about her a little more when in the late 1980s and early 90s I had a long-term boyfriend whom I'd met at Sky News, where I then worked. He and Dad got along famously. The three of us would put the world to rights accompanied by vat-loads of alcohol well into the early hours of the morning. But he didn't really click with Mum. And everyone clicked with Mum. Ever since my schooldays my friends had commented on how friendly, welcoming and warm she was. But he didn't see the charm. She picked up on it and was nervier than usual around him. I thought she wasn't keen on him and he'd picked up on that. Which way round was it? And then we went to my cousin Jackie's wedding, where I was a bridesmaid.

We met Mum and Dad in Cambridge the day before the wedding. Mum was very agitated and emotional, but I put it down to spending hours in the car with Dad — they always arrived at each other's throats after a long journey together. I was a bit annoyed and embarrassed about her behaviour because my boyfriend was with me. On the day of the wedding Mum was close to tears most of the time. But it was a wedding, and it was her closest sister Auntie Mary's daughter who was tying the knot, so she was bound to be, I reasoned. She was distracted and jumpy and really not herself at all. Her behaviour was odd enough for me to remember that incident and single it out from the numerous 'off the wall' occasions with mum. She kept welling up and going off to the loo. It's her and Dad again, I thought — they're going through another bad patch. And then came the speeches. After the best man's monologue Mum stood up for the toast and her skirt fell down. Everyone laughed, I cringed, my dad said something derogatory, and Mum looked as though she was going to completely break down.

I found her in the loo sobbing and saying, 'I

170

don't know what's wrong with me.' No one did. She was only in her late fifties so we never suspected that anything was dreadfully wrong, but it was a weekend that stands out and one I look back to as maybe the first sign of an illness which, then, we knew nothing about. She struggled for a while after that and made frequent visits to the doctor to try and sort herself out. She was on hormone replacement therapy and I thought that might be messing her up. She was pretty desperate to get her positive outlook back and was referred to a psychiatrist, whose manner really upset her. 'All he keeps doing is to try and tell me it's something in my past. He's rude and cold, and I don't like him,' she told me. That episode spooked her out and made her feel even more desperate to find answers and a solution. Eventually she was advised to try Transcendental Meditation, which despite my disbelief, and David and Andy's — this was our mum, who'd dressed us up in our 'best' clothes to visit her trusted GPs and believed in the power of conventional drugs all her life — seemed to work. At least, we think it was Transcendental Meditation that did the trick, but as Mum told us she was doing 'incidental medication' we were never quite sure!

It's hard trying to track a consistent pattern of behaviour when you don't live with someone all the time. Having got through our teenage traumas and the usual agitations that plague most families relatively intact, I was very close to Mum and Dad and would head to Wales whenever I had a break in my work schedule, even though they'd look me up and down as soon as I walked through the door and ask what on earth I thought I was wearing and in Mum's case, 'when was I going to do something about that straggly hair?' Mum had a knack of winding me up by putting me down without meaning to. 'Do you think you'll ever work on real television?' she'd ask when I was at Sky News. 'Do you think you'll work for the BBC one day?' was the question when I worked for *GMTV*. It always prompted a curious reaction of feeling really angry that she'd said it and really unworthy that she thought I hadn't done well enough.

All of Mum's myriad behaviour traits made it hard to fathom how she was really feeling at any one time, plus her desire to always make other people happy masked a lot of her emotion. David, Andy and I teased her mercilessly when we got together, and because she seemed to take it and not get mad, we did it even more. Mum's kindly nature was always taken advantage of, but people loved her. She was the star of the show in Ocky White — 'Pembrokeshire's Leading Store', the local family department store, where she worked in Haverfordwest. She greeted everyone with a smile before regaling them with the highs of my career and coaxing them into buying things they didn't want. She'd often phone me in her lunch break. 'Hi, Toots. I'm in china today.' 'China?! What on earth are you doing there?' Some days it was, 'Toots, I'm in underwear.' It was only when she said, 'I'm in linens next week,' that I could be sure she was talking about departments in her beloved store.

Sometimes in her lunch break she'd write little stream-of-consciousness notes to me. I came across one recently.

Dear Toots,

It's a beautiful sunny day here and I've been very busy in the men's department. Just had a bit of lunch, a lovely jacket potato, your favourite, with cheese and butter. I won't want anything to eat tonight. Dad is fine, still busy driving his van around and taking the dog for walks. I might go to Uncle Tom's when I finish here today, then Dad can pick me up from there. Hope you are well and still enjoying work — looking forward to when you've got some time off and can come down again. Maybe we could go to Carmarthen and see what they've got in Marks and Spencers? Anyway, my Toots, must get back to work. Always thinking of you.

Mam x.

Mum absolutely adored Jeremy White, the store's boss, whom she called Mr Jeremy. If Mr Jeremy said it was so, then you'd better believe that it was. We shared many a family joke over Mr Jeremy, but he really looked after Mum and appreciated her loyalty and unique selling skills. He rewarded her by making her a buyer for the linen department. Well, you'd have thought she was on a royal visit every time she and Mr Jeremy took off to some supplier somewhere to select pillows, sheets and whatever else she thought would sell. She'd plan her packed lunch for a whole week beforehand and regale me with every detail. It was when, a few years later, she was taken off buying to return to selling that, now I look back, she often worried that she was making mistakes on the tills. It was around that time too that she had problems with her cashpoint card; she went into the Abbey National and always asked the staff to help her. But we thought that was just Mum being dense.

However bad, worried or depressed she was feeling, Mum's coach trips to see us in London continued. I loved having her to stay. Wherever it was — grotty bedsit (of which there were many), shared student house, my first one-bedroom flat, sharing a bed with me or sleeping on the floor if I was ill — Mum would be there. I find it really hard every time I pass Victoria Coach Station in London now not to well up and think of all the happy greetings and sad goodbyes that took place there. From the days when I'd scrape together pennies to get the bus and the Tube to meet her and take her back to some damp, grim hole, to the times when I drove there in my own car and took her back to my own flat or house, paid for by the unremitting work ethic that I'd picked up from Dad, that coach station always made my heart jump at the prospect of seeing Mum's smiling face waving at the window as the lumbering vehicle pulled in.

Mum was never alone as she disembarked, having extracted the life story — whether tragic, happy or in development — of the person she'd sat next to and shared her Welsh cakes with.

174

She'd introduce the stranger to me: 'This is so and so, poor chap, he's heartbroken because his girlfriend's left him,' or: 'This is so and so, she's in London for a university interview. I've told her all about your degree.' Yes, I bet you have, Mum, I would think as I smiled apologetically at her new-found friend. Once she shared a journey with a poor lady who'd been filled in on all our accomplishments. Top of the bill at that time was David, as he was at the Arts Educational Drama School in London. The woman was probably under the impression that David was the new Laurence Olivier by the time the coach dragged into Victoria after an eight-hour journey. David was meeting Mum that day, and when she rolled in she looked out of the window as usual and spotted David waiting for her. She was horrified at what she saw — instead of a clean-cut budding thespian, there was David with long, flowing, curly locks and clothes she disapproved of. How was she to introduce the son she'd been bragging about to this woman, when he looked 'like a tramp', as she put it? She didn't, that's how. She alighted from the coach with her travel pal, walked straight past David and bustled the woman out of view before coming back and asking David why he hadn't had a haircut. We've laughed about that incident for years. Her face when we challenged her and she knew she'd been rumbled, was like a guilty child's. It was at some of these coach-station rendezvous, now I look back, that it was clear that Mum was suffering, although we didn't realise the significance of the various episodes at the time.

175

On another occasion David and I both went to meet Mum, and when she saw us she just broke down completely. I think it was following an incident at home, which at the time we knew nothing of. It prompted my brother Andy to leave home. This all points to Mum's late fifties, which is when, looking back as always, things seemed to start going wrong. No one told David and me at the time, but there was a completely out-of-control ding-dong at home in Wales. Andy was a teenager with his own life, a bright boy who, like his brother and sister, looked as though he was going to waste his intelligence. He and Mum often clashed, just as David and I did with Mum, when she used to deliberately bang the hoover against our bedroom doors, before barging in and flinging the curtains wide open, while spluttering, 'You lazy madam/bugger; I've already cleaned the house and done a day's work while you've been in that bed.'

We were horrible teenagers. Mum loved us, but didn't like us at all. At the time it was all her fault for not understanding us, of course. With my own eleven-year-old who's starting to think his friends — definitely not his parents — are where it's at, I now completely get where she was coming from. At least David and I had each other, but Andy, having been on his own with Mum and Dad since they moved to Wales when he was seven, was brought up, more or less, like an only child, and he was finding it increasingly hard to cope with the usual teenage things and Mum and Dad's idiosyncratic relationship. Things were worsening between them, not

176

helped by the fact that Dad was made redundant from a TV firm he'd gone on to work for in Haverfordwest. He was fifty-three by then and, following countless job rejections based on his advancing age, he half-heartedly went right back to basics and set up his own business fixing televisions and video recorders.

He didn't have the heart to charge the going rate for hours of arduous, fiddly work and his heart wasn't in it either. His situation had exacerbated the frustration of never having achieved more in his life, and the thought of his lost opportunities along with his dignity, hit him hard. Mum was worried that they'd hit rock bottom, and on the day in question they were bickering and arguing as usual when Dad suddenly flipped. I don't know why this day as opposed to any other — whether Mum's obsessive nagging, whether he was particularly depressed, or just beside himself at Mum and Andy's constant squabbling — but he got hold of Mum and nearly throttled her, before doing the same to Andy. My little brother, then seventeen, packed a bin liner full of his stuff and left home. I think that marked the beginning of the end for Mum — and maybe for Dad too. Who knows? Mum cried and cried over Andy and regularly turned up at the door of his friend's house, where he was staying, and begged him to come home.

It's easier to look back and analyse the evidence than to weigh it all up as it's happening. The not knowing and the carrying on with life as though everything was OK have been sources of great regret, grief and guilt for me. 'Why didn't I notice that things were bad?'; or 'Why didn't she tell me?; I could have helped her much earlier than I did,' and 'If only I'd known that she was ill . . . ' still plague me every day. I guess the answer to all of them, if I'm brutally honest, is that I was getting on with my own life too.

18

At the end of 1993 I moved out to Los Angeles where I'd been promoted by *GMTV* from reporter to LA correspondent. Mum, Dad and my brothers came to wave me off from Heathrow airport just before Christmas. Despite reaching the ripe old age of thirty-two, it was the first festive season I'd ever spent without my parents. I'd left my beloved dog Bizzy, a handsome but mad and very highly strung Weimaraner, with them too following a tearful conversation in which I told them I was thinking of turning the job down because I didn't know what to do with Bizzy. 'Bring him down here — we'll look after him,' Dad said. So I did, and cried all the way back down the M4 to London — nearly 200 miles of misery and tears. Anyway, once in America I spent the festive season in New York with a lovely cameraman I'd hooked up with from work, and phoned home from the Empire State Building on Christmas Day. I kept in touch with home on a weekly basis, keeping Mum informed of everything that she hadn't seen me talking about on TV.

Less than a month after I arrived in LA, I was tossed out of my bed at around four thirty in the morning on 17 January 1994 by a massive earthquake, measuring 6.6 on the Richter scale. I say my bed, but actually I was sleeping on a mattress on the floor, having not had enough time to sort a bed out. Plates and cups slid out of my cupboards and smashed on the floor, the walls cracked, and sirens sounded all over town in the pitch darkness. I instinctively knew what it was despite never having experienced the ground opening up under my feet before. I phoned *GMTV* in London and then hurriedly got dressed and dashed down to my car and off to my office at the headquarters of America's NBC network in Burbank, all the way looking at the fires which had broken out all over the city. The journey there was eerie, dark and pretty damn terrifying, not knowing what to expect — but fully anticipating my car to fall into a crack at any moment. It's the weirdest sensation, being involved in an earthquake — suddenly one of life's solid, dependable certainties, the ground under your feet, is no longer predictable, rumbling and shaking and rocking buildings as you put one ponderous foot in front of the other. It's a spooky feeling which suddenly renders everything unreliable and dangerous.

I worked for hours on end, reporting live on *GMTV* and hoping that Mum and Dad would see me so they'd know I was OK. As the day went on phone lines were either down or completely overloaded with the volume of calls, so I hadn't been able to make contact with them. Sixty people died and nearly 8,000 were injured in the Northridge Quake. I witnessed a policeman's body being dragged from the ruin of a massive freeway which had split in two under him. I knew Mum watched *GMTV* every day to see what I was up to, so I took solace in the fact that she'd know I was OK. Probably the whole street would have known I was all right too because Mum would drag neighbours into the house, whether they wanted to or not, by saying, 'Have you seen my daughter? She presents breakfast TV.' Once I was in a queue with her in Tesco in Haverfordwest when she tapped the person in front on the shoulder. 'This is my daughter Fiona. She presents *GMTV*, you know.' Talk about wanting the ground to open up; I could have done with an earthquake right there in Tesco so I could disappear down a fault line without trace.

Back in LA I was having a brilliant time, working around the clock, driving my little Mazda MX5 convertible with the wind in my hair, the sun beating down on my head and the local radio station, KROQ, blasting out hits by Pearl Jam and Green Day. When you live in LA it's no longer the glamorous, untouchable town of movie legend, just your regular home town. It fast became my home town, and the regularity with which I'd bump into the same old faces at movie premieres that I reported on made it seem like a village, albeit that the inhabitants, such as Tom Cruise, Mel Gibson, Tom Hanks, Steven Spielberg, Cameron Diaz, Brad Pitt, et al., were just a tad more glamorous than the neighbours I'd left behind in Battersea. LA is a bit of a one-horse town if truth be told. Everyone, but *everyone*, wants to be someone they're not. Someone thinner, someone more attractive, someone younger, someone famous — someone who makes a living as an actor is what it all really boils down to. You tire of that quite quickly: the shallow values, the vacuous goals, the never seeing elderly people anywhere, unless it happens to be Clint Eastwood or Elizabeth Taylor (and she always turned up at least two hours late). So it was a blessing that I had my dear friend Neal to laugh with and to stand back and voyeuristically stare at it all from the outside in.

I met Neal when I went to cover my first Oscar ceremony for *GMTV* in 1993. He was assigned as my producer and we clicked from the moment we met. I was nursing a broken heart having split up from my Australian boyfriend — the one Mum wasn't that keen on — and Neal hadn't long been out of a serious relationship either. We sat in the Beverley Wilshire Hotel — the location for Julia Roberts' *Pretty Woman* — sipped heady margaritas, discussed our Oscar plan and then slowly dissected each other's life stories. Neal and I were real soul mates — whenever I think of him it makes me smile. His nervy pacing around, dragging on his umpteenth cigarette of the day, his direct questioning and sometimes hurtful honesty were all little quirks that I cherished. We relished work; both of us extracting huge satisfaction from breaking exclusive stories or getting access to someone no one else had managed to speak to.

One of our coups was grabbing Hugh Grant from right under ITN's nose when he was at the height of his fame having recently starred in *Four Weddings and a Funeral*. He'd arrived in

LA to do all the big chat shows after attending the London premiere with his girlfriend Elizabeth Hurley in her famous Versace safety-pin dress. They were the hottest couple on the planet at the time. Another was getting the only British TV interview with Michael Jackson's parents after he'd first been accused of child molestation. And then there were the Oscar ceremonies we covered — I think it was four in all. Thanks to Neal's intrepid contacts book, we were the first UK TV company to come live from the Oscars as the stars made for the after-show parties clutching their golden statues. He'd schmoozed Graydon Carter, the editor of *Vanity Fair*, who held the hottest party in town, and we got a prime position right outside the entrance to Morton's Restaurant, where the bash was held, tightly packed in with the big American networks and their larger-than-life big-mouth reporters, who thought they owned the world. I'd yell at *GMTV*'s control room as soon as I saw someone approaching, scream at the likes of Madonna, Nicole Kidman and Leonardo Di Caprio before yanking them over to our camera position to talk to them live on *GMTV*. Of all the stars I encountered in LA, I think my favourite has to be the edgy, nervy, slightly verging-on-genius/madness Mel Gibson. When he won best director and best picture for *Braveheart* in 1996 he handed me his two Oscars on his way into the Morton's party so that I could feel the weight of them. It was a pure Hollywood moment, and such a long way from the days when Mum would reassure me that, 'It won't always be like this.'

My Christmas present to Mum and Dad in 1993 was a trip to LA. When the big day arrived, 17 June 1994, I went to meet them from the airport with Neal, who had a bigger car than me for their luggage. I hadn't seen them for six months by then. They looked like two lost children. Goodness knows how they'd negotiated check-in, immigration and all the rigmarole of two international airports. Dad must have been the guiding light, because Mum couldn't even manage the down escalator let alone the vagaries of the baggage carousel. They seemed stressed and agitated and I thought, 'Oh here we go again, so much for my great expectations of a lovely time — already they're annoying me.' I felt as though I'd dragged them over against their will and I resented the fact that they made me feel like that. I guess I hadn't bargained on the fact that, despite Dad regaling us with his stories of living in Malta and Egypt and Mum jumping on a coach to Victoria at the slightest whisper of an invite, they hadn't been on a plane for decades. In fact I don't think Mum had ever been on a plane in her life. But when they're your mum and dad you expect them to be able to handle things. I compared them with Neal's parents, who (with his dad being a diplomat) have travelled all over the world. My parents were so totally unworldly, they hadn't even been on a package holiday to Spain and here I was dragging them across the Atlantic.

Neal and I bustled them into the car and then headed down to the coast at Malibu for something to eat at Gladstones, a huge buzzing wooden shack of a restaurant. Bizarrely, in the middle of tackling our mountainous plates of California's finest grilled grub, the TV screens lit up and a crowd gathered round to watch former American football idol O. J. Simpson, now suspected of the murder of his ex-wife Nicole Brown Simpson, involved in a low-speed police chase on the San Diego Freeway. His white Ford Bronco, driven by his friend and former team-mate Al Cowlings, was engulfed in a buzz of TV news helicopters until the chase ended hours later when Simpson returned home and gave himself up. My news nose knew that this was a story that *GMTV* would want back in London, but I was on holiday and I couldn't just dump Mum and Dad in the middle of Hollywood. Goodness knows who Mum would have ended up befriending if left to her own devices. So Neal dispatched himself to our office while I took my parents back to settle them into their hotel for the night, before rejoining him. It's a story I ended up covering until the culmination of the O. J. Simpson trial in October 1995, when following a 'Not guilty' verdict 'The Juice', as they called him, was cut loose.

I'd arranged for Mum and Dad to stay at the Hollywood Roosevelt Hotel, scene of the first ever Oscar ceremony. It looked as though it had seen better days, which was a good thing, as Mum would have been intimidated by too much grandeur. It was situated on Hollywood Boulevard, directly opposite the famous Hollywood Walk of Fame, but Mum was more impressed by the basket of fruit which had been left in their

185

room along with a warm welcome card. I didn't know what it was then, but there was a change in the dynamic between Mum and Dad, as though they were weary of each other, that they'd reached the end of the road almost. Mum was her usual sunny self, but in patches, and not nearly as effervescent as she normally was. I blamed it on the long flight and we soon embarked on a tour of the local hotspots.

We meandered our way through Beverley Hills and the beautiful bougainvillea-stained Hollywood Hills, to spot stars' houses, Mum's camera clicking away at every opportunity. We went to San Diego, down the coast to Malibu, to Santa Barbara, and to Universal Studios and Disneyland. In San Diego Mum walked arm in arm with Neal and found out every single thing about him. 'What a lovely chap,' she told me in a tone that meant 'He'd be ideal for you.' But I didn't see Neal in that way — we were definitely soul mates, but mates is how I wanted it to stay. We went to Neal's house for dinner, an affair so comfortable and casual that Neal tipped peas onto our waiting plates direct from the saucepan! Dad wasn't well. It was more than a jadedness; he was in physical pain, which we later found out was a deep vein thrombosis which had affected a particularly tender part of his anatomy.

There were lovely moments on that trip, particularly when Mum and I went to Disneyland on our own because Dad wasn't up to it. She was like a child, but I kept thinking that something in her had died and I didn't know what it was. One morning we went for a coffee and she was uncharacteristically distant. Her eyes were teary and she was nervy and agitated, playing with her hands. I felt again that I'd forced them to come to LA against their will, and I got cross because I didn't know what was wrong. 'I can't believe you've come all the way here,' I said to Mum, 'and you're miserable. You might as well go home if you're not enjoying it here.' Dad looked at her quite tenderly, as though he understood, as though he was glad I'd noticed. I can still picture us sitting there, a feeling of desperation around the table, not realised nor vented. When they went back I felt empty, not knowing what the 'something' was that was missing on that trip.

The next time I went home, for Christmas 1994, Mum had had all her photos developed. She'd written on the backs of most of them so she could remember where she'd been, to show off to her friends. Her handwriting was hesitant, her spelling erratic and she'd got some facts wrong — most of them, if I'm truthful. Again, we all laughed at Mum's eccentricity — at least that's what we thought it was. I've got those photos at home now and I look at the backs of them and guiltily wonder why we didn't realise that Mum's problem was more than being a bit daft at times. 'Holliwood Hills' is one phrase constantly misspelt and written in an odd mix of lower case and capitals.

Back in LA, life continued as one big delicious mix of work, play, eating, drinking, travelling and coveted nights on my own in my little redwood shack just off Beachwood Drive, which leads up to the famous Hollywood sign. I'd play Wagner loudly and light candles, drink wine and dream. Spookily I began to receive little parcels and cryptic notes, left at my gate, and which I tripped over as I bolted out in the morning. '*I hear you like Wagner — it seems you're even more interesting than I thought! I thought you might like to try some Mahler.*' I looked around and peered towards the house up the bank, which looked over mine. I was spooked out knowing someone had been watching me and listening when I was alone in my house. Several other packages arrived at random intervals; I never did find out who it was, but in the notes that accompanied various classical CDs he (at least I think it was a he) commented on how I parked, what I wore and where I shopped. Urgh! I never felt quite the same about that cosy little wooden refuge again.

And then just before Christmas 1995 a significant event happened, a significant event which I thought was a pain and an intrusion when I first heard about it. I was going home for two weeks and *GMTV* were sending a reporter to cover my leave. Neal and I were to meet him and fill him in on what we did, where he'd find things, what was expected of him, etc. We met in one of our favourite restaurants on Cahuenga Boulevard, where Neal and I had spent many hours. It wasn't the first time I'd met Martin Frizell. I'd certainly watched him presenting and reporting on TVAM and I'd bumped into him at Sky News when I worked there — he'd joined after TVAM lost its licence in 1991. Then he turned up at *GMTV* as chief correspondent in 1993. I thought he was arrogant, cold and aloof. We had an odd sort of professional relationship based on trading light-hearted insults and banter. So, let's just say, I admired him professionally. But that was it.

The man Neal and I shared dinner with on that fateful night in LA couldn't have been more different. The arrogant man was nowhere to be seen, and in his place was a very shy, private, actually quite vulnerable person who wasn't sure of himself at all. To my complete shock and surprise, I thought he was lovely. He wasn't my type at all to look at, but there was a dignity and a sensitivity about him that I found appealing. The more we spoke, the more my long-held impression of him faded away. I think he must have felt the same about me because when it was time to leave the restaurant he asked, 'Shall I come to yours for coffee?' 'No,' I replied, 'I'm leaving in the morning and I need to pack.' Just the fact that he wanted to was enough for me. I flew to London knowing that wouldn't be the last time I'd be sharing a meal with Martin Frizell. Despite his weird name.

19

In April 1996 I moved back to London. I'd spent two and a half years in Los Angeles and was keen to pursue some of the job offers which had been winging their way over the Atlantic; I'd also been told that I was to stand in for Anthea Turner, who then presented *GMTV* alongside Eamonn Holmes, while she was on holiday. Eamonn and I had done a week of presenting *GMTV* live from New York, and our bosses liked the chemistry between us. We were like two peas in a pod in so many ways: both hated authority, both workaholics, both from similar backgrounds and both lumbered with the terribly frustrating habit of leaving everything until the last minute. We were made for each other!

Before all that took off though, I had to get used to being back home. It was weird being in my little one-bedroom flat again after renting it out while I was away. The first thing I did was buy a new loo seat! Once that very important problem was sorted I settled back into London life straight away. As most of it was consumed by work, it wasn't dissimilar to life in Los Angeles anyway, except that I didn't see the sun and Neal every day, and I missed that.

I was a general reporter again and the main fill-in presenter on the sofa. In June 1996 I was dispatched to Ascot to broadcast live from there on Ladies' Day. I rose at 3 a.m., got dressed in a flimsy wedding-type outfit and a stupid hat and met the crew at *GMTV*. We were all to travel in a minibus and it turned out I wasn't the only reporter on board; it was a two-reporter job and my travelling companion was a certain Martin Frizell. I'd seen him on and off since I'd been back, and we'd often ended up being the last two at the table after long lunches with our colleagues, but getting up in the middle of the night doesn't leave much time for carousing, so it was a slow-burn thing. Well, I thought it was a slow-burn anyway, but for all I knew he might not have considered it to be smoking in the first place.

It was freezing at Ascot early in the morning, and my flimsy outfit and ridiculous shoes were ill-suited for the nippy air and the damp turf. Martin and I sort of verbally snuggled up in between broadcasts — there was definitely a spark between us which our colleagues noticed too. On the minibus on the way home he sat next to me and asked me if I fancied going for lunch in our local area. By strange coincidence we lived a five-minute walk from each other in south-west London, so it couldn't have been more convenient. We went to my favourite local Italian restaurant, the same one I'd had dinner in with Mum, Dad, my brothers and my lovely future sister-in-law the night before I left London for LA. After our chilly start to the day it turned out to be a beautiful sunny lunchtime, so we sat outside and lingered and lingered. It was early evening and the restaurant was preparing for dinner by the time we left. I walked Martin back to his because I was too embarrassed for him to see my flat until he knew me better. It had been rented out for over two years and I hadn't unpacked half my stuff or even thought of decorating it. I didn't mind him seeing the new loo seat, but the rest, resembling a hobo's street collection, didn't bear inspection. I walked him to the gated entrance of his mansion block and pecked him on the cheek before enigmatically walking away. Well, I thought it was enigmatic anyway!

After that peck on the cheek things progressed really rapidly, so much so that we were having a drink in Covent Garden one lunchtime after work and Martin asked me to marry him. It must have been just four weeks since that first lunch alone together. It wasn't a bended-knee job or anything like that; it just sort of came up in conversation. I had never until that day believed in marriage, having had Dad telling me not to do it 'whatever you do' for years, and having endured two previous long-term relationships which I wanted to get out of once the whole heart-popping, stomach-churning honeymoon period was over. Both of them lasted over four years, but I think I was ready for the off after about two and a half years. I really couldn't see myself being with one person for life. So I told Martin just that. His reaction was pretty instant: his eyes filled up and he had to turn away. I was really taken aback. Cripes, this guy really does mean it, I thought. I felt terrible but I still stuck to my guns, even offering my thoughts on it being much better for long-term relationships if the two parties concerned lived in separate abodes.

Martin said he'd never wanted to get married before either, but, 'It's the first time I've ever wanted to commit myself to someone; to put it on another level.' This was a man who I'd once thought cold and arrogant; who'd spent most of his reporting career covering the biggest stories of the day; who'd dodged bullets and tank-fire in war zones — and there he was sitting alongside me at the bar, wearing a very big heart on his sleeve. He's a proud, very dignified man, so this was a huge admission for him. I didn't say yes, but after all the weeks I'd thought about him since having dinner in LA and in the few weeks I'd known him better back in London, I somehow knew that he was the 'one' that Mum had insisted I'd stumble across some day.

Mum's only dream for me (and herself and the relations and neighbours) was to have a wedding video of the happy day when I would walk down the aisle in a cloud of net curtain, accompanied by Dad muttering, 'Don't get married whatever you do,' all the while with a beatific, winsome smile on my face, walking towards the captured one. Mum would be in the front row, big beam on her face, camera at the ready and on the verge of doing or saying something completely inappropriate. It was the stuff of nightmares for me, but a dream for Mum worth a hundred times more than all those videos she'd taped of me on *GMTV*. I'd been treated to countless viewings of other people's weddings, usually her friends' daughters, in an effort to prompt a Cinderella moment out of me, but to Mum's utter disappointment it hadn't worked. The Big White Wedding was something that never ever made its way into my psyche; it was never an ambition, never a dream. I know it's hard to believe, given what I do for a living, but I hate being the centre of attention. The thought of being the star of some sanctimonious gathering of sniping relatives was anathema to me.

'Just like your bloody father,' Mum would say.

20

My fast-track relationship with Martin and the accompanying realisation that he was a perfect fit, despite the fact that we'd only been together for six weeks by then, meant that he was allowed to meet Mum and Dad, an honour only ever awarded to three men before. It was one of those occasions that again, when I look back, should have alerted me to the fact that Mum's behaviour wasn't right. I was already in Wales that weekend, a beautifully crisp-aired golden July day in 1996, and Martin was making his way down by car having had some commitment that had prevented him travelling down with me. I sat on a wall on the road into Haverfordwest just down the road from the railway station waiting for Martin so I could show him the way to Mum and Dad's. And anyway, I wanted to warn him of my parents' strange habits! Mum, as usual on a Saturday, was in China or some other exotic location in Ocky White's.

I met Martin and we went for a coffee so that I could prepare him for her onslaught on his life thus far. We picked Mum up and there was a tension in the air. Maybe it was me, I thought, worried that everyone would hit it off, that Mum and Dad would like Martin, that he'd like them. But it was Mum — she wasn't herself. Normally she'd have had the whole of Martin's life story laid out bare before the end of the five-minute journey home, but she didn't seem that interested. She was smiley, friendly, but her warmth didn't spread like it usually did. I became tense and went off both of them: Mum because she wasn't who I knew she was and Martin because he could have offered more conversation himself and therefore eased my angst. His shyness was one of his endearing qualities, but right then I could have coshed him for it.

I think we went out that night, because I'd anticipated we all might need a breather from the cloying atmosphere of being lumped together in a small bungalow with Mum and Dad sizing Martin up and vice versa. Mum briefly became herself before we went out, dancing around with her camera, making sure she'd got material to entertain her mates at Ocky White's. My brothers and I used to get so annoyed with Mum's paparazzo tendencies, but she's left a real family history behind that we'd never have had otherwise. I recently discovered one of the pictures she took that night. It was in a box full of memories, in Dad's flat, where I've taken most of the family photos. Now he spends hours poring over them, although he doesn't seem to know who anyone is any more. Anyway, Martin and I are sat side by side on the sofa, me with my head in my hands and a 'Mum, do you have to embarrass me?' look on my face, while Martin, with a benevolent smile, is gently looking at the camera. On the back of the photo Mum has written, '*Please return.*' She used to send photos to Auntie Mary, Auntie Brenda or Auntie Joan if there was anything to show off about, and I guess me finally finding a boyfriend and bringing him home was worthy of that honour. Then Mum had written, 'Fiona was annoyed at me takein pictures.' Mum never had difficulty with spelling, and seeing she'd spelt 'taking' as 'takein' made my stomach turn with the regret of not having realised that perhaps she was experiencing cognitive difficulties back then. But how was I to know? In 1996 Alzheimer's was largely perceived as a faintly amusing condition which old people had and which made them say funny things. A couple of years on from that first visit home with Martin, I was to embark on a very steep learning curve.

Anyhow, that weekend sticks in my mind as not being all it should have been because Mum was not all I know she could have been. Or maybe she couldn't any more. But we were all too tied up in our own worlds to notice. I often wonder why Dad didn't twig that Mum's personality was altering, but then they'd reached a point in their marriage when they were generally irritated with each other. Dad especially wouldn't go on holiday, wouldn't go to Mum's work dos, wouldn't do anything much with her by then. He'd drive down to pick her up from work some days, and they'd go for a ride in the car together occasionally, or in the work van that he now drove to deliver car parts to various local destinations. He worked long hours all for not much more than £4.00 an hour until the minimum wage was introduced in 1997. He often intimated that he felt he'd 'come to this', and that life didn't have that much to offer him.

Dad's attitude broke Mum's heart. We would play his indifference down and say, 'He's always been the same, Mum. He's never going to change now; you're just going to have to accept it.' But she couldn't, and as she sat alone among tables of other married couples smiling and laughing as usual, I think she was slowly dying inside. This may be a totally irrational thought, but I'm convinced heartbreak can in some way have an impact on the closing down of a mind. I know that Alzheimer's disease, simply put, is caused by protein plaques which damage nerve cells in the brain until it no longer functions properly, but I'm pretty convinced that environmental factors have their part to play too. That general atrophying of a relationship, an air of indifference from someone you love, leading separate lives and a feeling that the home is a lonelier place than anywhere else — all of these can grind away at the spirit until life is not worth living any more. Both of them were deeply depressed, and although we didn't fathom the exact cause of it back then, it was becoming increasingly obvious that something was wrong.

In December there was a family wedding. Clearly it wasn't mine. My brother David was marrying Sarah, his gorgeous long-term girlfriend. The night before the wedding we all gathered in the hotel in Richmond upon Thames where the nuptials were to take place. Mum and Dad had travelled from Wales, which usually, as we'd witnessed over the years, resulted in them being tense with each other by the time they arrived. Both Mum and Dad were edgy, and Mum was dreadfully pale, her face almost the colour of alabaster and clammy-looking. Dad seemed very vulnerable too. They were by no means old and frail — Dad was sixty-two and Mum sixty-four at the time — but there was definitely a marked change in them. They seemed older, somehow diminished, and Mum looked . . . well, just not like Mum — as if someone else had moved in. Nevertheless she managed to provide us with at least one comic moment.

David and Sarah had recently visited Wales to tell Mum and Dad that Sarah was pregnant. Mum would normally have been on the phone to all the numbers in her address book, announcing the fact that she was to become a grandma — a nana, as she wanted to be called — but on this occasion there was a muted response. Before she could even digest the wonderful news she was struck by the horrific realisation that they weren't yet married, so she didn't want the shameful facts to be spread, not even to Auntie Mary, who she'd usually have been on the phone to first. At the wedding we were sitting with Mum, Dad, Auntie Mary, Uncle Roy, Dad's brother Uncle Barry, his wife Linda and Mum's friend Auntie Joan and her husband, also called Roy. During the wedding reception, and I'm not sure exactly how it went, but I think Sarah asked Auntie Mary if Mum had told her the news. 'The news? No, what news?' enquired Auntie Mary. 'That David and I are going to have a baby,' Sarah replied, with a customary huge beam across her face. 'Of course they're not,' chipped in Mum, who'd obviously been eavesdropping and didn't like what she'd heard. 'No, of course they're not, are you, Sarah?' Poor Sarah didn't know what to say, but knowing Mum and her *ach y fi* ways, we all burst out laughing and teased her mercilessly until she saw the funny side too.

What an eventful wedding that was, because Martin, while all the old-fashioned tittle-tattle about the pregnancy continued, had decided to do something equally out-of-date and asked Dad if he'd 'mind very much' if he asked for my hand in marriage. Dad said, 'Of course not; welcome to the family.' Poor Martin.

21

As I've said, a wedding, never mind a white one, was not on my life list of 'Things to Do'. Even though I really felt that Martin was 'the one', I still had nagging doubts that I was cut out for a life-time commitment. So Martin drove the effort on and booked a Las Vegas extravaganza — £150 for the licence, the ceremony and a tacky limousine. We were to fly there later that month, December 1996. Despite still being of the opinion that I didn't want the trappings of a conventional existence at all, Martin had persuaded me that I should sell my little one-bedroom flat so that we could buy a grown-up house together too — well, I *was* thirty-five, hardly a sapling any more — so we spent a lot of spare time browsing around looking for furniture. The afternoon before we were due to fly to Vegas, we were in an antique shop after work, eyeing up a kitchen table, when my mobile rang.

It was Dad. Dad never made phone calls. Never. Ever. That's why Mum had her trusty notepad, for goodness' sake: to tell Dad all the things he didn't particularly want to know. Dad's voice was quavering. 'It's your mother,' he said, in a flat, sombre tone. 'What about her?' I replied with trepidation. 'She's got breast cancer.' Apparently Mum, who'd looked so ghostly and strange at David's wedding, had known something was up at the time, but hadn't said a word.

She'd been shopping in her local Tesco and spotted a mobile screening unit in the car park with the words 'Breast Test Wales' emblazoned on the side. For some reason she went in, maybe because in her forties she'd had a lump scare which turned out to be benign. Around one in every one hundred women screened in Wales is found to have breast cancer. Like most people, Mum thought that she couldn't possibly be that one person, so she was screened and didn't think any more of it until she received a letter saying she'd been called back as they had found something. At the wedding she knew all of this but didn't let on because she didn't want to worry anyone — no wonder she was pale and haunted-looking. We didn't have a clue about any of it until Dad's phone call in the middle of that shop; it was a huge amount to take in and I felt sick and unsteady.

Even if I'd been armed with my own notebook right then, I wouldn't have been able to write anything down — to see it all in black and white would mean it was true, and Mum just couldn't have breast cancer, could she? She did. And in a couple of days she was due at Neath Hospital to have a bone scan to make sure it hadn't spread. Fortunately, as we were supposed to be flying to Vegas to get married, without telling a soul, we had booked some time off work. We set about cancelling the flight, the hotel and the wedding straight away, and the day after Dad's call headed towards the M4 for the five-hour journey to west Wales. The following day Mum had her bone scan, but as Dad had work commitments, he carried on as normal, his sense of duty meaning that he would never let anyone down. Apart from us. Mum didn't drive, so I'm not quite sure how she would have negotiated the sixty-two-mile journey from Haverfordwest to Neath if we hadn't been there. I know she'd have found a way, or got a friend to go with her, but Dad's complete lack of care was unbelievable, and although I didn't tell him, I resented the fact that he just assumed that I would pick up the pieces.

The day we drove to Neath was grey, grim and grimy, and if it hadn't been, that's how we would have seen it anyway. It had been snowing, and had reached that depressing stage where the snow has almost gone, leaving behind dirty slush and patches of ice. Mum, as always, was in good spirits. God bless her, she couldn't let on if she was feeling any different because she wouldn't have wanted to upset anyone else. Martin parked the car and waited outside the bleak stone building while Mum and I trotted along arm in arm towards the out patients department. I think Mum was so happy just to have me home that thoughts of her predicament became secondary to wanting to make the most of having me there. We laughed and talked as we walked down the slope which approached the entrance and suddenly ended up in a pile on the floor. We'd slipped on the ice and pulled each other down to the ground, shrieking and laughing like two giddy children. That moment has remained in my mind as a very special one. It was as if we were suspended in a happier time for just that precious couple of minutes. If I'd known what lay ahead then, I'd have frozen that moment and protected it against the ravages of truth. That day though, there was at least some good news when, after the scan, the consultant told us that his initial feeling was that the cancer hadn't spread. Nevertheless Mum was going to have to go into hospital for a mastectomy, and it being Mum it couldn't happen at just any old time of the year.

We spent most of Christmas Day 1996 on a ward at the Prince Philip Hospital in Llanelli. Mum was recovering from her operation, but as usual tried to make us all feel as though it was really nothing at all. Something had left her though, an unfathomable something that meant her smile wasn't backed up with a feeling. David told me later she'd said to him that she didn't want to go on any more. 'I'm ready to go now, Day,' was what she said, suggesting that she knew that recovering from breast cancer wouldn't completely solve her problems. We gave her presents, chatted and joked, but there was an emptiness about Christmas that year, and although I still wanted to think that Mum would be with us for ever, I think she'd given up a little bit on life by then, a feeling which has become stronger with hindsight.

22

Hindsight — it's a word that crops up regularly when someone you love is finally diagnosed with Alzheimer's disease. 'In hindsight, she was acting oddly,' or 'With hindsight, it all seems so obvious that something was wrong,' are sentences that seem to raise their heads all the time. Now, for instance, I think back to something that Mum's dear friend Joyce, a neighbour, told me that Mum had said when she came out of hospital. 'Oh, don't worry about me,' she reassured her friend, 'I enjoyed it, and at least I've had a good send-off.' Joyce and I laughed at the time, but in retrospect that sentence seems loaded. I'm convinced now that Mum knew that breast cancer wasn't her primary concern. Hindsight is accompanied by a large dose of another word that features highly: guilt. One episode (in hindsight) that I should have picked up on at the time, and which still smothers me in guilt every time I think of it, is a restaurant outing while Mum was recovering from her operation at home.

Martin and I travelled to Wales and booked into a hotel — something that Mum was quite hurt about. We did it rather than stay with them because things had changed — there was tension in the house, the beds weren't changed or were dressed with sheets full of holes, and very often there was little or no food, again, all signs that I should have picked up on, but because my parents' relationship was so dysfunctional it was an easy screen for all that was peculiar and we put it down to that. They were so at odds with each other that I thought they'd had some sort of shopping stand-off which had resulted in neither of them buying food or really just bothering. Their house was no longer the welcoming home it once was, with Mum beaming at the door and ambushing us with a surfeit of home-made food. So we took them out to a restaurant, an idea which, from the beginning, we began to feel was wrong.

Mum was very tense and nervy, but then she'd just been through a traumatic time. Dad was fine with us — he was always pleased to see us and talk about anything really, as long as it wasn't personal — and quite protective towards Mum to begin with. I sat next to Mum, opposite Dad and Martin, and as the meal went on the conversation got round to Mum saying she wished she could have a television in the bedroom as she was spending more time in there resting after her operation. It was a request that had obviously been made before and which had clearly not gone down well.

Dad, for some reason, became irrationally angry and said he was not going to do it. I tried to mediate, but Dad was having none of it. 'But all you've got to do is carry the portable telly in there and plug it in,' I suggested. Dad wouldn't budge. I couldn't understand why he was being so insensitive. I was embarrassed for Martin too. I hadn't been with him that long — about six

206

months — and Dad was behaving really badly.

I held Mum's hands, which were shaking by then, and her vulnerability and hurt made my shock at Dad's manner boil over into red-hot anger. 'You're behaving like a bloody cold unfeeling Nazi,' I hissed across the table. I can't remember his response, but needless to say the evening didn't really recover from that low point, and they went home, Mum like a meek, shaken child, but still trying to put on a show of 'Everything's all right.' I knew it wasn't and I cried all night in our cold damp hotel room. I had never felt so angry with my father before. He was never exactly gushing over with emotion, but this was a new callousness that really disturbed me, a heartlessness that was quite shocking. I wanted to pick Mum up and take her away from it all, but she wasn't my child, she was my Mum, and anyway she loved Dad, despite it all. She always missed him when she came away on her trips to mine or Auntie Mary's, and she'd look like an expectant child when the phone rang, thinking it was Dad, maybe to say he missed her. He rarely did.

In March 1997, as a Mother's Day treat, we took Mum to Crufts at the NEC in Birmingham. I'd been asked by the PDSA if I'd come and do a photocall at their stand, and the first thing I thought of was Mum and her love of dogs, so I agreed to do it. Martin and I booked a hotel and arranged for Mum to get the coach to Birmingham and then a cab from the coach station to the hotel. We were really looking forward to her turning up armed with her big smile, and we didn't think anything of it when it started to get dark and she still hadn't arrived. Maybe the coach had been late leaving or was held up in traffic somewhere. As it got later and later we started to get concerned and phoned to check if the coach had arrived. It had and, what's more, it had arrived on time.

Well the cab must be stuck in traffic then, we thought, desperately trying to convince ourselves that Mum was on her way. There was nothing we could do — the coach had arrived but where was Mum? If I'd asked her to get the train, I'd have understood her lateness, but would have been even more worried. Mum didn't like the train because having to look out for the right stop meant she couldn't relax and enjoy the food she'd prepared to eat on the journey. If she'd got the train I'd have feared that she'd missed her stop amid a mouthful of homemade *bara brith* (Welsh fruit bread), but she didn't have to worry about a thing on the coach, only how to get to the taxi rank. It was so frustrating not knowing what to do; I phoned Dad just to check that she'd left. 'I took her to the coach station this morning,' he assured me.

Eventually, as we paced up and down outside the hotel, praying that every car that pulled up would deliver Mum to us, one did. A taxi containing a very confused driver who clambered out, opened the door for Mum, got her luggage out of the boot and declared, 'She didn't have a clue where she was going, it's been like *Twenty Questions* trying to work out where I was taking her to.'

'I'm so sorry; she's not used to taking taxis,' I limply explained, handing over his, by then, huge fare and an equally large tip. 'Mum, I told you what the hotel was called. And you wrote it down,' I scolded mildly. 'I know, but I just couldn't remember. I was confused,' she said with a helplessness that jolted me. She had the air of someone who'd had the life drained out of her — which she tried to hide, as always, with a smile that didn't entirely mask how she felt.

We were staying in a gorgeous hotel, one which would normally have prompted Mum to whip her camera out and arrange us in various positions, so that she had the evidence to show around to her colleagues at Ocky White's when she returned home. She wasn't excited at all. She was weary and her mind seemed to have been enveloped by an impenetrable grey fog. We sat around the dinner table trying to prompt some conversation out of Mum, when normally she'd have exhausted us with her questions and her tales of birth, marriage and death back home. She really wasn't herself at all and again the thought occurred that perhaps she didn't like Martin. But she didn't like anything — she didn't want to eat anything either, which was so unlike her. And she didn't look like herself. Her eyes had ceased to sparkle. Her hair wasn't as immaculately groomed as usual, her clothes not as glamorous. It must be depression, I thought, as I lay in bed that night trying to think of a way of sorting out her head once and for all.

The next day at breakfast it was obvious that Mum had tried to dress up in her sunny personality, but the mantle wasn't convincing. I could see that she wished she'd stayed at home but, on the other hand, I felt that if she had, she'd have wanted to be with us. That was the state of her mind, really not wanting to be anywhere. We set off for Crufts feeling deeply anxious. Once there I had my professional commitments, so I told Mum to wander off with Martin. And she did. Every time Martin turned his back, she wandered off and he had to go looking for her. He found her talking away to various dogs all over the arena, with a tear in her eye as though they were the only creatures that she could find comfort with. Once I'd finished with the PDSA I wandered around with Mum and found it just as frustrating as Martin had. Sometimes her conversation with the dogs' owners were inappropriate — in that it was naive and childlike and a bit overfamiliar.

If Mum was feeling tense, then so was I by the end of the day. I knew she was on tamoxifen as a result of her breast cancer and wondered whether that was playing havoc with her head. I was convinced that the HRT she took had caused her breast cancer and I was angry that her GP had put her on tamoxifen, another hormone therapy treatment, this time to block the effects of oestrogen, following her operation. She'd been put on it for the recommended period of five years, and nothing I could say could convince her that her doctor might be wrong in his slavish adherence to prescription drugs. It brought back memories of Mum dressing us up in our 'best' clothes to visit Dr

Miles and of her uttering the phrases, 'Yes, Doctor,' and, 'Thank you, Doctor,' over and over again, with a reverence reserved for no one else. The most common side effects of tamoxifen are fatigue, hot flashes (which Mum suffered badly), night sweats and mood swings. She had the lot. It *must* be the medication then, I reasoned, floundering around for reasons why she was becoming increasingly preoccupied and distant.

Martin and I rearranged our abandoned wedding for 7 May 1997. We flew to Las Vegas, stayed at the legendary Caesars Palace Hotel and got married at the Little Chapel of the Flowers with the limo driver, a man we'd never set eyes on in our lives before, as our only witness. I'd had my nails, hair, make-up — the whole works — done at the beauty spa at Caesars Palace all to the accompaniment of squealing exclamations, 'Ure geddin' MArreeeed? REEAlly? That's so cooooooAl,' a routine which I'm sure had been practised at least ten thousand times before.

I wasn't looking forward to getting married at all. Isn't that awful? But I told you, I'd felt that way since I was pushing dolls around in a pram and all the while eyeing up David's Meccano set with envy. I loved Martin, but marriage? It still wasn't on my wish list. That wasn't the reason that I decided to wear a black dress though; it was one that Martin had bought me — floor-length and tight-fitting — and I wore it because he'd chosen it, although not necessarily to get married in! We queued up to obtain our marriage licence at a twenty-four-hour bureau, a building not unlike the premises where I used to sign on in Hackney years before. We had to produce our passports, write the name of the person we were marrying and sign the form in pencil — and that was it. They could have rubbed it out and written Mickey Mouse or George Clooney and I'd have been none the wiser. At the chapel, a spookily white and pristine affair, the minister had a quick chat with us which mainly comprised a verbal push to sell us a flower package, a photo package, a video package 'or all three for a very reasonable price'. We decided to waive the lot for a very reasonable price indeed, engaged our limo driver to take photos with my camera and were led up the short aisle for the ceremony. The minister then addressed the congregation, which, as there wasn't a single guest in attendance, made Martin and I giggle at the absurdity of it all.

We celebrated with a Chinese meal — having turned down the tempting offer of a Toga Party and Roman Feast at Caesars Palace — played the slot machines and wandered around the neon strip, teasing each other that we had another forty years of marriage ahead of us before we both popped our clogs.

★   ★   ★

Back home we came to the realisation that we had landed ourselves with the tricky situation of telling our parents. We hadn't factored time in our few days off work to go to Wales and Scotland after the wedding to let our parents know, so we phoned them. Martin's mum and dad were thrilled, or Martin seemed to think they were. Martin's dad is a very gentle, lovely man, and he'd have just been pleased that we were happy. And although I'm sure Martin's mum would have like to have got dressed up for her eldest son's wedding, she didn't say so and offered her congratulations. I phoned Mum and Dad with trepidation, not because I thought they'd be annoyed that I'd denied them a big ceremony — Dad would have hated that and Mum would have suffered the headache of her life — but because I was a bit embarrassed; strange, I know, but I'd always joshed with Dad that I'd never get married, and I'd often told Mum, 'Look, I don't believe in it, no matter how many wedding videos you show me.' I guess I felt that I'd compromised my belief. I certainly wasn't going to change my name!

Dad was his usual accepting self; he's always just let us get on with things, never dumping his ego all over our plans, and if he was ever miffed at anything we did he didn't really impose his feelings — except when I gave up radiography and told him I was going to live with Joe! He loved Martin, knew he was a decent sort and was happy that we'd done the deed without the agony of having to get together with people he'd rather not see, in a church he'd rather not worship in. Dad was very anti-establishment, and I've taken on his views hook, line and sinker, hence the doubts about getting married. Mum wasn't delirious when I told her, which normally I know she would have been. Usually she'd have screamed with delight, asked, 'Have you got any photos, Toots?' before running off to find her dependable notepad. That day she was muted in her response, to say the least, and I felt a surge of guilt for having denied her her day in the sunshine as mother of the bride. I looked back to David's wedding and how unmoved she had seemed to be — but, I reasoned, that was because she knew she had breast cancer. Maybe she thought that I would eventually relent and do the whole white-dress thing and she was truly disappointed in my news. Whatever it was, I detected a coldness in her voice that disturbed me. 'Auntie Mary always said you'd run off and get married,' was her only real response.

It wasn't like Mum at all — and it was just the beginning of a series of episodes which, as my brothers and I often told each other, were 'not like Mum at all'.

23

Martin and I spent a lot of our time off in Wales. We'd often shoot down there for a weekend, take Mum and Dad out to see the sights of the beautiful Pembrokeshire coastline and treat them to a meal in the evening. Mum seemed, more and more, to be in a world of her own, and the relationship between her and Dad had reached a point of constant tension. When Martin and I went to visit we'd taken to staying regularly in a local hotel because at Mum and Dad's there seemed to be an air of desperation and decline. I feel terrible about that now, because the two of them could probably have done with us in the house to ease the stand off. I remember Mum saying, 'But why aren't you staying with us?' with a tone of hurt in her voice. It's only now that I've got children that I realise how hurtful it must have been.

It didn't help that Mum no longer had her job at Ocky White's — she'd been forced to retire because of her age and because, I think, she was making mistakes, which she'd never made before. Mr Jeremy, his wife and brothers put on a magnificent leaving event, taking Mum and me to an elegant Georgian hotel in the coastal town of Newport in Pembrokeshire, where they all said the most wonderful, touching things before presenting Mum with a gold bracelet. She was odd that night too though — happy but very flushed and as though her mind was dissembling. I blamed this on the drugs and on the contrasts in her life — outside the home where she was loved and appreciated, inside it where she was not.

When Martin and I took Mum and Dad out on a Saturday night, to our favourite restaurant in Fishguard for a meal, Mum would look distracted, her eyes cold and distant, as though she didn't really care what any of us had to say. She wasn't interested and she had always been so interested.

The worry about Mum and Dad was set against the scrutiny I was under at work. I sat alongside Eamonn Holmes from January 1997, following a storm in the newspapers over Eamonn's alleged remarks about his former co-host Anthea Turner. He's supposed to have called her 'Princess Tippy Toes', a name I'd never heard him utter. He said plenty of other things, mind you, but never 'Princess Tippy Toes'! I was due to make my full-time debut beside Eamonn in the first week of January, but it was delayed because of the furore over Eamonn's newspaper antics, which resulted in his suspension. Mum got Dad to set the video in anticipation every night, so I kept her updated every time I received a phone call, saying, 'It could be next Monday . . . ' or the like. When it finally came, and I can't remember the exact date, *GMTV* was under the microscope, following the stories of Eamonn and Anthea's less-than-friendly partnership.

The reason I say this is because if I hadn't been so immersed in work I could have spent more time with Mum and Dad. I could have stayed there and observed their relationship and their behaviour over a couple of weeks, but it didn't occur to me at the time that there was anything out of the ordinary. Mum and Dad had never had a lovey-dovey relationship — fiery is a more apt description. So 'could have' remains just that: I could have, but I didn't. Another notch on the 'Guilt' bedpost.

Mum continued to come and visit. She often arrived disorientated at the coach station, despite being delivered door to door and sometimes there was a palaver retrieving her luggage because she couldn't remember which bag she'd brought. Once she'd settled in, I'd always treat her to a proper cut, colour and blow dry at our local hair salon. She loved going in there and everyone knew her, so I would go off and do my shopping while she had her hair done and quizzed all the girls about their private lives. It still upsets me to think of this now, but on one of our trips to the hairdresser we were just about to open the door and go in and Mum stood in the doorway wringing her hands, and said, 'I don't want to go in there.' 'Come on, Mum,' I said. 'You always love having your hair done and you know all the girls.' She broke down and cried, clinging on to me and saying, 'I don't know what's wrong with me.' I do, I thought. It's you and Dad, and you're depressed. I finally persuaded her to go in and I sat there all the while she had her hair done, like I'd done so many times with the children. She was fine after that, not her usual self, a little shaky and teary, but fine, I convinced myself.

As a child it was a great treat if Mum let us count her sixpences. She saved the little silver coins in a gold caddy, and David and I would count them into piles of forty, which made a pound. I'd continued that habit with my loose change, and after we came back from the hairdresser and Mum had had a cup of soothing tea, she asked if she could count up my change, which I kept in a huge whisky bottle. I gave her plastic bank bags to put her piles of change in. It was only when she'd gone and I counted up one bag on the off chance that I realised she'd tallied them all up incorrectly. They were five-pound bags and there was £3.80 in one, £4.70 in another, and so on. I felt annoyed that she'd been so careless and that I'd have to count them all over again. I should have been more thoughtful and made the connection between this and the fact that she'd pleaded, 'What's wrong with me?' but I didn't.

In August 1998 Martin and I went on holiday to Barbados and a few weeks later I found out I was pregnant. Having always thought that I didn't want children, I wasn't exactly over the moon, but it had happened and was obviously meant to be, so I gradually got used to the idea. Very gradually. I was nearly five months' pregnant by the time I told *GMTV* and I still hadn't told Mum and Dad. Now that is not normal. But they were not acting normally and, as close as I was to them, I felt a distance between us. I'm finding it hard to reason why, and even harder to put into words, but I could

218

not bring myself to tell them. Part of my rationale was that I wasn't excited about it — realism has always been my thing and it got in the way of the cooing baby image. I kept imagining having a surly teenager around the house, and that thought, combined with my early starts five days a week, did my head in. But more than that, I felt Mum needed me, and by having a baby she'd feel I was deserting her. What screwed-up logic, but at the back of my mind I felt that my precious mum was fading away. Was it depression over her defunct relationship? Was it the effects of the tamoxifen? Could it be she was missing work? I thought it was all of them.

At Christmas 1998, as always, we dashed down to Mum and Dad's as soon as we finished work. We'd booked Christmas dinner at a fourteenth-century farmhouse at the foot of the Preseli Mountains in the heart of the Pembrokeshire Coast National Park, where we were also staying, so that Andy and his girlfriend could sleep at Mum and Dad's.

It was Christmas Eve and the fridge was empty. There was no drink in the house. The tree was up, but there were none of the usual over-the-top festive garlands and ornaments that characterised Mum's childlike relish at that time of year. I felt angry because Martin was with me and I felt embarrassed. I felt sorry for Andy and his girlfriend. And I really felt that it was a result of Mum and Dad's warring relationship, that the battle had been fought and an impasse had resulted which meant that neither of them would shop for the other. So they hadn't shopped at all.

We went out and got some wine and crisps. Mum sat in a chair as we ate them, looking at us with eyes that had left the room. I really didn't like her, and there was nothing I could do to make her want me to like her. She looked as though she couldn't give a damn about any of us, as though all the loving over the years had worn her down and she was left with nothing. It was quite obvious that I was either fat or pregnant, but nothing was further from my mind than telling Mum and Dad that I was going to have a baby. There was no emotion in the room apart from a tangible sadness.

On Christmas morning I phoned Mum to tell her that Martin and I would be coming round soon to exchange presents before we all went for our Christmas meal. She sounded as though she was disappointed in me, and her coldness took my breath away. I fumed as I opened the thoughtful presents that Martin had been so excited to give me and inside I felt empty. I missed my mum, the mum who on Christmas Day would be up before we were, singing and making magic with her love for us. We arrived at the house with no food, and opened presents. Thank goodness Andy was there, because he always finds the humour in everything, we all do generally, but I couldn't find it within me to summon it up that morning. I began to think that Mum had guessed I was pregnant and was hurt I hadn't told her. I felt a chasm had opened up between us and my mind was too full of sorrow to whoop about Christmas presents. The meal at the restaurant was fine — Andy and

Martin made sure of that — but I felt somehow dirty that I was keeping a secret from Mum, because she was too cold for me to tell her.

It was a cold day just after Christmas when finally, at a beachside pub in Dale, we broke the news to Dad. Mum had gone to the loo and we told Dad first because Mum's demeanour had repelled me again and made me feel as though I couldn't share the news with her, so we wanted to test the water. Dad didn't think there was anything wrong with her, mired as they were in nearly forty years of tempestuous marriage, and laughed off the fact that I thought that it wasn't necessarily a good time to tell her. When Mum came back we didn't say anything — I was struck dumb with sadness. I can clearly remember sitting there, nearly choking on my cheese and onion crisps, because they had trouble negotiating the lump in my throat.

Not being able to bear the tension any more, we went for a walk along the beach. I was cold, shivering and wretched, looking at Mum and hating her. I walked behind her feeling that no daughter would have had this kind of dilemma over telling their mum that they were pregnant. Gradually, as we walked, I put my arm through hers and told her. She smiled and made all the right noises, but it wasn't the mum who would normally have walked along the beach beaming from ear to ear and collaring strangers to inform them of the good news. Once again I travelled back to London with a very heavy heart. Poor Martin. It seemed as though every time we went to Wales my parents made me cry.

24

On 28 May 1999 my first son Nat was born at the Chelsea and Westminster Hospital in London. For someone who had never wanted children, I immediately fell head over heels in love with this wailing little bundle. I wanted to tell Mum, to let her know that I realised how much she loved me now that I'd experienced the overwhelming animal instinct of protecting that little boy from any troubles that the world might fling at him. Well, I say little; he was actually a whopping nine pounds, three ounces! I phoned Mum.

Unusually, Dad answered. 'Hey, Dad, it's me. I've had the baby — it's a boy!' I announced. 'Aah, congratulations, that's great,' Dad replied with an understated warmth. 'Do you want to speak to your mother?' Mum came on the phone. 'Mum, it's me; I've had the baby — it's a boy!' There was a silence and then words that I still can't repeat without choking up: 'Never mind,' she said. 'Maybe the next one will be a girl.' In that moment someone could have shot me and I wouldn't have felt more torn apart. I was injured. I lay in bed with the baby that night, held his tiny naked body to my chest and cried and cried. I hated her. But I loved her so much and I wanted her to love my little boy too.

At home we were festooned with flowers — the doorbell rang throughout the day with more beautiful arrangements and presents being dropped off, but I was looking only for the one that never came — the one from Mum and Dad. It was evident that whatever was going on at home in Wales was consuming my parents, and the outside world wasn't impacting on them very much at all. Eventually though, Mum said she was coming to see us. She travelled on the coach from Wales, as she'd done so many times before, to come to London and lend a hand with her new grandson. Martin went to meet her from Victoria while I, rather than enduring the kerfuffle of getting the baby ready, stayed at home tidying up and making sure everything was fit for Mum's arrival. Martin left on time, and it was about twenty minutes to Victoria from our house, so when an hour and a half went by I began to think that Mum's coach was late.

Then the phone rang. 'Hi, it's me,' Martin announced. 'What does your mum's bag look like because she says it's not here.' 'What do you mean it's not there?' I replied. 'Did it go in the hold?' 'According to the coach driver, who's now your mum's best mate, it did,' Martin assured me. 'Well it must be there then,' I added unhelpfully. Mum came on the phone, sounding vague and confused. 'Which bag did you bring, Mum?' I enquired. 'I don't know, Toots.' 'Is it the grey and red one?' I asked, knowing that was the holdall she usually brought on her trips to stay with me. 'I don't know,' she replied, sounding as though she didn't care either, that it was all too much to deal with. Martin came back on the phone. 'The coach driver's been telling me how she talked to him all the way here,' he related, 'and how he knows about all of us.' 'What does he know about the bag then?' I asked impatiently, frustrated that I wasn't there to sort things out. 'Hang on, he's just told me there's one bag left, but your mum swears it's not hers.' 'Get him to open it up and see if Mum recognises her stuff,' I suggested. They did. And she did. And three hours after he'd left the house to pick her up, Martin arrived home complete with the villainous bag and a timid-looking Mum carrying a bunch of bedraggled carnations.

It wasn't the way I'd hoped it would be. I'd imagined Mum being cock-a-hoop about the birth of my child. I'd dreamed of her arriving with her huge smile and rushing to pick up her new grandchild. It didn't happen that way at all. She peered at the baby, sat down and held him, but her mind was somewhere else. She looked very flushed and sweaty — the effects of that bloody tamoxifen again, I assumed — and her eyes were sort of vacant. Her visit to help out with her grandson ended up being a huge strain, it was like having two new children. Mum couldn't even use the toaster or make a cup of tea, let alone take the baby out in the pram. At night she'd wander into our bedroom and ask where she was. She thought everyone was talking about her, and her eyes, which always twinkled and smiled, became permanently cold and dark and blank during this period. Being busy with a new baby, I didn't twig that she was seriously ill. I thought she was depressed maybe, and at times — and it pains me to say this — I thought she was jealous of the baby. Stressed up to the eyeballs with my two new charges, I once told her to 'stop being selfish and attention-seeking'. I didn't know that she was desperately sick. She was only sixty-five, and although she'd recently beaten breast cancer, it didn't occur to me that something might be medically wrong. I put it down to a combination of her feeling her nose pushed out by my new baby, her now toxic relationship with Dad and the drugs she was taking.

One afternoon my brothers and their partners came round to see us all and I felt very emotional, having been putting up with Mum and what I thought was an uncharacteristic self-obsession and a very young, hungry baby who didn't like sleeping much. We were in the garden and I slipped into the kitchen to get some drinks and was greeted by Mum sitting at the table alone saying, 'No one's interested in me.' Another sign, I thought, of her jealousy over the baby. I felt wretched and very hurt that she'd reacted so badly to me having the grandchild that she'd been egging me on to have for years. When we were out shopping I wrestled with Nat, the buggy, the shopping, Mum and strangers cooing over the baby and saying, 'Ah, it must be so nice to have your mum down to help you.' I felt like screaming every time the baby yelled, because I couldn't cope with the feeling that Mum had let me down. When she went back home I cried as in retrospect, I felt guilty that I'd been a bit harsh on her. Was it me? Or was it her? I was emotionally drained and couldn't fathom it out.

After four months' maternity leave — I hadn't dared take more, having been made to feel that someone else would occupy my seat next to Eamonn on the sofa if I took too long off — I went back to work. I clearly remember that first morning, stepping out of my soft, marshmallowy baby world into the harsh light of 4 a.m. starts and the heartbreak of kissing my little boy goodbye, when I was all he'd ever known at that time of the day. I travelled into work gagging on the lump in my throat, peering through the tears that pricked my eyes and fervently wishing that I could stay at home to look after my tiny son.

Martin was still *GMTV*'s chief correspondent — just after Nat was born he'd taken off for Bosnia to cover the war there and didn't return for nearly a month. We didn't know where he would end up on any single day, so our lives were a mixture of tiredness and unpredictability, all mixed up with a small baby and two parents who were making each other terribly miserable. At least, that's what I thought.

During that hectic time I still looked forward to Mum coming down. Mum and Dad continued to rub together, and to rub each other up the wrong way, and the next time Mum came to visit she was a nervous wreck. I took her to get her hair done as usual, and she wouldn't go into the hairdresser's. She broke down and cried on the doorstep again. Once in there she recovered enough to smile and chat to the girls in the salon, and I took the opportunity to go and get some food in for tea. 'Please don't let her go anywhere,' I pleaded, 'I'll be back before she's ready.' Mum was a bit nervous about London and wasn't familiar enough with the streets to be able to navigate her way around, so I told her to stay put even if she was ready before I returned. I arrived back earlier than her expected finish time, but there was no sign of that big smile in the room.

'Where's my mum?' I enquired, assuming that she'd gone to the loo or something. 'Oh, she's gone; we finished earlier than expected,' was the nonchalant reply. I could have strangled that girl right there and then. I raced out of the door, as much as you can race with a buggy in tow, and frantically looked up and down the road for Mum. I knew she was vulnerable and not in a healthy state of mind, and the longer I wildly dashed around searching for her smile, the more I thought I might never set eyes on it again. And then there it was, there she was, like a child who had no knowledge of the worry she'd caused. She saw me and her smile lit up the whole street as she waved at me as though we'd previously arranged to meet like this all along. I wanted to tell her off and shout, 'Why can't you be like a mum, not a child? I've got a child now. You're supposed to be my mum, his nana, and you're more trouble than he is!' But I didn't; I just thought all those things. And hugged her.

On that same visit I'd arranged a treat for Mum. I'd been offered a couple of tickets for *An Audience with Cliff Richard* at the ITV studios, just down the stairs from *GMTV*. I didn't normally like going to celebrity gatherings, but I thought Mum would love to see Cliff. We got there just as the pre-show drinks were ending, which was fortunate because Mum, with the inhibitions of a child, kept going up to famous faces and saying, 'I know you, don't I?' She wouldn't normally have done that. And she did it in a charmless way, not like her at all. She reached out for June Brown, famous for her long-standing portrayal of Dot Cotton in *Eastenders*, and I had to apologise for her, feeling mortified. Lovely Gloria Hunniford looked at me with sympathy when Mum was similarly overfamiliar with her.

As we descended the stairs to the studio, ITV's boss at the time, Charles Allen, stopped me to say hi, and Mum blurted out, 'Do you work with Fiona then?' 'I work *for* him, Mum,' I intercepted with haste. But her mind had already wandered. I gave Charles a sheepish look and scuttled away with Mum as quickly as I could. Once we were in the studio we were sat alongside Charlotte Church's stepdad James. Again Mum was over-familiar in a way she wouldn't normally be. She was always warm and friendly, but this was different. I was so on edge I couldn't tell you what happened on stage that night, but halfway through the show I wanted the ground to open as Mum stood up and reached out towards Cliff like some crazed, obsessive fan. She wasn't herself at all — that phrase again — and I was really worried. I knew she'd been seeing the doctor regularly, so I convinced myself that she must be in good hands. And, if truth be told, I didn't want to allow myself to think anything else, because I had enough on my plate already.

Just after returning to *GMTV* following my maternity leave I'd been given a prime-time entertainment show on ITV called *OK! TV*. So, just a few weeks after I went back to the sofa, I was getting up at 4 a.m., doing the show, returning home by about midday, feeding the baby, getting made up and changed all over again and sometimes filming until 2 a.m. the following morning. I received about an hour's notice of my first big assignment for the first show of the series, which was to debut on Friday 3 December 1999 — an exclusive interview with Victoria Beckham at Asprey, the luxury shopping store on London's Bond Street. When I took the call I was dressed in tracksuit bottoms, hair scraped back and just about to breastfeed Nat, who was only five months old. How was I going to feed him and transform myself into someone glamorous enough to stand alongside Posh Spice all in the space of an hour?

I don't know how I did it, but I got changed, made up and, as it was at short notice and I hadn't had time to arrange child-care, bundled Nat into the car with me and sat praying that it would all work out, all the while wondering if I'd taken on too much. Of course I had, but thanks to Victoria's mum Jackie, who was looking after her six-month-old grandson Brooklyn in a room at the back of the store, I managed to concentrate on the job in hand. She offered to look after Nat while I got on with my work, so I left him gurgling away next to Brooklyn on a very posh carpet in a very grand room, while I went to speak to Victoria for a rare interview in which she told me, among other things, that David was so obsessive that he ironed his socks. It's funny what you remember, but at the time, with barely any sleep to speak of, it's a wonder I could remember anything apart from setting my alarm clock.

You might wonder why I took on so much work when all the while my heart was tugging me home. The truth is that I either stayed at home or worked. There was only one job like mine, and I had it. I didn't have the option of saying, 'I'll take a year off and then I'll be back and perhaps work part-time,' because someone else would have been in there like a shot and there would have been nothing to go back to, meaning I'd have to start all over again or change career. My work ethic, instilled in me by Mum and Dad, meant that there was no chance of me completely opting out, and my job, being what it was, meant that I had to completely opt in again. Despite the guilt and the misgivings.

By Christmas 1999 we were desperately in need of a rest and some relaxation. In the event it didn't turn out that way as we'd all, including Mum and Dad, arranged to spend Christmas Day at David's in-laws in north London. Malcolm and Maxine, my sister-in-law Sarah's parents, had always treated me like part of the family on my visits back to London from LA. Before travelling to Wales to see Mum and Dad, I'd look forward to wonderful Friday-night family gatherings at their house, which was always stuffed full of food, drink and laughter.

We piled round there a little while before Christmas lunch was served. Mum and Dad were already there and they looked agitated. Oh God, I thought, this is going to be tense. Mum was very flushed as usual, the tamoxifen having now been complemented by antidepressants. Clearly the doctor was trying to sort her out, but all she'd say was that she was on Seroxat, an antidepressant known for causing suicidal tendencies. She had that cold thing about her and the distance between us set me on edge. Why does she have to be like this? I thought. Can't she make an effort on Christmas Day? Dad and Mum seemed to have a knowingness between them. A knowing it was over? A knowing that they'd have to get on in company, at least for today? I didn't know what it was, just a 'knowing' which none of us knew. They paid no attention to Nat or to their other grandson, David's son Zak, and I felt the now familiar hurt of them being more engrossed in their own misery than of gaining pleasure from their children's happiness.

Finally, after all the worry, the frustration and the convincing myself of the various possible causes of Mum's deterioration, there was a breakthrough very early on in 2000 when by chance I found out that the doctors suspected she had Alzheimer's disease. Apparently she'd been visiting her GP for months. I knew that she'd been to the doctor on several occasions because of the medication she was on, but didn't realise that she was going with a regularity that suggested that she was desperate to find a reason for her change in personality. She hadn't told us because, as one of the symptoms of Alzheimer's is short-term memory loss, she couldn't remember having been there, let alone what the doctor had told her. Ludicrously, her GP was prevented from telling anyone else of her predicament because of patient confidentiality rules. So she was the only one who knew. I only found out because on a visit to Wales I noticed appointments in her diary all written twice or three times over in bold capitals as a desperate aid to her failing memory. One of the appointments was for a memory clinic.

I asked her about it, but she couldn't tell me why she'd been there. I went with her to her doctor and tried to convince him that he'd got it wrong. I didn't even really know what it meant to have Alzheimer's. Wasn't it something that old people got? Like Grandma? But Mum was only in her sixties. He obviously didn't know what he was talking about, I figured. He didn't realise that Mum and Dad had fractured, that she was depressed, that she had been prescribed the wrong drugs. Mum never actually said, 'I've got Alzheimer's,' so we persuaded ourselves that she hadn't. It was all going on two hundred and odd miles away from us and our busy lives with babies, jobs and lack of sleep. And, well, your parents are supposed to just get on with it, aren't they?

If only I'd realised how much they weren't getting on with it. How incapable they were of getting on with it. Happy New Year.

25

GMTV got harder, and not just because I was doing two jobs, one at either end of the day. My lovely old sparring partner Eamonn had taken against me a bit because Martin had been appointed editor of the show. Rather naively, I guess, we thought that because everyone at work knew Martin and respected his professionalism, there'd be no problem if he actually got the job. We didn't expect him to get it, but because I was working and we had a seven-month-old baby, his peripatetic schedule was getting harder to deal with and he thought he might as well apply for it. I can understand why Eamonn might have felt a bit compromised having to answer to Martin as editor, but I was hurt because, knowing me as well as he did, he didn't speak to me openly about how he felt. We never fell out, but I sensed that he'd created a distance between us, which upset me and was hard to combine with everything else that was going on in my life.

In grabbed moments, when I was wondering how to deal with it all, I went on the Internet to find out as much as I could about Alzheimer's. Back then the information wasn't as vast or enlightening as it is now, but the one fact that leapt off the screen and made my mind swim was that Alzheimer's is terminal. Desperately I looked up the symptoms. There was no mention of being tearful or depressed and detached like

Mum. When I looked up depression though, all of Mum's symptoms were listed, fuelling my conviction that the medics had got it wrong. Thank goodness. It must be depression then. I grasped at that glimmer of hope. Meanwhile Mum's visits were becoming more disturbing. Sometimes we heard terrible noises coming from her room 'because,' she told me, 'I keep seeing things in my sleep.' She was suffering night terrors, followed the next day by raging paranoia. She was sweating, there were involuntary facial movements and she was agitated all the time. She was seriously suffering, but the fact that I'd decided it had to be clinical depression instilled me with hope. I was livid with her doctors.

Unknown to me, Mum had been visiting a day centre a couple of times a week. Because her short-term memory was broken she couldn't retain information, so I now knew nothing of her daily life, when before I'd been treated to each and every little moment of her day. Dad had never phoned us anyway, and that didn't change, plus he clearly had no interest in Mum's life whatsoever, so he didn't let us know a jot of what was going on with them. In truth, I don't think I wanted to hear it anyway. One Friday after *GMTV*, I bundled the baby in the car and drove down to Wales in order to speak to the specialist who suspected that Mum had Alzheimer's. I was going to fill him in on Mum and Dad and depression and how he'd got it all wrong.

He was situated at a day hospital and I had the shock of my life when Mum walked into the waiting room crying and saying 'I shouldn't be in a place like this; they're all old here. Tell them there's nothing wrong with me.' Apparently she'd been attending the day centre for two days a week. I felt gutted, guilty, angry that I didn't know. 'She's so lovely,' one of the carers said. 'She's so desperately unhappy, but always manages to smile at everyone.' If only she'd known that at home Mum was receiving no care at all. Dad didn't understand, didn't want to understand, because I suspect he thought that Mum was behaving in a deliberately annoying way, just to aggravate him. It was a desperate situation. I certainly felt desperate. I was tired, not happy at work, felt guilty about Mum, guilty about Nat, angry with Dad, and that it was all my fault.

Never mind, I thought. I'll see the doctor, sort out the nonsense about Alzheimer's and make sure she gets better once and for all. The consultant told me that Mum had taken two memory tests and that the latest one had showed a marked decline. She'd also been screened for vitamin B12 deficiency, which can lead to symptoms similar to those of Alzheimer's. Unfortunately, that had come back negative.

'But I don't think you understand,' I said in desperation. 'Mum and Dad have a really awful relationship and she's clinically depressed; it's not Alzheimer's.'

'She didn't know the name of the prime minister in the memory test. She couldn't tell the time. She didn't know what day it was,' he insisted.

'She might not know who the prime minister

is and she's confused because she's terribly depressed. She keeps crying. 'Mum,' I asked, 'what's the time?' It all came out in a frantic want for it all to be all right, for the consultant to lie. For him to say, 'OK, I believe you. It's not Alzheimer's.' But he didn't. Mum was looking at her watch and didn't say a thing.

I remember so many episodes from that dreadfully dark time: Mum crying at a carnival that she, Nat and I went to in Narberth because, although she talked to countless people who knew her, she couldn't remember who most of them were. I recall her breaking down on a supermarket trip because she'd forgotten why she was there and where the bread aisle was. We both chatted away to a pair of old family friends by the frozen foods and she clung to me afterwards, asking who they were. She'd known them for years. And now she didn't know them at all. I remember her crying and crying and being unable to speak when I phoned her. I remember her staying with David and weeping because she thought her three-year-old grandson Zak hated her. I remember Nat and I staying in a holiday cottage in Wales for a week one summer and Mum weeping and begging me to take her there with us because Dad was working until late and she was scared in the house on her own. I remember her obsession with getting her bank accounts in order, as though she knew she was going to be leaving behind the hard-won money that she'd hidden away for so many years. I remember her phoning me at 3.00 one morning, sobbing, and pleading, 'Please help me.' I remember all of these things, but she couldn't remember much at all. Her voice was crushed, almost drowned in grief, as she told me she'd forgotten how to make cakes. Ever since we were tiny children squabbling over who was going to lick the mixing bowl clean of the yummy, gooey mixture, my brothers and I could rely on the cupboards being packed full of Mum's home-baked treats. They weren't made with a recipe, just with the passion of making us happy. When I heard her say that she'd forgotten how to bake, my childhood drained away, and I knew that I'd lost my mum.

And that wasn't all I lost. In the middle of it all I lost a baby too. I trudged into *GMTV* one morning, feeling as low as low can go, was briefed for the programme, walked down the stairs and felt a surge of blood leave my body. I was nine weeks' pregnant. I knew what that loss of blood signified. And I knew that it was meant to be. How could my body cope with having a baby with all that was going on? How could it handle happy hormones when misery ruled my head? It couldn't. I made my excuses at work and went back home, where the baby, and the happiness that it would have brought into our lives, simply washed away down the toilet.

The following week a columnist in the *Daily Mail* wrote a story about how I'd gone into work and stomped out like a prima donna without presenting the programme because I'd read something that she'd written that morning and didn't like it. I don't normally phone journalists — as long as my loved ones don't believe what

237

they write, they can say what they want — but I was devastated that she had turned a very personal tragedy into a lie. I phoned her and very reasonably, through stifled sobs, told her the truth. She just went, 'Hmmmm,' as if to say, 'So what? Do you think I care?' I lay in bed sobbing for my lost baby and for my mum, who was also lost to me. In the end I got a lawyer on to the paper, and had to suffer the ignominious trial of a hospital examination so that I could prove to the paper that I'd had a miscarriage. Bastards. I felt like phoning my mum, but couldn't because she wouldn't have understood.

I knew then that all the sun she'd brought into our lives had gone and all that was left was a grim, dark day.

26

By Christmas 2000, I'd had my fill of dealing with Mum and Dad. I was exhausted, emotionally wiped out and couldn't face another Christmas fraught with emotion. If I was to be able to cope with everything throughout the coming year, I had to have a break from them. I'd only ever spent one Christmas away from Mum and Dad and this was to be my second; I did it with a heavy heart but with the knowledge that if I didn't I was going to go mad too. We went to Scotland, and on the way I phoned Mum's GP, as she wasn't eating. She'd been put on the Alzheimer's drug Aricept, which for a while seemed to pull her together a bit, but she was struck down by its side effects, which included severe stomach cramps. I didn't know this at the time, because no one told me. She was permanently depressed, agitated, tearful and full of hopelessness, but she always made the effort to smile, so that she wouldn't worry us. It didn't work; I was constantly concerned about her and angry at Dad, because he should have been her main carer. She desperately needed warmth, love and affection, and he wasn't providing any of it. Whenever I spoke to Mum's doctor, I hoped he was going to say, 'she's getting better,' but he never did. Even when I said, 'She seemed fine today — she was laughing with me,' he remained stuck in his realism, while I looked to a future where she'd got herself back again.

Mum was staying at David's for Christmas, while Dad remained at home on his own; it's the way he wanted it. I talked to David on the way up, and like me his conversation was full of denial. 'Oh, she's having a great time, laughing and entertaining us with her funny ways, she's fine,' he promised me. We both lived in a world where we were sure that one day she'd be back, and then we could sort her and Dad out, and everything would be fine. I'd even taken her to look at flats, convinced that if the pair of them lived apart she'd make a miraculous recovery. She'd sit in the car and shiver with trepidation while I scanned one-bedroom apartments. Little did I know that, far from being able to live an independent life, by Christmas the following year she wouldn't be living much of a life at all. I hugely regret not spending that Christmas with Mum, but I was not to know then, laden as I still was with hope, that that time of year would never hold the magic that Mum had brought to it ever again.

Maybe I should have realised that she would never be well again when on New Year's Eve I phoned her from Scotland and discovered that she'd spent the last day of that year looking through her photos, trying to hang on to her memories. When she heard me she broke down, and then in a whisper and with her voice quavering she choked, 'I just wish life was still as good as it was when you were children, Toots. I don't know what's wrong with me, but I'm never happy now, like I was then.'

240

I found her diary for 2000 recently, the only one left of all the diaries I'd bought her every Christmas from the age of eleven. She kept them meticulously up to date, but there are blank pages throughout this one, as well as lots of doctor's appointments which I knew nothing of at the time. On 1 February she'd written, '*Audrey and I at doctor 10.10.*' The writing was a mix of lower case and capitals and scratchy-looking. Four days later on 5 February the writing is much worse and she notes: '*Bean [sic] shopping with Phil. In a bad state.*' There are many entries with the addendum '*wrong day*', such as on 17 February, when she wrote, '*Went down to meet the girls — wrong day. Shall go again tomorrow.*' The writing varies throughout: fine on good days, I guess, and all over the place, reflecting the state of her mind, when things were worse. There are some thoughts where the writing is the same all the way through with maybe just one word in capitals, as though she'd had to search for it for a while before writing it down in big letters to confirm that she'd managed to recall it. On Friday 31 March she'd written in capitals, '*SHORT MEMORY LOSS*' (it should have been short-term memory loss) as though she was trying to consolidate it in her mind.

During this time, Mum did all she could to carry on as usual, even though '*Too ill*' was becoming an increasingly regular entry in her diary. She worked a couple of days a week in a Paul Sartori charity shop, a short walk from the house, when she could. She even managed to go and visit Auntie Mary on 9 April. I remember it well, because she was supposed to be coming to stay with us and I couldn't handle it because I was in the middle of a terribly stressful battle with a Sunday newspaper which had sunk its vicious lying talons into me. They were even trying to intercept my post so I spent most of my days, in between work and childcare, on the phone to lawyers and Martin, who had to put up with me crying down the phone while he was dealing with his own stressful situations at work. I dearly wanted Mum to come and stay but didn't know how I was going to do it all.

Auntie Mary, a rock as always, persuaded me that she would look after her sister and that I could come and visit, so I met Mum at Victoria coach station and took her to King's Cross for the train to Cambridge. I climbed on board to make sure that she was sitting near people who were also getting off at Cambridge so that they could remind her to do the same. She looked like a scared, lost child when I left her, and I phoned Auntie Mary to make sure that she would scan the coach to look for Mum when she met her off the train at the other end. I'd never felt so low. I knew she wasn't in a fit state to embark on a train journey on her own, but I wasn't in a fit state to look after her either. I wanted to give everything up, right there and then.

All through my working life, like Dad I suppose, I'd taken pride in never taking a day off unless I really couldn't even crawl in. But during that period the grief, the guilt and the exhaustion stole so much of me that I didn't have much in reserve for emergencies. I can remember waking up at 4 a.m. some mornings and feeling so weak and battered as though I couldn't face the me that faced the public. I couldn't put on an act, even though Eamonn could make me cry with laughter just by looking at him some mornings. One week after I'd taken Nat to Wales to referee the hopeless situation between my parents, I felt achy and miserable, rising for work as usual, and leaving the warmth of Martin and my little boy behind on the Monday morning. I felt very vulnerable; I was tired, emotionally spent, and with no time to take it all in. I also had a huge strap of pain across my back. But work was a tonic, I guess, a place where I had to forget that my mum had forgotten almost all she ever knew. As the week went on I became weaker and weaker, all the time fighting the need to give in, until one morning I woke up and couldn't face the day ahead. I had shingles. My immune system was completely run down with exhaustion and emotional shock. I had to take three weeks off.

Most days I just lay in bed, depressed, feeling hopeless, worrying about my absence from work and that I wasn't able to look after Mum. When I returned to *GMTV*, I was down to a size 6 and still losing weight through a grief that went on and on. I didn't want to go out anywhere. Poor Martin spent months turning up everywhere on his own because I needed the refuge of home. I got into trouble at work for refusing to go to professional engagements such as the National Television Awards; I turned down jobs and guest appearances on other TV shows; and I can remember lying on my bed one day, feeling there was nothing to look forward to when my agent phoned to say that she'd had a request for me to guest on Jonathan Ross's Radio 2 show. I simply couldn't face it. I worked, worried about Mum, looked after Nat, I tried to sleep. I felt that it was all down to me and I drove myself crazy trying to cope with it all.

In the summer of 2001, Martin insisted that he and I should go away on our own — away from everyone and everything. Our wonderful friend Gwyneth, who'd become part of our family after looking after Nat since he was six months old while I was at work, stepped into the breach and took over the reins while we were away. I couldn't face the guilt of being absent for more than a few days. But we needed to be on our own, to escape the unrelenting sadness, to regroup, recuperate, recover.

In the autumn of 2001 I discovered I was pregnant again. Our joy was marred by the fact that Mum was becoming increasingly aware that something catastrophic was happening to her. My lovely, happy, smiling mum was fast disappearing, despite her efforts not to worry anyone. I tried to tell her she had something wrong with her head and we were trying to get it all fixed. It was heartbreaking knowing that in reality there was absolutely nothing that anyone could do. It's one of the worst things about Alzheimer's: the lying, the cajoling, the pretending it might be all right in the end. The alternative is to tell the truth, with its utter lack of hope.

My days towards the close of 2001, were peppered with calls from social workers who were keeping an eye on the situation between Mum and Dad. Dad had been sent on an anger management course following a previous incident when he'd lost it with Mum early on in her illness. He'd been told to take the dog for a walk if he felt he couldn't cope. This time they decided that Dad needed some space, so they organised for Mum to go into respite care for a week. I think they didn't want to worry me, so they said they were doing it so that they could sort out her medication. As Dad and Mum were barely communicating, I was in touch with all the arrangements for Mum to go into respite. I told her she was going in so that they could have a close look at her and finally sort her out. I believed it myself. They'd find out it was depression and they can sort that out and then she'd be fine again, and we'd just have to try and patch up Mum and Dad's broken relationship. If she didn't have Alzheimer's, anything was possible, I reasoned.

The day we took Mum in was one of the saddest episodes in the whole sorry saga. It was a nice place, as those places go. She had her own room, which looked out over the Milford Haven Waterway; but it may as well have looked out into hell because that's what Mum thought it was. She didn't want to stay there. I bought her flowers to make it nice, chocolates to munch on, and we took the portable telly from the kitchen in so that she had some company. She didn't want any of it. She didn't read any more, she

245

hadn't knitted for a couple of years, and the TV no longer held her troubled gaze. She sat in a chair and I tried to tell her that this was best for her, just for a week, and then they'd be able to give her the proper medication she needed. We sat in that room, Dad pacing around and offering nothing in the way of reassurance to anyone. Martin had Nat and was entertaining him at a children's farm nearby so that I could get on with dealing with my parents. 'You all just want to get rid of me,' she suddenly said from nowhere, her eyes dark and cold. 'How could you do this to your own mother?' I felt hurt, I felt angry, I felt like crying. I felt that everything was resting on my shoulders and I wanted to scream. But most of all I wanted my mum back.

The day Dad and I left her there and she stood crying and waving weakly, begging us not to leave her there, still wakes me up at night with a jolt, hoping it didn't happen. But it did.

During her stay I phoned every night. It was only a week but it seemed like an eternity. She cried as soon as she heard it was me. She was scared of the other people there, most of whom were a lot older and in the advanced stages of dementia. She was frightened when they banged on her door at night and walked into her room. 'Please help me get out of here. I shouldn't be here. I'm not old and there's no one to talk to,' she pleaded. I spoke to her carers at the end of every call, and they talked such common sense, always reassuring me she was in the best place. 'But she's depressed. They think she has

Alzheimer's, but it's clinical depression,' I'd try to convince them — and myself. 'Have you worked out what's really wrong with her?' They told me that the doctors would let me know what was going on. Of course they already knew, so by the time the week was up nothing changed at all.

Christmas had proved to be a focal point in the chaos that engulfed us in those torturous years. In 2001 Mum, Dad and Bizzy the dog came to stay with us, and on Christmas Day my brothers, their partners, David's mother-in-law, my nephew Zak and my little boy Nat all played at happy families, even though Mum not being herself cast a cloud over the whole affair. She didn't eat and spent whole chunks of time just sitting and staring ahead and I wished we were alone together so she didn't have to deal with the pretence that everything was jolly. The mood was compounded when on Boxing Day Dad took Bizzy for a walk and while off the lead he was hit by a car. Dad disappeared for ages — we were worried about him so Martin went to the common to search for him while I looked after Mum. He couldn't find him. Later there was a knock at the door. When I answered there was a concerned-looking policeman alongside Dad carrying an injured Bizzy in his arms — 'I was worried about your dad,' the officer told me, 'he seems very disorientated. He's obviously upset about the dog, but he couldn't really tell me anything.' Apparently they'd found us because Dad had said 'Fiona Phillips' was his daughter and the local police knew where I lived. The next day we loaded the badly injured Bizzy, who'd by then been seen by a vet, into the back of Dad's car. Mum was visibly confused and anxious as she got in for the long journey back to Wales.

27

Wales was the destination for Mum's seventieth-birthday celebrations in April 2002. I'd had big plans for that occasion — a huge party with all her friends and relations — so that she'd finally, *really* know how very, very much loved she was. In the event she didn't even know what day it was, so my brothers and their partners, Dad, me and Martin took her to a favourite Italian-run country inn for a meal. It was a wretched occasion, where when she tried to smile, she cried instead. She didn't eat a thing, and her birthday cake, sitting on the table representing a happiness which none of us shared, felt like a stand-up comic at a funeral, a grinning impostor that we all wanted to smack in the mouth.

After work one day, a couple of weeks following this trip to Wales, Gay Phillips, the *GMTV* presenters' secretary, called me at home to say she'd received a phone call from the police in Haverfordwest because there'd been an 'incident' at my parents' house. Oh God. Mum had driven Dad to breaking point again and I was going to have to sort it out. I felt overwhelmed. Dad lives with Mum, I reasoned, while I'm pregnant and with a toddler to care for, work and my poor, selfless Martin to neglect, yet I'm the one doing a ten-hour round trip most weekends to keep an eye on Mum, while he gets on with a voluntary job he's taken on, driving

249

elderly people to and from hospital appointments. The fact that he couldn't do the same for his own wife was an irony not lost on my brothers and me. I know now that it must have been his escape from a world that was falling in around him, but at the time I just saw him as an uncaring, heartless brute.

This latest crisis nearly sent me over the top. I called home and Mum answered. When she heard my voice she broke down. 'Get him on the phone,' I fumed, livid that I was having to deal with them when he should have been caring for her. 'What the bloody hell have you been doing?' I spat. 'She's f***ing ill — don't you realise?' I'd never sworn at my dad like that before, having remembered the punishment I'd received for saying 'bloody' to him when I was a child. 'I'm bloody ill too,' he swore back at me. But I was too upset to believe him.

On 14 May 2002, after pacing around our home from 2 a.m. and running into the bathroom every time I had a contraction so I wouldn't alarm Nat, our second son Mackenzie was born, just half an hour after we arrived at the Chelsea and Westminster Hospital. I remember feeling the flatness of knowing that neither Mum nor Dad would be jolted out of their misery by my news. I don't recall phoning them, although I must have; in fact there's not much I recollect about that pregnancy, it being consumed in a torrent of work, caring for Nat and my parents. I do recall sitting in the kitchen after arriving home from work and devouring tins of Cadbury's Smash instant mashed potato slathered in puddles of butter and topped with a river of melting cheese. Those indulgent moments were snatched from a life which had no space in it at all: no time for friends, for relaxing weekends, for each other. I was sick of explaining why I was never available — I just couldn't fit any more in, with two tiny children to care for, as well as two adults who may as well have been children, who were living well over two hundred miles away.

★ ★ ★

It was around six weeks after Mackenzie was born that I received a phone call saying Mum had broken her hip and was in hospital. Apparently the dog had jumped up and knocked her over and Dad had lifted her into bed. When she woke up in the morning she found that she couldn't move. As soon as I'd finished work for the week, Martin, as he'd done so many times, drove us all down to Wales. I went straight to the hospital, armed with Mackenzie, who was hungry. What I saw when I got there completely kicked me in the guts. I was floored by the sight of my Mum lying in bed, her body jerking with the most alarming involuntary movements. I felt leaden-headed, as though all the denial of the past few years and the hope that it had brought had clubbed me and brought me to my senses. My mum was dying. For the first time I could see it. It finally dawned on me that what she had was irreversible. Mackenzie was screaming as though he could sense the feeling in the room. Before long my lovely Auntie Mary arrived, full of life as ever, but we both knew that we wouldn't be sitting around a table, sipping tea with Mum, and crying with laughter over something hilarious that she'd quite innocently and unknowingly said, ever again. When Dad arrived, he looked at Mum and said 'Good God' in a voice hushed by the shock. We left him on his own with her.

As Mum started to recover from her hip injury, we discovered that she'd lost the capacity to speak properly. From being able to talk, albeit at nothing like the rate or clarity that she used to, Mum was now able only to give out a series of sounds mixed with the occasional word. Her frustration was tangible. She cried for her lost voice. We were simply devastated. When she'd been admitted to hospital no one had told the doctors that she had Alzheimer's, so they had put her under general anaesthetic, and it had proved to be too much for her body to take on top of everything else. It had greatly accelerated the effects of the disease and we knew that Mum was on the long, downward path. I was furious, but helpless. Once again there was nothing I could do.

28

Mum was moved to the South Pembrokeshire Hospital in Pembroke Dock for rehabilitation, where on one of our visits, Dad announced, 'I don't want her home again.' Poor Mum, I couldn't bear it. I knew it would be down to me and I didn't know where to begin. David and I went on a joint visit; we sat on her bed and brought her nice clothes and tried to reassure her, although there was really nothing to look forward to for any of us. We told her that she couldn't go home as it was best for her to go and live in a place where people would look after her. It was like telling a child they were going to boarding school and that they'd never see their parents again. We were all desperate for someone, something, to help us out of our despair. If only Dad would have her back, we could arrange for carers in the home, meals to be delivered — we had it all planned, except we knew it was the end of the road with Dad. I couldn't believe how callous he was being. How had it come to this? My dad was tossing my mum aside, like she was a stranger. But then she was a stranger now. She wasn't the mum we'd grown up with and loved. Sometimes though those bits came back fleetingly — and they were worth waiting around for. Sadly Dad didn't think so.

David set about getting a list of all the care

homes near Dad; meanwhile, Martin and I worked out a plan that would allow for Mum to come and live with us. We figured that if carers helped us out every day, we could manage it. I told Auntie Mary and she said, 'You can't do that, chick; it'll ruin your marriage, and it's not fair on the children. You've got your lives to think of now.' But I still couldn't help feeling that Mum deserved our care, not the care of strangers and whatever anyone said, whatever anyone continues to say, I will never rid my system of the guilt.

As soon as we could, David and I bombed down to Wales for a tour of Pembrokeshire's residential care homes. We took Dad, as it was his decision that had made it necessary. I only hoped he would visit her, so that some of the responsibility of my weekly M4 dashes would be alleviated. As I imagine it does with most people, the homes confirmed my thoughts that I really didn't want Mum to be institutionalised — to live in one room, with the only variation being to sit in a circle with other residents, around the telly. Most of the places we visited were unwelcoming and depressing. And then we found Fairfield, a home just a mile from Dad's that was bright and clean. The matron, Nimahl, was friendly and efficient, but the clincher was a resident well into her eighties, who looked at us and said with a big beam across her nearly toothless face, 'You can't get a drink around here and I'm desperate for a gin.'

At home Mackenzie had severe eczema, which started at the top of his head and ran right down to his toes. His sheets were spotted with blood every morning and he woke around six times a night. I went to bed at 10.30, was up again at 11.30 and right through what was left of the night, until my alarm went off at 4 a.m. I didn't really discuss my private life in any depth with my colleagues at work, but Eamonn would often tell me during our post-programme gossips in his dressing room, 'You're seriously depressed; you need to see someone.' I told him and myself that I wasn't and that everything was really OK.

In October, after changing my diet countless times in case my milk was causing Mackenzie's eczema, plus episodes with soya milk, goats' milk, no wheat, no tomatoes, no red fruits at all, and experiments with every natural remedy and skin application under the sun, we had to take him to Great Ormond Street Children's Hospital to get him sorted out. The remedy involved wrapping him from head to toe in bandages every night before we put him to bed. It's probably not surprising then, with the zombie-like state I was in, that I have forgotten the trauma of taking Mum to her new home for the first time. All I know is that the last photo I took of her was on Christmas Day 2002.

It was the first Christmas without Mum. Dad's whole appearance bore the weight of a life that he'd given up on — his eyes were full to brimming and he hardly spoke at all. We all went to the home on Christmas morning and we took two pictures: one of Mum with Dad and my brothers, and one of Mum with me, Dad and either Andy or David. I haven't looked at either until now because it's too upsetting. Mum is sitting on a chair with her head bowed, while we're behind her, grinning but with blank eyes. I didn't take another photo of my mum from that day on. It wasn't her. My mum had brimmed over with love for us, and her naive optimism, her acceptance of everyone and her interest in them had made us feel that the world was a wonderful place. I wanted to remember the happy lady with the big smile and the joie de vivre, the ability to bring a rush of warmth into a room and the gift of making people smile. That was my Mum.

Mum gradually disappeared more and more as time went on. It was murder trying to juggle my frantic life with thoughts of her in that place fading away on her own, coupled with a tugging need to speed along the M4 to see her as often as I could. It was hell knowing that strangers were looking after her, however caring they were — how could they possibly look after her as those who loved her would? If I could have called it would have helped, but she couldn't handle the phone and her speech hadn't recovered following the hip operation. What followed was over three years of just watching our mum suffer without being able to help. I raced up and down to Wales, sometimes with Martin and the children, sometimes on my own, sometimes with one of the children while Martin had the other. The first year was the worst, with Mum pleading with me to take her home every time I left to embark on the long journey back to London and another week full of work, children

256

and guilt. Each goodbye was the same: my heart breaking as she begged me to take her home, then I'd wait until she was distracted and go without looking back. I felt wretched each and every time I climbed into the car and dared not tune into a music station on the radio for fear of crying all the way home.

There was one man whose wife was in the home with Mum. He was there each time I visited, and the staff told me he came to see his wife every day. It filled me with sadness for Mum that Dad didn't go near the place unless I physically went round to get him and delivered him to the doorstep. Mum was often agitated by his presence: sometimes she would glance at him with a stern stare and a dark look and on other visits she was simply indifferent. I always left them on their own for some time together, but Dad was out of the door after a few minutes, not knowing what to say or do. He told me he couldn't 'face seeing her like that'. Mum's relations, in particular my Uncle Tom, Auntie Audrey, Auntie Cenlais and Uncle Ron, were constants in her life, as they had always been when she was worried that there was something wrong with her.

Auntie Audrey was a saint, sorting out Mum's precious Abbey National affairs for her and sometimes accompanying her to the doctor. Mum's diary for the year 2000 is peppered with entries such as, '*Audrey came with me to see the Dr*' and '*coffy with Audrey*', with the strange spelling and handwriting a reflection of how she felt — jaggedy and all over the place. On

257

Tuesday 1 August there's a particularly poignant entry: '*Fiona and I had a lovely time in Carmarthen.*' I remember that day vividly because Mum was very weepy on the way there, saying she was not like everyone else — I'm '*twp*' (stupid). I took her to Marks & Spencer to get some new clothes and she took her top off in the middle of the shop with no sense of inhibition at all. I felt angry when people stared and I was so deeply sorry for her loss of dignity. The last entry in that diary was thirty days after that, on Thursday 31 August, when she wrote, '*Mary is coming down.*' And that was it, a blank diary after that, after all the years of diaries I'd bought her every Christmas, 2000 was the year they stopped. She was sixty-eight. And there we were, two years later, in that home where Dad never came.

29

We could have given up on Dad. But we didn't. So every time I travelled to Wales I'd call him to say I was on my way and, depending on how he felt, I'd either see him or I wouldn't. Sometimes he'd say, 'I'm busy — I'll phone you back,' and didn't. Other times I'd just go round and collect him and take him to see Mum, so that he didn't have the choice of rejecting us both. Sometimes we had a lovely time together, but I was always on tenterhooks as to whether he'd want to see me or not. Acceptance or rejection — that was it with Dad. We felt his true personality had been exposed by Mum not being there to screen him and couldn't believe how uncaring he was. I was constantly on a mission to make my dad want to see me, to be interested in my children, just to be a loving dad.

Even though Mum was in a home, not saying much and never smiling, I still found it hard to acknowledge that she was never going to come back to us, and every time she had a lucid moment — such as when she looked at Dad when I took them on a visit to Uncle Tom's and suddenly declared, 'You've never cared for me' — I wondered if she was still in there somewhere. On the one hand I hoped that she was, yet I also prayed that she wasn't, for the horror that knowing what was happening would bring her.

The pressure of looking after everyone and holding down work continued to take its toll on me. Although I just got on with it at the time, there was one standout incident which made me wake up to the fact that I was probably teetering on the edge. Mackenzie must have been about two at the time and he and I set off for Wales, while Martin looked after Nat. I'd been so busy all week and had a hundred things on my mind, so I flew around like a mad woman, chucking things in the car before we went. We had got to the beginning of the M4, near Heston, when my puncture light went on. It often did that when all the tyres actually needed was air, so I drove into Heston services, parked by the air machine and found I didn't have any 20p pieces. I got Mackenzie out of the car and took him to the service station to get some. Got back, put them in the machine — nothing happened. Went to call the AA and my phone was dead. Walked into the Travelodge and asked if I could use their phone as it was an emergency. Waited half an hour for the AA, still fretting over the fact that my phone was out of energy. The AA man came and put some air in my tyres. Drove further up the M4 and the puncture light went on again but decided to drive on doing no more than 60 mph if I could help it. Mackenzie and I needed the loo, went to another service station. He went first, and I handed him the car keys as I went after. I heard a *plop* — he'd dropped the keys in the loo. I stood up with a start and the automatic flush whooshed my keys around the U-bend. I got down on my knees and plunged my arm into the loo, up to the elbow and felt around the slimy bend. And it was there, on my knees in a grubby cubicle, with my arm half-submerged down its waste-stained toilet bowl, that I just broke down and sobbed, trying not to alarm Mackenzie but feeling as though I really couldn't take any more.

Eventually we resumed our journey, went to Kwik-Fit in Carmarthen on the way and arrived at Mum's feeling like I'd been in the ring with Mike Tyson. She was in a very agitated, dark state — kept wandering off and pacing up and down the corridor. I tried to get her back in her room, all the while worrying about Mackenzie. I finally coaxed her to sit down and she leaned forward and hit Mackenzie. I felt like screaming. I felt for my mum. I felt for Mackenzie. I felt like running away from it all.

The worst thing about those visits, apart from witnessing Mum's decline, was the lack of privacy. The home had no specialist dementia care and the residents were a mixed bunch of elderly and infirm, some with cognitive powers intact and a few who had Alzheimer's or some other form of dementia. Mum was the youngest there, but she was also one of the sickest. There was little compassion in the other residents, and they tutted if she did something wrong and stared at us when we sat together. I had to go there because I couldn't bear Mum being alone, but the visits were never satisfying, as there was nothing I could do to make things any better.

In December 2005 I received a phone call telling me that Mum had had a fall and broken her hip again. I arrived at the hospital and she was unconscious. Dad hadn't been anywhere near and she didn't even have a nightie with her. I phoned Dad and he said, 'I'm busy fixing my bike.' 'Shall I come and get you then?' I volunteered. 'No, it's OK. I'm busy,' he replied matter-of-factly. That's it, I thought. That really is it. And I felt I'd finally lost him. I went to buy Mum a couple of nighties and looked at the other people in the store thinking what happy, carefree lives they must have.

That was the beginning of the end for Mum really. One day as I walked into the home after my long journey I heard a terrible heart-piercing scream. It sounded like someone who was deeply disturbed and it went right through me. It was my mum. I went and held her in front of several pairs of staring eyes and she looked right through me as though the misery she was suffering was my fault. The scream may have been because of the pain she was suffering following her hip operation, but to me it sounded more profound than that, like a final, desperate cry for help. She never walked again after that hip operation. I insisted that she receive physiotherapy at the home and the advice, in so many words, was: what's the point? Why prolong the agony? David and I went to the home together and they asked if she became ill again, would we like them to resuscitate her. David said no, but I couldn't let go of Mum without trying and maybe that was selfish of me.

30

The weekend of 6 May 2006 I sat with Mum as she lay in bed, breathing thin slivers of breath and moaning, tearing my heart into a thousand tiny pieces. Her misery was deep. Her existence shallow. I wanted to grab her pillow and smother her. I wanted to smother her desperate descent into indignity. I wanted to smother her misery. I wanted to smother my mum. I was alone in her bleak room. Alone because there was none of her in it, just a body that didn't now hold any of the essence of my mum. I could easily have killed her there and then. I could easily have killed my mum. And that's what stopped me. In the eyes of the law I would have murdered her. In anyone else's eyes I would have relieved the misery, the pain, the suffering, the indignity. But as I didn't want my sons to have a murdering mother or my husband to have a murderous wife, I didn't kill my mum. A week later, on Saturday 13 May 2006, I wrote this as the lead in my *Mirror* column. It followed a vote by the House of Lords to reject a euthanasia bill:

People who pretend to care about life know nothing of a long, drawn-out, undignified death. If they did, the House of Lords would have voted for the Assisted Dying for the Terminally Ill Bill yesterday. My mum is dying. She told me she wanted to die five

263

years ago. Alzheimer's has been killing her for at least nine years. For me she really died when she wasn't herself any more, but now her body's slipping away too. I've written before about her battle with Alzheimer's. I say battle, but there's no fighting this big clout of a disease, which whacks you down and leaves you helpless and terrified. Many of you who've written to me with your experiences already know that it wrecks lives. And not just the victim's. It is devastating for their families who are drawn into the long, tortuous descent into death. That's why, although her body is still here, unable to move, talk, eat, see, or pretty much do anything except to draw in shallow breath, I would really rather she had been at peace before the years of suffering. Some religious people though, supposedly caring souls, seem to feel nothing for the pain of others. 'Suffering can be good for us,' says the Reverend George Curry, chairman of the Church Society, who disagrees with assisted death. Suffering a broken relation-ship, the death of a loved one, hardship or injustice can all teach us valuable lessons in life, but what is the point of the suffering of a terminally ill person? That's just plain cruel. That's why we have our pets put down. Because we don't want them to suffer. Legislating for euthanasia would make it lawful for a doctor to administer lethal drugs as long as the terminally ill patient had signed a written request, was judged by two doctors to have no quality of life, and was likely to die within six months. In the meantime my mum continues to fade. We have asked doctors to make her comfortable but not to prolong her living death. For now that's all we can do.

I wrote that on Thursday 11 May 2006 for publication in the *Daily Mirror* on Saturday 13th. On the 14th it was my younger son's fourth birthday. I was numb with the strain of it all: Mum, Dad, children, work. I always make a huge fuss for the children's birthdays, because it's only when you become a mum that it finally kicks in just how special birthdays are. But I can't for the life of me remember what we did on Mackenzie's fourth birthday.

That night I fell into bed, and as usual couldn't sleep. The phone went at around midnight. It was the care home, and someone on the end of the line was telling me that Mum was not good. They'd said that a lot over the previous weeks and I'd sped down to Wales many times (literally, I'd gathered a precarious nine points on my licence) thinking that this could be 'it'. I put down the phone and agonised and agonised until my alarm went off in the morning to get me up for *GMTV*. I was going to go to work until I thought, But what if this *is* it? What if that's it and she dies while I'm smiling away on television? I phoned work, told them I wasn't coming in and got in the car. That familiar, long, now-hated journey. I hated the people who looked after Mum, because I should have been doing it. I hated the silence from Mum. The memories of us talking and talking and talking. And I hated arriving and the smell and the noises, the signing in, the moaning, the television, the windows that needed washing, the sticky carpets, the chipped furniture, the lack of privacy, my mum's horrible room. I hated it all for not being good enough for my mum.

When I arrived she was in her room, just lying there. And I knew it was the end. I kissed her and knew I was never going to take her on our much-discussed coach trip to Holland to see the tulip fields, that we'd never ever talk and talk and talk, never laugh till we fell over. That she'd never smile that 'It'll be all right, Toots' smile ever again. I sat on her small single bed, with the rubber sheets and the cheap pillows, and I wanted to scream for all her pain and the tears, for the not being able to help, for the guilt of handing her over to someone else's care when she'd loved and cared for me so much. For the guilt I knew would never leave me, for all the horrible things I'd ever said or done, for not letting her know every day that I loved her. I wept inside and held Mum's hand and cradled what was left of her. I sat with her all day and the next day until, in the late afternoon, David phoned and told me to 'go home to your boys. Mum went years ago.' And Nimahl came to the room and said the same. I phoned Martin and, ever the selfless gentleman, he said, 'You do what you think's best; we're all fine here.'

So I left, and it hurts like hell even writing this, but I left, and of all the things in life that I regret, it was that I went. My mum died on her own a few hours later. I've blanked it out until now telling myself that she wouldn't have let go if I'd stayed, that she'd have held out until I went back to the hotel to sleep, so that even if I'd remained in Wales that night she'd have died on her own. I hate Alzheimer's for that, for wearing you down over the years, so that when it really is the last goodbye, you're too worn out to stick around for it.

Isn't it awful, but I can't remember Dad much in this whole scenario. It's sad to admit, but as far as we all were concerned, he'd become a bit-part player appearing, as he did, not to be bothered, nor to care. Not long before Mum died, I did collect him, telling him that she probably wouldn't be around for too much longer. He sighed a deep sigh and said nothing. As he entered the care home we had the usual embarrassment of him shuffling awkwardly and saying inappropriate things like 'I hope I don't end up in a place like this' within earshot of the residents and staff. When I took him into Mum's room he didn't know what to say or do, or where to look. He wanted to go home not long after he arrived. His presence angered me. I was cracking up and he was so detached.

After receiving a phone call from Nimahl, saying 'She's gone' not long after I arrived back home, I phoned Dad and could tell that he was crushed that she'd gone. His voice was reduced to a whisper as he said, 'I'll go and see her now.' I phoned David and we discussed the practicalities of what we had to do next. And I phoned

Andy and rather harshly announced, 'Mum's dead.' They were all the words I had left, but it raised a smile as Andy said, 'Oh, cheers,' at my directness. Martin came in from work and I wanted to collapse all over him and sob, but the boys were still awake, so I saved the grief for myself. In my diary on 16 May I drew a heart with a tear falling from it and wrote underneath, '*My Mum.*' I couldn't bear to write '*Mum died*' or '*Mum's dead*' or '*Mum passed away*' or whatever; there isn't a nice way to write it or feel it. All those years of guilt and agony, of telling Mum that the doctors were looking for something to fix her, of travelling up and down the M4, of feeling beyond disappointed in Dad, of testing Martin to the limit and allowing no time for myself at all, had culminated in this. Mum was gone. Even though she already had. And I was angry that there'd been several big cut-off points, rather than one huge one that I could react to with proper grief.

That feeling of knowing you're never going to see someone you love and cherish so much, ever again is a stomach-churning realisation which hits you last thing at night and first thing in the morning. And then never really leaves you.

31

I returned to Wales with David, where we got on with arranging the funeral and phoning Mum's friends and relations. At the funeral directors' we were told, 'She's in there, we've looked after her and made her look pretty.' Dad was the first to go into the Chapel of Rest to say goodbye to Mum. He came out looking completely gutted and announced, 'She looks bloody awful.' David and I winced at the inappropriateness of his comment and went in to say our own farewells. He was right: she looked awful. David and I held on to each other as we choked up and said, 'That doesn't look like Mum.' And it didn't, and in a way that was comforting. We knew that the mum we adored had gone years ago.

The funeral was beautiful, with a choir singing the Welsh hymns '*Calon lan*' and '*lesu Tirion*' that Mum had sung herself at school and to us as children. There were tears, but because the service embodied Mum's fun-loving spirit, there was lots of laughter too, especially when the reverend retold a family anecdote about Mum, with her typical knack of using the wrong vocabulary, saying that said she had been to a bisexual hairdresser, instead of a unisex one. Martin captured her mischievous personality in his reading, which he ended with Dylan Thomas's poem 'Do Not Go Gentle into That

Dark Night', but if she could have seen who the second reader was, Mum would have burst with pride and got her camera out: Mr Jeremy, the boss she worshipped at Ocky White's! We were so touched that he agreed to do it.

Outside we all looked at the flowers and read the messages. I'd organised our family flowers and had chosen an arrangement for Dad along with a card which I asked him to write. He's never been one for words; Mum often despaired that he'd sign her anniversary or birthday cards 'Phil x', and that was it. On this card he'd written, 'Your love and friendship brightened my days and made my life so much nicer. Rest in peace Amy, my darling.'

The next day, 24 May, Dad, my brothers, my sister-in-law, Martin, me and my Auntie Mary and Uncle Roy gathered once more at Narbeth Crematorium to bury Mum's ashes under a fragile silver birch sapling. Its delicate fronds rustled in the wind as we stood on a slope looking at the baby tree and at the wooden box which contained all that was left of Mum. We had the best of her in our heads. And in our hearts. And in her little grandchildren, whose mischievous behaviour brings her spirit alive every day. We stood there — me numb, Dad dumb and broken — as the minister conducted the final goodbye. I can't remember the order, what the weather was like, but there's one indelible image I'll never forget: Dad took hold of Mum in a box, placed her in the little rectangular hole which had been dug in the ground at the front of the tree and then fell to his knees and kissed that precious box. If only Mum had been alive to witness it. To receive it. A kiss in death to replace all he'd never told her in life. Whatever we all felt about losing our mum, he was the one who had to go home hand in hand with remorse. Grief-stricken with his inability to communicate love and affection. I often wonder what he made of the poem delivered by the minister somewhere in that beautifully tragic little service. It was written by the American poet Isla Paschal Richardson. It's called 'To Those I Love'.

If I should ever leave you whom I love
To go along the Silent Way,
Grieve not,
Nor speak of me with tears,
But laugh and talk of me
As if I were beside you there.

(I'd come . . . I'd come, could I but find a
    way!
But would not tears and grief be barriers?)
And when you hear a song
Or see a bird I loved,
Please do not let the thought of me be
    sad . . .
For I am loving you just as I always have.

You were so good to me!
There are so many things I wanted still to
    do . . .
So many things to say to you . . .
Remember that I did not fear . . .

It was just leaving you that was so hard to
    face.

We cannot see Beyond,
But this I know:
I loved you so . . .
'Twas heaven here with you!

Gregory Peck chose this poem to say goodbye to
his mate Frank Sinatra at Ol' Blue Eyes' funeral
in May 1998. With all its good intentions it
was just what we needed that day. At the end
of the service Dad just walked off. I can't recall
whether he said goodbye to anyone. I just
remember him walking off on his own, fists
clenched by his sides as if they carried all his
emotion for him. My brothers and I watched
him go.

32

On Monday 29 May I went back to the red sofa. I felt at home there. Life was carrying on as normal, as it has to. People care, but they've got jobs to get on with, news to deliver, a programme to get on air. I walked in at 5 a.m. as usual, discussed the day's programme, trudged down the familiar stairs with their view of the Oxo Tower and St Paul's Cathedral silhouetted against the rising sun and went into my dressing room and cried my eyes out. I cried for it all being normal when it wasn't. I cried for never having got round to arranging for my mum to come and visit *GMTV*. 'Oh Mum, I'll make sure you come in soon, I promise,' I always said. But I never did.

I can't remember who I sat beside that day, but I think it was Andrew Castle and I think I sat on that sofa outwardly smiling and immersing myself in other people's lives. Andrew was a great comfort to me — we often talked about our mums. He'd lost his mother after a long, drawn-out battle with illness which resulted in her eventually going blind. He understood how I was feeling and that I had to smile for the camera when I felt like looking at it and saying, 'I want to go home.' For some reason Westlife always reduced me to tears when they appeared on the show during the years that Mum was ill. My mum would have loved Shane, Kian, Nicky

273

and Mark. They'd come into the category of 'lovely boys — why can't you meet someone like that?' And that's why they made me cry when they sang. Corny? You bet. But mums and grans as well as young girls love those Westlife boys, and they made me think of Mum. You wouldn't have wanted to see the off-camera mess I was in when they came in in 2004, just over a year before Mum died, and sang 'You Raise Me Up'. Inconsolable doesn't even begin to describe it. I think it was pretty obvious when the cameras were back on Andrew and me that I'd had a bit of a private moment. I can't remember what we said, but I know that Andrew was brilliant. His eyes had welled up a bit too. I don't think he'll forget Westlife in a hurry either.

Back in that first week at work after Mum died I had to sit down and compose my weekly column for the *Mirror*. They'd asked if I'd write about my mum, and to be honest my head hadn't been full of anything but, so I gladly let it flow. I wrote the article on Thursday 1 June, my deadline day, sobbing in my study, which was awash with letters of condolence from complete strangers who will never know how much their words helped me. This is a truncated version of what appeared in the paper on Saturday 3 June. It sort of made sense of it all for me.

This afternoon we're going on a tour of Stamford Bridge to celebrate my son's seventh birthday. At home, Chelsea balloons and birthday cards line the shelves alongside the scores of sympathy cards I've received following the death of my lovely mum, Amy. Life and death, all on one shelf.

The children, in their innocence and excitement, are life-affirming, but even they can't shake me out of the bubble I've been cocooned in since hearing that Mum has gone.

The pain of her passing has left me reeling. I go to bed thinking of her, wake up thinking of her, feel guilty when I'm not thinking of her and torment myself for not realising she was ill when, in her mid-60s, Alzheimer's first got a grip on her big personality.

I feel as if I've been punched a hundred times. I don't want to speak to anyone other than family, and because life is carrying on as though nothing's happened I feel like screaming, 'But I've lost my mum!'

Right now everything means virtually nothing. But despite it all I feel she's with me now more than she was over the past few years when her illness took away who she was.

Now I don't remember the ravaged shell of a person she became. I can see only her huge smile and feel her huge heart. My image of her is of her arms wrapped around my brothers and me, plastering us with love.

It makes me cry to think I'll never feel that again, and yet I've been crying over Mum for at least seven years. That's how long Alzheimer's has had her. She hasn't been an active part of our lives since she lost the ability to communicate. We've already mourned the loss of her phone calls, hugs, reassurances, and her gigantic pride in us.

At times I've willed her to let go, to find peace — even though selfishly I wanted her to hang on for as long as she could. Once, when we were alone, she was screaming with pain, exhausted but unable to sleep for spasms that ran through her body. I seriously thought of ending it for her then.

Since Christmas, when she broke her hip for the second time, I've gone to sleep with my phone by the bed, dreading the call to tell me she'd gone, yet not wanting to miss it. At midnight on Sunday May 14, it rang. 'Your mum's condition has deteriorated considerably,' said the nurse. Almost relieved she was still there, I tried to go back to sleep, but couldn't.

When my alarm went off as usual at 4 a.m. on Monday I got up like a robot, showered, got in my *GMTV* car and completely choked up. 'What am I doing going to work when my mum could be slipping away?' I asked myself. I got out of the car and into my own, phoned work and headed for Wales.

When I got there Mum's eyes were already gone. I lifted her eyelids but her eyes were dead. She was breathing, and that was all.

In some ways I took comfort in the fact that the pain and suffering seemed to have ceased. I sat for hours just looking at her and telling her all the things I'd said a thousand times. Things she hadn't under- stood for a long time. Things I wish I'd said when she was the mum who I thought would be around for ever.

I tried to sound happy when I phoned the children to tell them I wouldn't be home that night. The next day she was the same. I sat by her bed until a wonderful nurse, who's become extended family over the years, said, 'Why don't you go home to your boys? Your mum went years ago.'

I know from your kind messages that so many of you have suffered the heartache of losing your mum. As most of you say, it changes your life for ever. I think it forces you finally to grow up. But even though I'm no longer a child, I still want my mum.

Life is carrying on as if nothing's happened and I want to scream, 'I've lost my mum!'

I have two huge white boxes full of the letters and emails and cards which I received following Mum's death. Some people found out because *GMTV* explained my absence from the sofa, some read short reports in newspapers, while others read the piece I wrote for the *Daily Mirror*. I spent hours in my little room, numbly reading those messages — the comfort of strangers, in a way so much more comforting than the cliched words of people close to you, who often don't have a clue how to deal with bereavement. I will always be truly grateful. They helped me no end.

★   ★   ★

Life is never ever the same once your mum goes. No one on this earth could ever love you more than your mum. No one could be more proud, more devastated when things go wrong, more ecstatic when wonderful things happen. My mum had lost those emotions long ago, so I'd had to learn over the years that she was ill to get by without her complete immersion in my life. I felt guilty that I'd ever thought or said over the years, 'Oh Mum, do you have to keep ringing? I told you that the other day.' The phone hadn't rung with that chirpy, happy voice on the other end for too long. Whenever anything amazing happens to me now, it's just another thing that's happened. It doesn't mean the same now that Mum's not there with her notepad writing every detail down, before digesting it then screaming, 'You're interviewing the prime minister?!!' or, 'Tony Blair's asked you to do what?!!', or whatever it was I'd told her. It was unbridled love, pride and joy. And only your mum feels that unconditional love for you. And I miss being able to give her that joy, being able to make her proud and happy and ecstatic. Because she loved me like no one else ever will.

33

During those dark months following Mum's death I often recalled the words of the carers who looked after her and who tried to make me feel better when I told them that I felt I should give up everything to look after Mum. 'You're doing all you can; she's not going to get better, and you can't give up your life. Your mum wouldn't want you to do that either,' they'd tell me. I clung on to those words so often when I felt the pull of mum and the weight of my conscience. To tell the truth though, amid all the grief and regret, I was a little relieved when Mum passed away. The special lady who'd always brought so much love and laughter into my life hadn't smiled for years. She'd cried. A lot. And screamed, and begged for help. But I couldn't help her, and the guilt that came with that, as you'll understand by now, nearly drove me mad. I didn't miss going into that care home. I didn't miss having to leave her when I drove back to London to be with my family. I didn't miss imagining her there on her own when I should have been with her. I missed her desperately though. But I still had Dad.

I'm trying to recall the next time we saw him after that little service at the crematorium. When he'd dropped to his knees to kiss the remains of Mum, whom he'd not kissed for years. I realise now that it's easy in a marriage to do that. But the remorse and the regret and the sense of waste of a love that could have been so good if he'd let it, must have weighed heavy on him. It's hard to put together a chronological account of how Dad coped because we didn't think he cared that much. He'd not been to visit Mum in the care home — unless I picked him up and dragged him in there — in the three years she deteriorated there. His lack of concern had been shocking, and the dad that I worshipped had become a source of great pain and frustration to me. His many rejections, his inability to show Mum any warmth when she so desperately needed it, his bizarre, seemingly unfeeling, impenetrable demeanour made me want to cut him off to relieve the pain he was causing. 'You have to accept that he's never going to be who you want him to be,' my brother David told me again and again. He'd removed himself emotionally from Dad long before, as had Andy, but I couldn't let him go.

In the July, after Mum's death in May, I went to stay in Wales before the boys broke up from school, so I could spend some time with Dad. Just me and Dad, when before it would have been the three of us. I felt that he didn't really want me there and I felt guilty for not being Mum. I took him out for coffee and his eyes were constantly misty and on the point of overflowing. I couldn't understand: why all the emotion now, when it would have been of so much help when Mum was still alive? He talked about her as if she'd only just left him. As if she hadn't been in a care home for three years. As if

280

he'd visited her every day, and now she was gone. I hated his self-indulgence, his all-too-late emotion and I'm almost reluctant to admit that I felt he deserved some of those tears, but I loved him all the same. Even though he didn't once ask how I was feeling now that I'd lost my mum, even though he didn't thank me for doing everything for Mum because he hadn't done anything, even though, as always, it was all about him. I pitied him and I'd always respected him too much to pity, but now I pitied him for not having the wherewithal to get over his mother's lack of love and emotion, for not being able to show it to anyone else.

I did have some lovely times with Dad during the time Mum was in care though, although never consistently lovely. When I arrived from London, I'd phone him and pick him up so that we could go somewhere. The house wasn't welcoming, it was a mess — stuff everywhere and as time went on increasingly strange objects hanging from the front door (a black skeleton) and the walls (a menu from Gladstones, the restaurant I took Mum and Dad to in LA) and my Southampton FC FA Cup Winners commemorative mirror which was down from the loft and perched on the radiator in the hall along with a newspaper cutting of former star player Mike Channon, whom I'd worshipped in my teens. It was as though he was trying to recreate memories. I stayed in a hotel on my trips down, as Dad gave me the impression that this was his house and that he didn't want the nuisance of someone else around. Often I'd drive straight to the hotel from London and he'd come and meet me there. The staff got to know our little arrangement and teased, 'Where's your boy-friend tonight then?' if I ate on my own because he was 'too busy' to come. On our 'dates', he'd always bring the subject around to Mum, and his eyes would brim over as he gulped back his emotions and said, 'She was a lovely lady, just a really nice person.' When he left to go home, I'd sometimes say, if I didn't have my car, 'Can you come and pick me up at 10 a.m. tomorrow?' 'Yes,' he'd say, full of certainty. But he never came. It's only now that I know — he forgot. I recall thinking it was odd that he didn't turn up because he'd never let me down in that way before, but with Mum's death still fresh in all our minds I put it down to that.

Having spent the past few years living Mum's life, in respect of her bank accounts and other financial investments that she'd squirrelled away, and having to deal with the fact that she hadn't made a will and all the time administration, frustration and stress it used up, I knew that we had to get Dad to make a will. I'd got him to sign an enduring power of attorney, having been unable to do the same with Mum — she got very upset every time money was mentioned and treated David and me as if we were Bonnie and Clyde. It meant that I could administrate Dad's affairs if he became incapable of doing so.

David and I drove to Wales, met Dad, with his eyes full of tears and his fists clenched by his sides, and took him to the solicitor. We sat and listened as the lawyer explained what he needed to do, and then left the room so that Dad could give his instructions in private. David and I wandered outside into the sunshine, thinking Dad would be in there for some time. About ten minutes passed and we were called back in to see the solicitor on his own.

'I'm afraid your father is incapable of making a will,' he declared. 'He can't remember all of your names and he doesn't recall his own address.'

'Well, he is grief-stricken, very depressed; our mum only died a few weeks ago and he's finding it really hard,' I replied.

'Sorry, I can't let him make a will in his current state of mind.'

So he gave Dad a will form to take home and fill out when he was 'less confused'.

A while later I opened an envelope addressed in Dad's distinctive handwriting, and inside the envelope — no note or anything — was the partially completed last will and testament. He'd filled the date in as the *Twentieth day of Saturday 2007*. His mind's going, I thought, as I peered at Dad's writing, which had a look of hesitancy about it. He hadn't completed anything else, apart from jotting his savings account number next to my name. At the end of the document, written in type, was, 'I wish to be cremated and my ashes to be buried with those of my wife.'

I received all sorts of worried phone calls from Dad during that period and took over the payment of his car tax and insurance, and sorted out the many other documents that he couldn't understand. On 21 October 2007 a letter with the envelope written in handwriting that I knew, but with a sort of feathery look to it and jotted out in a mix of block capitals, lower-case and cursive, plopped onto the doormat. It reminded me of Mum's erratic squiggles in the diary I'd found. It dawned on me that something might be very wrong. It wasn't just the address on the front of the envelope that set my mind whirring, but also the words: '*Fiona & Martins address*', followed by our address complete with correct postcode. It was a sign that I recognised, an indication that something was not right, that his mind was behaving over-meticulously in an effort to get a grip on things. He was writing his thoughts down in order to hang on to them, hence the '*Fiona & Martin's address*' as an instruction to himself.

I opened the envelope and inside was the cut-off front of a cheap old Christmas card — he never sent them, so it must have been one he received — on the back of which he'd written, '*Thank you for the card. Please forgive me for my tardiness. Love you all. Dad.*' I'd recently sent him a birthday card and I think his reply was a desperate cry for attention, maybe because he knew that something was wrong with him, as he'd never made a habit of writing to us before. Despite my misgivings, I was still convinced that Dad's behaviour was an extension of his very often odd ways, probably exacerbated by grief and remorse. After all, surely there was no way that he could have the same illness as Mum?

It's hard to recall when it became more than that; more than odd behaviour made worse by grief. Or rather, when we finally clocked that it wasn't odd behaviour at all, but Alzheimer's disease. How long had he had it? Is that why he had been so indifferent towards Mum when she needed him most? Was it why he had turned me away so many times, saying he was 'too busy' doing something or other? Was it the reason he didn't want us to come to his house? Was it why the policeman who had brought him and Bizzy back to my house over Christmas 2001 had said he was 'disorientated' and couldn't answer anything? Was it why he'd said, 'I'm bloody ill too,' when I accused him of not looking after Mum? Was it the basis for why he didn't seem to have much sympathy when she was recovering from breast cancer?

And then I received a phone call from his GP. 'We're slightly worried about your dad, because I got a call from the pharmacist saying he's turning up every day to collect a prescription that he's already picked up.' 'Yes, I think he's finding it hard to cope with Mum's death,' I replied. 'No, no, we think it may be more than that. He has some cognitive difficulties.' 'Yes, but he's depressed,' I said, knowing that the pattern we'd gone through with Mum was starting to repeat itself. 'You don't think it's Alzheimer's, do you?' I questioned with a note of incredulity in my voice. 'Yes, I think it could be.' I really didn't believe it. Yes, we'd made mistakes with Mum, convinced that she was depressed, but Dad was definitely suffering with depression. He'd been prescribed mirtazapine, a known antidepressant, because he couldn't sleep at night. Of course he was depressed, I tried to persuade myself, all the while knowing that Mum had been on antidepressants too. Still, Dad certainly couldn't have Alzheimer's — just when I was getting my life back in gear after the miserable years of witnessing Mum's withering away, just when we thought he was getting on with life, albeit a bit depressed. I told David and it sounded like I was repeating a bad joke, so we carried on in our denial until I knew we couldn't any more.

In March 2008 I went to Wales for a weekend with Dad. He was cold, he was odd, he was addled, and I resented the fact that I'd left my family behind, only to be offered a grudging greeting after driving for five hours. I took him out to a seaside pub and he perked up a bit, talked about Mum, and I felt good that he seemed to be enjoying himself. He was charming to the young staff in a bumbling, giggling, talking-nonsense kind of way. I drove him home and hesitated by the door in case he didn't want me to come in. But he did. And I could see why he hadn't wanted me to before. He was living in squalor, the whole place littered with mess and rubbish, dirty dishes, a grubby mattress and sheets in the middle of the living-room floor, books stacked high in the kitchen, rotting food in the fridge — it was a picture of desperation.

'Oh Dad,' I gasped, 'we've got to get you out of here.' 'It's fine,' he mumbled as I set about trying to make it cleaner, tidier. When I left — it was a Friday night — I said, 'I'll phone you in the morning, and then I'll come round and we'll talk about what we need to do. OK?' I think there was a sense of relief that I'd unearthed his secret. 'See you tomorrow,' he said with a smile.

Tomorrow never came. I rang and rang. No answer. I bashed on the front door. No answer. The same on Sunday. So I posted a note through the door. I found it when I was sorting Dad's house out with David. '*Hi Dad*,' it read. '*Called round again! No answer. Please keep my phone numbers* [I wrote them here]. *I will try and sort something out, so that you can move nearer us. Please look after yourself; I'm always on the end of the phone if you need anything. It was lovely to see you on Friday. All my love . . .* '

A few months later, after agonising over whether it was fair to uproot Dad from his home, I did, with the help of my Uncle Barry, 'sort something'. In the interim Dad would one minute say, 'I've got to get out of here,' and the next insist that, 'I'm not going anywhere.' I knew there was no way he could stay in Wales, so in the end I had to make the decision for him and we moved Dad to Southsea, where he's in a warden-controlled complex, happily losing his mind. Thankfully his experience is a better one than Mum's — he's generally in high spirits and content, but can't string a sentence together, which frustrates him. He bangs on his head when that happens and walks around going 'Quack, quack' when he can't find the words. It's been difficult, with phone calls saying he's gone missing, calls from the police at 2 a.m. saying they've found him nearly frozen to death and calls saying he's lost his keys, wallet — you name it. Perhaps one of the saddest things about Dad's

Alzheimer's is that he doesn't read at all now, doesn't even think of it. There's no point, his mind can't take it in at all. My dad, who got me hooked on reading from such an early age by telling me I could do anything if I read, now can't read himself. That's not my dad.

One day we were together, doing our usual performance of cat-and-mouse around the supermarket — the moment my back is turned to reach for something from the shelves, Dad wanders off somewhere else and I have to scuttle off after him before he disappears — when my phone rang. It was the *GMTV* press office letting me know they'd had a phone call from a newspaper saying they'd heard that my dad had been picked up by the police. He had, because he'd got lost again. They were intending to do a story on it. I looked around and chased after Dad while saying, 'They can't do that — it's not in anyone's interest. He's a seventy-four-year-old sick man and he deserves his privacy.' I rounded Dad up and my colleague said, 'OK, I'll phone them.' I was furious and felt awful for my poor dad, that they thought that an elderly, ailing man who gets lost a lot because of his illness deserves to be splashed across a national newspaper. The next call I received was that the newspaper was 'going to go' with the story despite my protestations.

I had to deal with it so I rushed Dad home, made sure he was OK and got into my car to make calls to a barrister to try and stop the story. I'd driven down after work that morning, leaving the children to be picked up from school by a childminder, and as I sat there after my phone call, mulling it all over, I thought, I can't do this any more. Dad was great company that day, as he mostly is now — he's affectionate, calls me 'darling' — but my phone was ringing all day, I was dogtired after getting up at 4 a.m., weary when I thought about having to do the same the following morning and I was stressed out about having to leave Dad to make those phone calls and then drive back to London. It was that feeling again: never having time to do anything properly. Later that summer I resigned from *GMTV*.

Now my time with Dad is a pleasure, tinged with sadness because he's ill, and with regret that we were so tied up with Mum's illness that we didn't realise that he was ill too, probably for some years. It just didn't occur to us that they could *both* have Alzheimer's. I'm not with Dad every day — I can't be — but when I am, we've got time to do things properly. He has a brilliant team of carers who look after him on a daily basis, all of whom say he's 'so sweet', 'a gentleman'. One of 'his girls' left me a note very recently, in which she wrote, '*It's always a pleasure to call on your dad; he always has a smile and is often laughing!*' That is all we could wish for. I wonder if Mum is looking down and laughing too.

34

Thursday 18 December 2008 was my last ever day on the *GMTV* sofa. It was the end of the most amazing career roller coaster, which started with a phone call back in June 1992, when I was having a day off from my job as a reporter at Sky News. I was hoovering my tiny one-bedroom flat in south-west London having been down on my knees scrubbing at a yellow takeaway curry stain on the carpet. My hair was clamped up in a messy twist at the back of my head and I was dressed like a slut. I only just heard the phone ringing above the noise of the hoover and my stereo blasting out Annie Lennox's *Diva* album.

'Hello, my name's Lol Ingham,' said the friendly voice on the other end. 'I'm deputy editor of *Sunrise*, the new breakfast programme which is taking over from *TVAM* in January next year. We've seen you on Sky News — I take it you're happy there?' 'Er, yes,' I replied, 'but I'm freelance so . . . ' I wasn't quite sure where this was leading. 'Well, the editor, Liam Hamilton, would like to see you, can you come in for a chat?' 'Yes, when do you want me to come in?' 'How about some time today.' 'Er, yes, that's fine,' I lied as I fingered my slimy hair and glanced down at my scruffy clothes. I put the phone down, jumped up and down and phoned Mum. She was at work at Ocky White's and didn't have her notepad with her. I had to explain over and over again, and as I wasn't quite sure what it was I'd been asked to do myself, it was a conversation that didn't make much sense. 'A new job, Toots? Does that mean you'll be on the BBC?' 'No, Mum, it's ITV, not the BBC. Oh well, never mind,' she responded and, as usual, I could have strangled her. Anyway I think she was pleased, but what about? I hadn't been offered anything yet. And I never would be if I didn't get a grip and get a hair wash and get out of the door. I remember what I wore: bright yellow jeans, a black top with stars on, a black leather waistcoat-type affair and black Chelsea boots — it was fashionable then, honest! Anyway, I went in for a cup of tea and a chat, and sixteen years later I was finally saying goodbye to *GMTV*.

When I woke as usual at 4 a.m. on that Thursday just a week before Christmas I felt strangely calm — odd, but calm and not too emotional, thank goodness, went through the usual shower, get dressed, kiss the boys and out-the-door routine and . . . I couldn't believe it! My last day and they'd forgotten to send my car. There was a *Mirror* photographer, Roger Allen, outside waiting to take pictures of me leaving the house for my last early-morning journey to that tall white TV tower on London's South Bank. 'I'll give you a lift in,' Roger offered. But not before he'd snapped me in jeans, baggy jumper, baseball boots, rat's tail hair and no make-up — not a look that photographs well. I phoned the office, told them what I was doing and got into the photographer's car.

When I arrived, for the first time in all those years I wasn't fully briefed on the programme. I had a few interviews to do, but nothing taxing, and Abi, my producer, was doing her best not to appear shifty and to pretend that it was just another day. Which it was, only it was my last day, and I'd feared it for the past three months — what if I couldn't put a sentence together with the sentiment of it all? What if I was feeling so emotional that I bottled it all up and wasn't emotional at all? What if . . . ? Oh, so what?! It's only a job.

In the end I mostly held myself together, thanks to my lovely colleague Ben Shephard, who was an absolute rock and a lifeline that day. He must have had huge great bruises on his right thigh given the amount of time I spent clutching it for reassurance. I felt OK about going though, knowing I'd had a good innings and feeling in my heart that it was for all the right reasons. I couldn't believe the send-off that my lovely colleagues gave me. There were filmed messages from Gordon Brown, David Cameron and Nick Clegg, from Frank Lampard, Take That, Kate Winslet and Bruce Forsyth and the *Strictly Come Dancing* judges. My old mates Status Quo sent me their usual cheek. Cheryl Cole and Girls Aloud came in to say goodbye. James Blunt sent me a good luck note attached to his latest album and David and Victoria Beckham wrote me a lovely letter, as did Cherie Blair. There was also one from her husband Tony who wrote, 'You were and are a superb professional, but also one of the nicest people I met in my time in UK politics.' If only Mum could have showed that one off! And then there was Donny. How can I forget Donny Osmond, who drove through snowstorms to get to a studio in Nevada to say goodbye to me, despite the fact I'd ravished him last time he was in? There were speeches, there were gifts and flowers and emails and cards and balloons and photographers and tears.

Then, puff! It was all over. And I went home to the warmth and privacy of my family, hopelessly hoping that Dad had been watching and wishing that I could phone my mum.

Acknowledgements

It truly is a miracle that my wonderful husband is still around after the years of neglect endured while I juggled children, parents, work and writing this book! I still never make enough time to let him know how very much I love, respect and appreciate him, but I do. To my gorgeous little boys, Nat and Mackenzie, who brightened up the bleakest of days with their naive curiosity, their laughter and cuddly love and for still talking about 'Nana' even though she was so fleetingly in their lives. And my brothers David and Andy — my best friends — for all the memories, the never-ending psychoanalysis and the love and support.

My mother's wonderful relatives kept me going when I sometimes felt I would have to give everything up to be with her. Special thanks to my Auntie Audrey, whom Mum relied on so heavily when she feared that she was losing her mind and to my Uncle Tom, Auntie Cenlais and Uncle Rhon who carried on visiting Mum when virtually everyone else had given up. Huge love and thanks to my 'second mum', my wonderful Auntie Mary, whom Mum adored and I still do and lovely Uncle Roy, her husband. My Uncle Barry, who always sees the funny side of life, provided laughs and immeasurable support in helping me to move my father from Wales to Southsea, where he still pops in to check on Dad every week. If Mum was still here she'd want to say thank you a hundred times over to her friends from Ocky White, especially 'Mr Jeremy' and his family, whom she worshipped. Thank you too, to the over-worked, underpaid, but truly priceless carers, especially Nimahl and Rosemary, who put my mind at rest so many times when the guilt of not caring for mum myself threatened to overwhelm me. And to Sarah and the staff at The Wolfscastle Country Hotel for being a welcoming second home on my bleak solo trips to Wales and Andrew at the St Brides Hotel in Saundersfoot for so often being family HQ when we travelled down to deal with Mum and Dad.

To all the wonderful friends I made during my time at *GMTV* — too many to mention, but so many special bonds were formed working in the middle of the night for all those years and they will never be broken. Helen Hand, you are not only big-hearted and thoughtful, but your make-up makes me look a hell of a lot better than I deserve to — thank you!

My friends at the *Daily Mirror* — Richard Wallace the editor, Shiraz, whose ear I bend every Thursday, and Peter Willis, a great mate and often trusty advisor, have been much-valued constants in my life and have supported me no end through thick and thin — thank you. And my heartfelt gratitude to you, Piers Morgan, for having the faith to give me my *Mirror* job in the first place and for telling me that I should write a book, although I don't think you meant this one!

Jan 'The Duchess' Kennedy, Vicki Mellor and

Sian Smyth, you are like best friends and family to me and have so often picked me up and driven me on when I've questioned my ability to do so. Thank you, and Jonathan, for persuading me to write this book and for putting me in the hands of Trevor Dolby whose editorial advice has been impeccable and whose company I've relished. I'll have to work again with you, Trevor, so that we can go out for lunch and gossip! Thanks also to Amelia, Nicola and Penny at Random House for all their help.

My dear friend Amanda Searle, who has heard so often the phrase 'I can't, I've got to write my damn book,' just to let you know how much I value your friendship.

Neal, I don't need to tell you . . .

Debs, my lifelong friend. I miss you. I hope you read this, and then you may understand why I never had the time.

And Dad, I love you. Even if sometimes you don't know who I am.

Other titles published by
The House of Ulverscroft:

GLORIOUS GRANDPARENTING

Gloria Hunniford

Grandparenting is not what it used to be, but as the grandmother to nine wonderful grandchildren, Gloria Hunniford knows about keeping up with them. In *Glorious Grandparenting* she shares her ideas on what to do when the grandchildren come to stay, and how to keep pace with them as they grow older. For many grandparents these days, life isn't always easy. In this book Gloria speaks to those who feel 'taken for granted' as a childminder, have conflicting views on childcare or, sadly, have become separated from their grandchildren. She looks at the controversial lack of legal rights for grandparents and offers advice and guidance on handling these emotive issues.

THE RELUCTANT TOMMY

Ronald Skirth and Duncan Barrett

In the First World War, like many other tommies, Ronald Skirth fought in the trenches, endured shell shock and somehow survived. But Skirth's story is extraordinary: on the Flanders battlefield he came across the dead body of a teenaged German soldier. The boy was just like him; in his hand, a photo of his girlfriend who looked just like Skirth's sweetheart, Ella . . . Skirth resolved never again to help take a human life. He altered the trajectory of guns to fire harmlessly, and, at great risk, carried out smaller acts of sabotage. Despite suffering breakdowns and amnesia, Skirth continued his peaceful campaign, lived out the war, and returned to marry Ella. *The Reluctant Tommy* is the story of a man who stuck by his principles in impossible circumstances.

THE MAGNIFICENT SPILSBURY AND THE CASE OF THE BRIDES IN THE BATH

Jane Robins

A young woman marries and before long drowns in her bath. There's no sign of a struggle or suggestion of foul play. In the dark opening months of the First World War, Britain became engrossed by the 'Brides in the Bath' trial: a story of murder, played out in the lodging houses of seaside towns, in the confines of married life, reaching its horrendous climax in that most intimate of settings — the bathroom. The nation turned to a forensic pathologist, Bernard Spilsbury, to explain the deaths. This was the age of science. In fiction, Sherlock Holmes applied a scientific mind to solving crimes. In real life, would Spilsbury be as infallible as the 'great detective'?

WEST END GIRLS

Barbara Tate

Barbara Tate was twenty-one when she escaped from her loveless home to the forbidden streets of Soho. London after the Second World War would never be the same again. There the naive Barbara met the beautiful and capricious Mae. When she takes a job as Mae's maid, she imagines she'll be housekeeping. But down a shabby back street Barbara discovers the secret lives of Soho's working girls . . . In an astonishing world of fierce friendships, bitter rivalries, dangerous men and desperate measures, Barbara soon learns that taking the punter's money and making tea are just the essentials. She will need to be nursemaid, protector and confidante to impossible, adorable, self-destructive Mae.

SEAGULLS IN THE ATTIC

Tessa Hainsworth

Tessa Hainsworth used to have it all —
except time, peace of mind and leisure to
enjoy the fruits of her labours in her executive
job with The Body Shop. One momentous
spring, she and her husband decided to start
again — and *Up With the Larks* describes
Tessa's first turbulent year, adapting to her
new life in the remote South West. Now, in
Seagulls in the Attic, Tessa reveals that
despite being a fully-fledged member of the
community, life is no easier. Being part of
small-village life isn't always straightforward.
Yet the reality of financial downsizing and
learning a whole new way of living hasn't
lessened Tessa's natural exuberance and sense
of fun — instead they help her to turn all the
hardships to her advantage . . . eventually.